THE PSYCHOANALYTIC MOVEMENT

Rethinking Theory

GENERAL EDITOR

Gary Saul Morson

CONSULTING EDITORS

Robert Alter
Frederick Crews
John M. Ellis
Caryl Emerson

THE
PSYCHOANALYTIC
MOVEMENT

The Cunning of Unreason

Ernest Gellner

Northwestern University Press
Evanston, Illinois

Northwestern University Press
Evanston, Illinois 60208-4210

Copyright © 1985, 1993 by Ernest Gellner. First edition published in Great Britain by Paladin in 1985; second edition published by Fontana Press, an imprint of HarperCollins Publishers, in 1993. Northwestern University Press edition published 1996 by arrangement with HarperCollins Publishers Ltd., London. All rights reserved.

Printed in the United States of America

ISBN 0-8101-1369-4 (cloth)
ISBN 0-8101-1370-8 (paper)

Library of Congress Cataloging-in-Publication Data

Gellner, Ernest.
    The psychoanalytic movement : the cunning of unreason / Ernest Gellner. —
Northwestern University Press ed.
        p. cm. — (Rethinking theory)
    Originally published: London : Fontana Press, 1993.
    Includes bibliographical references and index.
    ISBN 0-8101-1369-4 (cloth : alk. paper). — ISBN 0-8101-1370-8 (pbk. : alk. paper)
    1. Psychoanalysis—History. 2. Freud, Sigmund, 1856–1939. I. Title. II. Series.
BF173.G382 1996
150.19'5'09—dc20   96-17329
                                                                                  CIP

The paper used in this publication meets the minimum requirements of the American National Standard for Information Sciences—Permanence of Paper for Printed Library Materials, ANSI Z39.48-1984.

CONTENTS

To Susan

Aschenbach taught a whole grateful generation that a man can still be capable of great moral resolution even after he has plumbed the depths of knowledge . . .

Thomas Mann, *Death in Venice*

ACKNOWLEDGEMENTS

In writing this book, I have received invaluable help from my wife Susan and my secretary Gay Woolven. Katie Platt, Andrzej Lodynski and Declan Quigley, successively research assistants in the Philosophy Department at the LSE, have been extremely helpful in securing bibliographical documentation.

Various drafts of the book were read by John Hajnal, John Hall, Robin Ilbert, Ian Jarvie, Hilda and Jose Merquior, Declan Quigley, John Watkins, Justin Wintle, Gay Woolven and my son David, and I benefited very greatly from their comments and criticisms. Justin Wintle was a patient, supportive and stimulating editor.

I am much in the debt of Adolf Grunbaum, who allowed me to read various of his works, mainly prior to publication. I have learned a very great deal from them. Since I completed this book, his own *The Foundations of Psychoanalysis. A Philosophical Critique* (Berkeley, 1984) has appeared. His main interest is to link psychoanalysis to the philosophy of science, whereas mine relates it to its place in social and intellectual history. Consequently, where I disagree with him (and I do not think the disagreements are deep), I have not pursued the matter very far. I have also benefited from unpublished papers by Frank Cioffi, Yehuda Elkanna, Peter Urbach and Nigel Walker, and from hearing the delivery of another paper by Percy Cohen.

It will be obvious to readers that my general philosophical approach owes a very great deal to Karl Popper, whether or not I agree with all his ideas. But owing to the pervasiveness of his influence, I have refrained from referring to him on each occasion. If I am much influenced by his views on the nature of rationality and science, my ideas on the social conditions and consequences of science and rationality are as pervasively and obviously influenced by Max Weber, but once again I refrained from the pedantry of invoking him on each single occasion. When it comes to the manner of relating ideas, practices, institutions, values and communities to each other (a topic which takes up much of the book), my procedure owes almost everything to the dominant style of social anthropology as practised in Britain, though I refrain from singling out individual models.

It goes without saying that only I am responsible for the views expressed.

Ernest Gellner
Froxfield, 1984

INTRODUCTION TO
THE SECOND EDITION

The Enlightenment believed that the age of tyranny and superstition was due to be replaced by an age of Reason and Liberty. Mankind had lived under oppression and false belief: these were to go, and their heir was to be a social order in which truth would prevail and guide human life.

In the event, only two men were destined to articulate secular religions, capable of securing a wide following and offering a kind of secular salvation, comparable in its totality to that which had previously been offered in the literal sense: those two men were Karl Marx and Sigmund Freud. It is interesting to compare their systems: there are both similarities and contrasts.

Both of them are more than merely a theory: they are, in effect, an account of the central human predicament, a recipe for its remedy (partial or total), and hence, by implication, a morality. Each includes the occurrence of either faith or disbelief in itself amongst the phenomena it describes and purports to explain. For Freud, opposition to his own theories, whether in the course of therapy or in the abstract, is a sign of Resistance; for Marxism, opposition to its views is part of that very process of class conflict which is its own central theme. The possibility, generously exploited, of such explanation of dissent marks off these theories from ordinary scientific theories, which are admitted by their proponents to be subject to extraneous judgment not under their own conceptual control. Substantive truth trumps merely procedural propriety, which can well be under the control of nefarious forces, and which, on its own, is insufficient, and which in conjunction with real illumination, is really redundant. So, in both cases, authority or power within the system trumps evidence. In the case of psychoanalysis, it is the authority of the therapeutic practitioner which is decisive; in the case of Marxism, it is the authority of the forces which make for the liberation of mankind from the alienation imposed by class conflict and the political oppression and ideological blinkers which are its corollary.

The practices which, in both cases, render these systems eligible to function as religions are also what in effect excludes them from genuine science. In each case, the central idea or thesis of the system – the crucial role of class conflict in human society in one case, and the crucial role of the Unconscious in the other – is in effect treated as a Revelation; the subordinate clauses of the system, concerning the role of upholders and supporters of the central thesis, make it possible to discount and overrule all objections. One is somehow simultaneously taking part in an inquiry, in which rival claimants are subject to the verdict of evidence, and in a moral battle in which one *already* knows the identity of the Champions of Good and Evil, and where the need to succour Good and combat Evil trumps procedural principles applicable in the other arena.

So there is a marked formal similarity between the two systems. But there are also important differences, notably in the more specific nature of the salvations offered by each – differences which presumably help explain the diverse and contrasted fates of the two visions. In each case, the nature of the salvation offered is, naturally enough, linked to the diagnosis of that human predicament from which we need to be saved.

In the case of Marxism, man is alienated from his true essence – fulfilment in free unconstrained work in harmonious co-operation with his fellows – by the existence of unequal, asymmetrical relations to the means of production, engendering classes and class conflict. The historic and collective overcoming of this uniquely powerful and significant great hindrance of the good life will automatically engender a healthy society, free both of exploitation and its protector, oppression. This central intuition, if only it were valid, would free post-revolutionary society of any need to worry about procedure or safeguards. Human society would be safe in the hands of the Guardians of Human Liberation (in the original version, this was to be the Proletariat, and in the more catastrophic Leninist variant, the Vanguard Party).

Freudianism possesses the formal equivalents of all this. The human predicament is perceived differently: it is not engendered by any specific form of social organization and the manner in which it handles production and resources. It arises from the general condition of the human psyche, under any social order, and the fact that we are subject to unconscious conflicts and repressions which, *ex hypothesi*, we neither perceive nor understand, nor can control. Unlike Marxism, Freud offers no total liberation from the old version of the human condition, only a partial (but very significant) mitigation. It is not merely partial, it is also individual: It occurs on single occasions, as a result of a single, not a collective, operation, and one which leaves the wider world unchanged.

The difference in their respective theories of salvation has had tremendous consequences for the fates of the two visions. In a sense, and for a time, Marxism has been incomparably more successful: it became, in effect, a major world religion, the official creed of numerous societies including a superpower. But correspondingly, its collapse was at least as dramatic. It promised not therapy but economic success and power, and when these demonstrably eluded it, and were conspicuously bestowed on its rivals, it could not live with so conspicuous a refutation. For some reason, it did not possess the capacity conspicuous amongst literal religions, that of surviving the day on which prophecy fails. Its collapse has been near-total and general. It is true that the faith survives, formally, in China: but there are grounds for believing that what the Chinese leadership is really doing is finding its own, distinctively Chinese, path to dismantling communism. It prefers not to emulate the Russians, but to liberalize the economy whilst maintaining authoritarian order in society and politics. This does not arouse one's admiration or sympathy, but it does look like being more effective . . .

Freudianism was different. From the very beginning, it had within itself a certain tendency towards political quietism. Salvation lay in adjustment, a term which, in effect, depth psychology introduced into the moral vocabulary of modern man. By implication or overtly, it preached acceptance of the external social order, which turned out to cause a measure of embarrassment during the Hitler period (was that regime also to be accepted by the inwardly well-adjusted person?).

Whilst in a sense total and all-embracing, certain forays into the attempt to offer Theories of Everything notwithstanding, Freudianism focuses on one zone of life, man's inner feelings, and consigns the rest of life to a zone of the profane. This zone is of course in the last analysis (and penultimate analyses as well, if it comes to that) controlled by the sacred area where everything is really decided, the only area which truly matters. Nonetheless, secondary and subordinated though it is, this profane zone does exist. It can be inhabited, enjoyed, explored, when the sufferer is not preocccupied with the real and ultimate drama. In fact, such a relaxed enjoyment is even commended, its possibility is a sign that the crucial battle has not gone too badly . . . This, I think, is part of the explanation of why, in the end, psychoanalysis has fared well: the existence of a profane area of life permits escape into it, 'routinization', which means that the faith is not permanently exposed to the searching demands made upon a creed which is ubiquitous and permanently, as it were, in top gear.

Both theories have failed in their predictions: Freudianism does not offer a privileged path to mental health, any more than Marxism leads to economic performance and social co-operation. Freudianism is somewhat better equipped with falsification-evading devices than Marxism: the notion of the Unconscious, be decreeing that things are never what they seem and that the decoding of their real significance is under control of those properly initiated (the equivalent of the Vanguard Party), really makes sure that testing can never take place from the outside. To test a theory you must be able to recognize a counter-example, and you cannot do that unless you are licensed to characterize examples (thereby becoming fitted to see whether they are indeed *counter*), which *ex hypothesi*, you are not. The notion of the Unconscious in effect de-operationalizes all concepts, thereby making it impossible for unbelievers to characterize objects and decide whether or not they fit in with a given theory . . . The corrresponding theory of knowledge within Marxism is not quite as central to the vision as a whole. It can be and is attached to it, it can be derived from the central ideas of Marxism and made to appear as its immediate corollary – but for all that, the epistemology of false consciousness is not quite as central to Marxism as it is to Freudianism. In a sense, Freudianism *is* a theory of false consciousness.

However, I do not think it is either their falsification, or their skill at avoiding falsification which explain the differences in their respective fates. Marixism over-extended itself, it insisted on a public salvation, it in effect sacralized the whole of life, notably the economic sphere of Marxist societies, and it could not live with squalor and defeat in that zone. By contrast, Freudianism in practice sharpened the distinction between the sacred and the profane: for people 'under analysis', reality isn't quite real, only what happens inside the session really counts. The external world acquires a shadowy quality, a kind of period of *sursis*, of suspended emotional animation between two periods of communication with reality, *within* the analytic session.

So a number of times over, Freudianism and its derivatives have benefited from a certain modesty. No attempts at transforming the human condition or revolutionizing the whole of society: only at mitigating individual conditions. The wider world is not its testing-ground, but rather, an escape or refuge from the examination of the strong claims made in one zone only, namely in the affective state of the individual psyche. So an extensive profane zone remains, in a way insignificant for the true believer, but its reality is not denied, and it is not, in practice, refused a life of its own. Amongst the more educated strata of the developed world, Freudian ideas now live on, not so much amongst the covens of the formal Freudian elite, as in the vast world of 'counselling', which has probably taken over a lion's share of the pastoral care, of guiding and solace for those who are in inner crisis. Freudianism and its central ideas live on not as a dominant system linked to the central authority of a society, but rather as one of those ideological subsystems providing special services – above all, solace and support for the unhappy – which are not adequately catered for by the main and official social vision. To understand our world, we must understand how these ideas and their institutional and procedural props work. The most visible part of this iceberg is perhaps the movement which had started it all: understanding it helps us understand its derivatives. This is what the present volume attempts to do.

ERNEST GELLNER
April 1993

I

BACK TO NATURE

Our curiosity is naturally prompted to inquire by what means the Christian faith obtained so remarkable a victory over the established religions of the earth. To this inquiry an obvious but satisfactory answer may be returned; that it was owing to the convincing evidence of the doctrine itself, and to the ruling providence of its great Author. But as truth and reason seldom find so favourable a reception in the world, and as the wisdom of Providence frequently condescends to use the passions of the human heart, and the general circumstances of mankind, as instruments to execute its purpose, we may still be permitted, though with becoming submission, to ask, not indeed what were the first, but what were the secondary causes of the rapid growth of the Christian church?

Edward Gibbon, *Decline and Fall of the Roman Empire*

GIBBON'S PROBLEM

Psychoanalysis, like Christianity, is a founded or historic rather than a traditional system of beliefs and practices. It has an even more precise point of foundation than Christianity. Neither the identity nor the existence of its Founder is in doubt.

It made its entry on the world's stage as a set of new and definite claims. The speed of the acceptance, partial or total, of its message, by at any rate a significant proportion of those to whom it was addressed and who it could reach, was astonishing. The question which Gibbon asked about Christianity applies equally to psychoanalysis: by what means did the new vision obtain so remarkable a victory?

The present volume intends above all to offer an answer

1

to this question, one which should be internally coherent, and compatible with the established facts.

The objection which Gibbon anticipated to the very inquiry itself can of course, and most certainly will, also be raised against this version of it. Are not the truth and importance of the ideas contained in the message sufficient to explain its impact? This objection can be raised against the present inquiry with a double force. Gibbon mentions only the positive factors which can be expected to lead people to embrace the true faith. The case of psychoanalytic ideas is more complex. Not only does the truth of the ideas themselves exercise a positive attraction, but also, as is well known, the system of ideas also contains, as an integral part of itself, an explanation of the occasional failure of those ideas to secure conviction. The idea of *resistance*, which leads people in some circumstances to reject the ideas in question, explains the occasional failure or delay of conversion as cogently as the truth of ideas can explain their eventual success.

In fact, it may even seem to do it a little *more* cogently: the unconscious forces which, according to the theory, have such a strong hold over us, but which apparently can recognize and fear (even in anticipation and at a distance) the doctrine which understands and may eventually tame them – these forces clearly have every incentive to resist, by all the formidable and elusive hidden means at their disposal, the acceptance of those doctrines. So perhaps the problem facing the historian of psychoanalytic ideas may even be the inverse of that which faced Gibbon and indeed any historian of a true belief: is he not redundant precisely when attempting to single out the social factors obstructing the recognition of truth? Has he not been anticipated by the theory itself? Does not the convincing evidence of the doctrine itself explain, better than anyone else can, its occasional failures?

Be that as it may: whether this problem is the obverse or the accentuated, reduplicated form of the one which Gibbon described, there can be no doubt about a certain parallelism between the two situations. The manner in which we shall endeavour to cope with this issue, with the interaction of social and psychological causes and of valid reasons, will emerge as we proceed. In the meantime, note the existence of other styles of exposition. There are at least three such styles:

1. *Internal or Hagiographical.* This works through a narrative of how the various discoveries came to be made. The narrative is formulated in what might be called 'achievement' language: it looks back, and retrospectively describes how that which is now known (or assumed) to be true, came to be recognized, often in the face of enormous odds. Stories of (literal) saints and heroes are told in this way. This style has enormous pedagogic attractions: the stories convey the values of the believing community, the identification of the True and the False, of the Good and the Bad, not by overtly affirming them as such (which might on occasion arouse suspicion and even rejection), but *en passant*, through the tacit and pervasive identification of the Goodies and the Baddies within the story. The listener, stirred by the account of the adventures (be they physical, moral or cognitive) of the hero, thrilled and frightened by his hairbreadth escapes, exhilarated by his eventual but oh so perilously and narrowly attained success, absorbs the values of the narrative unconsciously, simply by identifying with the hero. Angered by his enemies, thrilled by his courage, he does not much attend to the merits of his cause, but rather absorbs them in passing. A good proportion of the favourable accounts of psychoanalysis take precisely this form, and are often told through fragments of the Life and Passion of Saint Sigmund.

2. *Eclectic.* This is characteristic of manuals of psychiatry which see psychoanalytic ideas or techniques as one set of options among others, among the tools available to the psychiatrist.

3. *Hostile.* This concentrates on the failures or deficiencies of psychoanalysis, notably its conceptual or methodological weaknesses. Of such charges, the best known and most important is that psychoanalysis consists of a self-maintaining,

3

self-confirming set of ideas (and/or practices), such that it 'comes out right' whichever way clinical or experimental evidence happens to point.

The present exposition attempts to answer a problem – just how did the astonishing psychoanalytical revolution in our ideas come about – a question which cannot possibly be resolved if one is content to remain largely within the bounds of any one of these three styles. The second and third styles, whatever their merits, are in a certain way even more inadequate for the purpose at hand than the first. The eclectic approach, whether or not sensible as a practical strategy, misses out the coherence and unity of the psychoanalytical vision, and what might be called its world-filling exhaustiveness. It can pervade and dominate a person's world in a way not open to therapeutic techniques in isolation. The third makes it rather difficult to propose any plausible solution to our central problem – unless one holds that *any* self-maintaining circle of ideas whatever, if well equipped with devices for evading falsification, will have a *succès fou*, which alas is not the case. I certainly do not believe this to be so. It is very easy to construct self-maintaining circles of ideas, and not all of them prosper. If we accept the legitimacy and importance of the question concerning why some systems of ideas (whether true or false) do on occasion acquire a kind of magic for those exposed to them, then we must seek an explanation which does not rely on circularity alone.

It hardly needs stating why the internal or hagiographical approach also cannot be sufficient. The ideas of the movement itself constitute data, indeed supremely important data for us: but they cannot be allowed to prejudge how their truth or falsity (and it could be either or both) contribute to the success of the intellectual system in question. The factors we shall look at will be drawn not merely from the domain which is the primary concern of that system, namely the human psyche: but we shall also look at two other domains – the intellectual history of mankind, and the wider social organization and ethos of our time.

4

It seems to me the first principle of the study of any belief system is that its ideas and terms must be stated in terms other than its own; that they must be projected on to some screen other than one which they themselves provide. They may and must speak, but they must not be judges in their own case. For concepts, like feelings and desires, have their cunning. Only in this way may we hope to lay bare the devices they employ to make their impact – whether or not those devices are, in the end, endorsed as legitimate.

SOME BASIC FACTS AND QUESTIONS

Psychoanalysis is a theory, a technique, an organization, a language, an ethos, an ethic, a climate.

> To us he is no more a person
> Now but a whole climate of opinion
> Under whom we conduct our differing lives.

So wrote W. H. Auden about Sigmund Freud.[1]

The aim of this book is to offer an account of how, within the span of less than half a century, this system of ideas could conquer so much of the world, at any rate to the extent of becoming the dominant idiom for the discussion of the human personality and of human relations. It will endeavour to do this by relating its central ideas and practices to the major social and intellectual changes of the time. The system is very closely related to its period, often in ways its practitioners do not fully understand. We will not attempt a detailed account of the life of Freud and of the development of the psychoanalytical movement: that could not be done in so short a space, and has been done by others.

Nevertheless, for quick reference and by way of background, some of the key facts are presented here.

Sigmund Freud was born in a middle- or lower-middle-class Jewish family in southern Moravia (now part of Czechoslovakia) in 1856. The family moved to Vienna in

1860. Freud graduated in medicine in 1881. Four years later he secured a university appointment in neuropathology.

During the 1880s and 1890s Freud's views gradually developed and crystallized. His relevant work was carried out at the frontiers of neurology and psychopathology. The question of whether or not he 'progressed' from a neurological bias towards an autonomous 'psychodynamic' view of the human personality, is an issue which continues to haunt Freudian exegesis. What is not in doubt is that his attention was turned towards the psychological, as opposed to physical, elements in certain illnesses. Nevertheless, he did write, in 1895, a *Project of a Scientific Psychology* (not published till 1950), which, while foreshadowing many of his theories, also gives them a firm physical or rather neurological basis, and which is much invoked by those who uphold a physicalist interpretation of his system. Those who like their Marx non-scientistic, turn to the young Marx; those who like their Freud scientistic, turn to the young Freud.

After toying with methods of hypnosis and suggestion, he developed, between 1892 and 1898, the alternative method of 'free association' for exploring the psyche of patients. This method, or should one say its institutionalized practice, is one of the main pillars of psychoanalysis. Those eager to interpret this development in terms of his own theories, will note that the first occurrence of the word 'psychoanalysis' took place in 1896, the very same year as the death of Freud's father. The real point of entry of psychoanalytic truth into the world, comparable to the birth of Christ, or that great moment in the 1840s when the young Karl Marx allegedly perceived that Hegelianism was but a coded economic history of mankind, took place in 1897, with Freud's own 'self-analysis'.

This led to such crucial doctrines as that of infantile sexuality and the Oedipus Complex. His admirers have emphatically qualified this self-analysis as heroic, and held it to be a great moral as well as cognitive achievement. It is not entirely clear why this particular piece of introspection should not be doomed, like that of other men, to self-deception, but instead be classed as heroic and veridical –

unless the reason is that its findings are valid, which to outsiders seems somewhat circular reasoning. The findings of that self-analysis were congruent with theoretical ideas towards which Freud had been groping anyway. From within the movement, however, the self-analysis is seen as an independent confirmation or origin of these ideas.

There is an Eastern European Jewish story about a *Wunder-rebbe* (a miracle-performing rabbi) who, caught one Friday evening far away from his home, was unable to reach home before the beginning of the Sabbath (during which travel is forbidden). But he was undismayed and performed a miracle: to the left of the road there was *shabes*, to the right of the road there was *shabes*, but on the road itself there was no *shabes*! The point of the story is that if you yourself make up the rules of what is the truth of the matter, performing miracles turns out to be not quite so difficult. The same would seem to be true of the heroism and accuracy of Freud's self-analysis.

If the doctrinal moment of incarnation is best set at 1897, then the organizational commencement of psychoanalysis is perhaps best fixed at 1902, with the Wednesday Psychological Society, which then began its meetings in Freud's house, and which was destined to become, in 1908, the Psychoanalytical Society of Vienna. Men other than Freud (Federn and Stekel) began to practise psychoanalysis in 1903; Ernest Jones, Freud's crucial British disciple and eventual biographer, began doing so in 1905.

Psychoanalysis can briefly be described as a technique in which a therapist encourages a patient to 'free-associate', i.e. to speak out anything that comes into his head, encouraging and guiding him only with occasional questions and, later on, interpretations. The assumption is that this will in due course lead to the uncovering of the unconscious, 'repressed' mental contents, which could not have been elicited by any more direct approach; and that their extraction and recognition by the patient will have significant and beneficial therapeutic consequences.

Outward expansion of the movement began about the middle of the first decade of this century. Correspondence with the Swiss psychiatrist C. G. Jung started in 1906, and in 1907 Jung founded a Freud society in Zurich. The first Psychoanalytic Congress took place in Salzburg in 1908. A Berlin society was founded in 1908, a New York and a separate American one in 1911, during which year the first article about psychoanalysis to be published in France also appeared. Freud gave some crucial lectures at Clark University in America in 1909.

During the second decade of the century, the movement also experienced its first great, and most famous, fissions: Adler left in 1911, Jung in the course of 1913–14. Jung had been, as is very clearly evident from Freud's own emphatic statements, the *Parade-Goy*[2] of the early psychoanalytic movement. His rapid elevation angered Freud's earlier Viennese followers, but Freud made it plain that favouring Gentile entrants was politically essential for the successful expansion of the movement.

Freud continued to live in Vienna until 1938, emigrated to London after Hitler's occupation of Austria, and died there the following year.

The Psychoanalytical Movement as an international institution and organization, with its parallel rival movements headed by Jung and Adler, and later some others, really crystallized after the First World War. Its phenomenal and exponential growth has never been documented properly and with precision. Given its influence, this is odd and regrettable. We are dealing with nothing less than an intellectual, moral and terminological revolution, on an enormous, indeed a global scale. Changes in intellectual climate constitute something that is inherently elusive, and yet supremely important. It is probably best at this point simply to sketch or classify the types of institutional underpinning which this intellectual transformation enjoyed.

The Psychoanalytical Movement in the strict and narrow sense is well organized, with an international association grouping national institutes and societies, and with a clearly defined membership. Analysts undergo training under their auspices; with its completion, the licence to practise analysis is issued by these bodies, and the monopoly of this licensing is in general jealously guarded. The most important part of the said training is that the apprentice himself undergoes a 'training analysis'; its successful completion is the main precondition of graduation.

There are parallel and rival movements, historically connected with Freud and with his dissident disciples, and with partly overlapping doctrines and techniques, and with roughly similar organizational principles.

There is also the entire profession of psychiatry, which as such has no shared dogma, but which has in the main recognized psychoanalysis as one legitimate approach, among others, to mental illness and personality problems. Those psychiatrists who use psychoanalytical ideas and techniques range from fully committed Freudians to avowed eclectics, willing to use anything on a trial-and-error basis, as part of a wider bag of tricks. The amount and kind of initiation received by these partial practitioners varies, once again, from full and officially sanctioned training analysis to all kinds of short-cuts. (It must be added that in the early years of psychoanalysis, before the First World War, and prior to its full institutionalization, what counted as initiation, and justified recognition by Freud of a fellow-analyst, varied enormously and would seem on occasion to have been perfunctory.) The degree to which psychiatrists use psychoanalysis can vary from sustained use of the technique, to simple use of the terminology in characterizing a patient's condition.

Furthermore, there is an enormous, fluid and uncharted world of 'psychotherapy' and loosely related movements and techniques, such as 'group therapy' (a kind of poor man's psychoanalysis, where the attention, and the cost, of a therapist is shared with an entire group). Roughly speaking, the central movement endeavours to retain the label 'psychoanalysis' for its own properly licensed guild members, and hopes that those outside it will content themselves with the unpatented 'psychotherapy'. This outer world of fringe depth psychology and therapy contains countless sub-movements, distinguished by technical idiosyncrasies or by syncretism with other systems of ideas, or identifiable simply by the identity of their leaders or their location.

This world is enormous, protean and volatile. A study published in 1959, and incomplete even then, lists thirty-six different kinds of psychotherapy. Another work, by L. Wilby, published in 1977, reports that there are no fewer than 200 conceptually distinct psychotherapies.[3] In France, under the leadership of Lacan, a sub-movement flourished which constituted a kind of Maoist cultural revolution within psychoanalysis – repudiating regularity of time-tables and of licensing. Sessions could be arbitrarily brief, and analysts were to be self-appointing . . .[4]

This world is of the utmost importance for the understanding of our society and its intellectual and moral climate. While the sociology of contemporary religion in the narrower sense is reasonably well explored and documented, this psychotherapeutic world, whose vitality and impact on people is probably greater, remains largely uncharted. Part of the reason for this strange contrast is perhaps that religious faith proper is now so lukewarm that the practitioners of religion are willing to cooperate with research, and indeed welcome it and often indulge in it themselves: the demonstrations of the social role and usefulness of their faith and ritual is the closest they can normally get to establishing its truth and importance. Practitioners of depth psychological cults, on the other hand, have a more genuine and straightforward conviction of the validity of their own ideas, coupled with a distrust and dislike of inquiries which are redundant if they confirm the faith, and positively harmful if they subvert it. They have on occasion refused permission to bona fide academics to carry out research. Freud himself is on record as holding that empirical research into his own ideas is redundant because they are already so conclusively established, but that it can do no harm. His latter-day intellectual progeny are no longer so sure about the second point, and do not generally welcome investigation.

Finally, there is the even more elusive and intangible, but at least equally important, phenomenon of the permeation

10

of the language and literature of our society by Freudian ideas. It is doubtful whether this could be summed up in any quantitative or precise manner, yet it would be useful if it could be perceptively described and characterized.

The range and scale of these phenomena are astonishing. The rates of exponential growth always transcend and astonish the expectations of the human mind. Moreover, once properly articulated in words, the whole vision evidently became airborne, and was and continues to be capable of seeding itself effectively across astonishing physical and cultural distances. There has been nothing like this since the spread of the potato and of maize, and this diffusion was even faster and may have deeper implications.

But this phenomenal diffusion would hardly have been possible had the system of ideas in question not satisfied some deep and pervasive social and intellectual need. The specification of just how the intricate and elegant structure of that system fitted in with the distinctive social and intellectual condition of mankind in our age, is the central aim of this book.

THE LAST ANGEL

The great pre-industrial and pre-scientific civilizations, especially perhaps the Western ones, tend to see man as half-angel, half-beast. Perhaps there was an earlier stage when he was more at peace with himself and his instinctual drives, and possibly the angel-beast tension does not characterize all great literate civilizations with the same intensity. However, there can be no doubt but that, with their severe ethics, influential clerisies and codified expectations, these civilizations do have a marked tendency towards a kind of dualistic and demanding vision. Freud himself commented on it with some eloquence in *Civilization and its Discontents* and *Moses and Monotheism*. And certainly the civilization which engendered modern science and industrial society itself as a whole, was very much given to the beast–angel dualism, and the arduousness of the struggle it imposed may well have played a crucial part in bringing forth our modern world.

This dualistic vision caused great torment to those condemned to live with it:

> Oh wearisome condition of Humanity!
> Borne under one Law, to another bound:
> Vainely begot, yet forbidden vanity,
> Created sicke, commanded to be sound:
> What meaneth Nature by these diverse Lawes?
> Passion and Reason, selfe-division cause:
> Is it the marke, or Majesty of Power
> To make offences that it may forgive?
> Nature herselfe doth her owne selfe defloure,
> To hate those errors she her selfe doth give.[5]

None the less, anguished though it may have been, this vision had one or two marked advantages. It provided a validation for the rules and values towards which men were obliged to aspire. They contained an answer to the question – why must we strive and suffer so? These higher values were tied to the better parts of the total cosmic order, and to the better elements within man. So there was an answer to the difficult question – why must we strive and suffer so? – an answer which linked the obligatory and painful endeavour to the overall picture; and as long as the picture retained its cogency, the demands retained their authority, even if anguish was the price.

But there was a further and very important advantage: the picture also provided an idiom and an explanation for all the forces within man which were *opposed* to the higher and purer elements. However much the Lower Aspects of our nature might have been reprobated, their very existence was not denied. Quite the reverse: the devil had a recognized place in the scheme of things. His power was treated with respect. No one who found him within his own heart had any reason to feel surprised. We had been warned.

However, with the coming of modernity, the total dualistic picture, of which divided man was a part, lost its authority. The twin currents of empiricism and materialism destroyed it, and replaced it with a unitary vision both of nature and man. Henceforth, nature was to be one single system, subject to invariant and neutral laws, and no longer a stratified system whose ranked levels in nature, society and man were to symbolize and underwrite our values. If materialism/mechanism is a great leveller or unifier, so is empiricism: at its root is the idea that all things are known in basically the same way, and nothing can have any standing greater than the evidence for its existence, and evidence is assembled and evaluated by *men*. Thus, obliquely, through the sovereignty of *public evidence*, all authority, sacredness, absoluteness are gradually eliminated from the world.

This modern vision was codified by the great thinkers of the European eighteenth-century Enlightenment. Perhaps the greatest exemplar of this type of view was David Hume; at any rate, he is certainly the one most relevant here. Like other thinkers of his age, he was under the impression that he was talking about man as such, rather than expressing the vision of an age. His *Treatise on Human Nature* gave a profoundly *un*-dualistic account of man, and one continuous with nature. Far from aspiring to a more-than-natural status for the highest elements in man, Hume's accounts of both abstract thought and of morality were profoundly of this world: ideas were but the aftertaste of sensations, morality was but a matter of feeling, feelings which in the end serve our collective convenience.

With the coming of a unitary vision of the world, man had to return to nature, to be seen as part of it rather than as the fruit of the intrusion of something higher, divine, into the world. Possibly the main agency of this renaturalization of man was the theory of knowledge, which acted as the Great Leveller by insisting that man was known, and knew himself, in the same way as he knew anything else – through his senses. Sensations were the universal building blocks, the ultimate material, of everything. So duality was overcome: the old cohabitation of Angel and Beast was replaced by Hume's famous 'Bundle of Perceptions'. The elements from which this bundle was assembled were exactly the same as those of any other object of nature, and were simply

13

accumulated by the senses. So there was no further reason to assume special, extra-territorial status for humanity within nature. That creature, assembled from such fragmented, transparent and hence basically innocuous elements, I shall on occasion call the 'Bundleman'.

And here we come to one of the greatest, most curious paradoxes in all the history of thought: this renaturalized non-dualistic man was, in a curious way, *more*, not less, angelic than his strife-ridden, anguished predecessor, with his double citizenship in the divine and in the animal, 'borne under one Law, to another bound'. Man now seemed very much at home in this world, and there seemed no good reason why he should not be at peace with it. Reading David Hume and Adam Smith, one might gather the impression that both the lusts and the guilts of the human heart are quite transparent to itself, at any rate in Scotland. (A little later, James Hogg, the author of *The Confessions of a Justified Sinner*, made it plain that this was not so; but he had little influence on academic psychology.) How did this astonishing beatification of man come about?

Hume was the supreme exponent of the empiricist vision, and one who explored its problems. One of his most famous, and also most misleading statements is: '*Reason is and ought only to be the slave of the passions.*'

Anyone not familiar with Hume's thought might well suppose, on reading this remark out of context, that Hume's vision of man was something like that of Dostoevsky, that he saw man as possessed by dark, tortuous, mysterious, perverse and uncontrollable passions. Not a bit of it. To understand properly the true nature of the famous Humean enslavement to passion, you must conjure up a different picture altogether. Imagine yourself floating in a boat on an artificial lake in a landscaped park, say one designed by Capability Brown. The currents of the lake are the passions, and you are indeed their slave, for the boat has neither oars nor rudder. If reason be the captain, it is a totally powerless one. The vessel will follow the currents, for there simply are no other forces that can impel or impede it.

Will they propel the boat to its destruction, in some

maelstrom or cataract? Not at all. These currents are mild, the shores of the lake are rounded and slope gently. The currents may take you to a picnic on an island with a grotto or, alternatively, to a musical performance of Handel on one of the shores . . . With such passions, who would not gladly be their slave?

All that Hume meant by the celebrated 'enslavement to the passions' was that the desires which impel our conduct could only be engendered by *feelings*. 'Reason' (perception of fact or of logical relation) could never on its own produce a preference for one thing over another. It could only note incompatibilities or select optional means. In that sense, but in that sense only, the boat was oar-less and rudder-less; and in that sense only, reason was powerless.

But the feelings which took over all responsibility for our aims and values, basically and simply for lack of any possible rival, were themselves of a very gentle and sensible kind, like the mild currents of our small artificial lake. This was a corollary of conceiving man (and everything else) as constructed out of the atomic elements assembled by outer and inner sense: sensations and feelings. The Bundleman was a gourmet crossed with an accountant, with a touch of compassionate sensibility thrown in. He conducted his life by studying his palate and seeking to arrange for its greatest satisfaction, and his imaginative sympathy for others inclined him to favour their satisfactions too, if to a somewhat lesser degree than his own.

A fallacious argument underlay all this: because only experience gives us evidence about the world (which is probably true), and experience comes in little bits (most questionable), therefore the only correct model of human conduct is one which sees it as the result of the accumulation and combination of introspectible feelings and sensations (totally false). This picture, endowed later with quite spurious tough-minded third person terminology such as 'Stimulus and Response' (henceforth SR), continued to haunt the tradition of 'scientific', empiricist psychology and does so still.

This tradition too has its compulsiveness: those who

15

adhere to it are under the sway of the faulty inference *from* the plausible view of the cognitive sovereignty of sense experience, *to* the absurd conclusion that explanatory models of human conduct must be in terms of elements similar to 'sensation' or 'stimulus'. The inference is quite fallacious, though an entire movement in psychology (Behaviourism) is based on the failure to see this.

But what concerns us here is not the roots of the behaviourist error, but its consequences. The idyllic, gentle-passion theory found in Hume, is in effect transmitted by it to the entire and rather influential tradition of academic 'empiricist' psychology. Man's behaviour is seen as a set of responses to given stimuli: the task of psychology becomes to identify the links between these stimuli and responses. Psychology becomes a search for a kind of algorithm linking stimuli to responses.

Yet it offered the new image of man, the mirror for secularized, literally *naturalized*, man freed from the dualistic doctrine and the endless inner battle between Beast and Angel. Unfortunately, the picture, which should have been cheering and relaxing, brought its own tension with it. The trouble is very simple: anyone who has the least sense of what it is like to be a human being knows perfectly well, and without any shadow of doubt, that the Hume/SR account of man bears no relation whatsoever to the facts.

But it was, and partly remains, the official or dominant psychological doctrine or assumption. Yet we also know, each of us, with as firm a certainty as we can ever have of anything, that it is false. What happens when the official doctrine says one thing, and what everyone instinctively knows to be true is quite another? The French have a couple of good phrases for this: what results is the dualism of *pays legal* and *pays reel*.

In French, this suggestive and opposite terminology arose from a political situation in which the official, overt political institutions did not correspond, at least in the estimation of some, to the real, genuinely felt sentiments and loyalties of men. But there is, especially in the modern world, a *pays reel* and a *pays legal* of the human mind, at least as sharply distinct and deeply opposed as French state and society once were. The *pays legal* is the rather atomistic, calculating, introspectively accessible gourmet-accountant, whose presence is (erroneously) held to be entailed by an empiricist theory of knowledge. The *pays reel* is the nature of our feelings, drives, relationships, as we know them to be, from the often bitter experience of actually being alive. One of the main clues to understanding the significance and impact of psychoanalysis is very simply this: it provided both an idiom and a justification for recognizing the *pays reel*. The more it was denied, the more an unconvincing *pays legal* was affirmed, the more clamorous the *pays reel* became emotionally. But it lacked an idiom and a doctrine. Anyone who provided it with a convincing idiom, rationale, and institutional underpinning, was bound to receive a reward.

The *pays legal* in the meantime consisted of the forcefully imposed survival of a demanding dualistic morality, sustained incoherently and unconvincingly by the doctrine of the Last Angel – that most implausible of ethereal beings, the self seen as assembled from the fragments of limpid consciousness, the innocuous gourmet-accountant, the Bundleman. But if we are bundles made up of quite harmless elements, why do we suffer so?

THE HARBINGER OF THE *PAYS REEL*

The paradox arose because the empiricist tradition, in its determination to make man part of nature, had made him more, rather than less unrealistically ethereal; he now seemed purer and more transparent than he had been when partly divine, or at least when touched by divine creation or design. The Bundleman was more innocuous than the Angel/Beast. The thinkers of the empiricist tradition had supposed that the only way to exclude the supernatural from our understanding of man was to insist that all knowledge came through the senses and in no other way. To turn the limits of the senses into the limits of sense seemed a sound way of ensuring that man was made of

17

natural materials only. It was supposed that the supernatural elements had to enter by supersensory channels; so if these channels were blocked, the alien elements and demands could no longer make their entry, and the result would be a man made of terrestrial materials alone, and responsive only to human and humane imperatives.

It is hard to imagine a more bloodless and unrealistic account of man. Should one be more appalled by the implausibility of this picture as an explanation of the twisted, devious and turbulent creature we actually deal with, or by the anaemia and complacency of this picture as a model of what man should be?

Many writers have noticed the incongruity between this model and reality. But there is one thinker in whose work this insight plays an absolute central part: Friedrich Nietzsche.[6]

Nietzsche, like Søren Kierkegaard, appeared in philosophy at a moment when the style of exposition of some thinkers at least was undergoing a fundamental change. He was influenced by predecessors like Schopenhauer who still wrote – even if they wrote very well – in an academic, science-emulating style, on the assumption that precise propositions were being propounded, and this, rather than tone and manner, was what mattered. In Nietzsche there is a shift to inconsequential, sometimes incoherent aphorism, and to a great deal of irony. The starched dress of formal argument, demonstration and precision is abandoned.

This change of form was no mere affectation. The new form genuinely reflected a change of content. Part of Nietzsche's message was that under the formal argument of a thinker there was a man whose deep emotional and situational concerns were reflected, or camouflaged, by the formally presented arguments. If this was indeed so, there was no point in practising such deception oneself; and Nietzsche, most consistently (thereby also giving licence to his marvellous literary talent), proceeded to turn upon the real psychic meaning of thinkers and intellectual traditions, while dispensing with the pedantry of much formal documentation or argument. The representatives of the empiricist, unwittingly-angelic, 'bundle-of-perceptions' theories of man were favourite victims of his irony.

It is a pity perhaps that Nietzsche did not concentrate on some major representative of this school, such as David Hume or Adam Smith; but nevertheless, the criticism strikes home. One might pedantically object that the British moralists invoked not stupidity, as Nietzsche suggested, but imagination, compassion and benevolence as the mainspring of morality. But to say that is to miss the point: 'stupidity' is the rhetorical exaggeration for a valid point. The empiricist or associationist account did indeed altogether miss the deviousness, the cunning, the camouflage and inversion, the envy or resentment, which underlie so many of our 'moral' reactions.

We have given an account of the peaceable, innocent, guileless, not to say anaemic Bundleman of the empiricists, suggesting that he had emerged almost by accident, through a faulty inference: the thinkers of the Enlightenment had wished to see man in terms of nature only, without supernatural intrusions; and because empiricism was a naturalist theory of knowledge, they quite mistakenly concluded that man must be made of, and actuated by, only such elements as figure in the simpliste version of the empiricist account of knowledge (i.e. the elements that appear on the 'inner screen' of sensation).

But in fact, the guileless Bundleman was accepted and welcomed not merely because he was the corollary of a mistaken inference: there were also more positive reasons for accepting so rosy a vision of man. Optimistic social doctrines such as the natural harmony of interests, the feasibility of a social order built upon consent, with only minimal coercion (or even none at all) – these doctrines were also in the air in the eighteenth and nineteenth centuries. The picture of the harmless and guileless bundle fitted in with these starry-eyed expectations, and they in turn seemed to provide a kind of confirmation for a psychology engendered by the empiricist picture of knowledge.

If this picture is deeply suspect, if it is but the *pays legal* of the Enlightenment, what is the truth of the matter, what is the *pays reel*? Nietzsche was not a coherent thinker and never properly codified the alternative. This would have been contrary to his style and spirit; moreover, it is doubtful whether the alternative he sketched or hinted at was or even could be fully consistent, and formal exposition would have laid bare its inner strains. But it is important to try and pin down this alternative vision, to codify it and make it precise – while admitting that this procedure may misrepresent in detail, and certainly in spirit, the intentions and style of the author to whom it is being credited.

These views about the *pays reel* of the human mind, which may I think legitimately be extracted from the works of Nietzsche, can be formulated and enumerated as follows. I shall henceforth refer to the ideas on this list as the Nietzschean Minimum (NM for short).

1. *Instinctuality.* Our real satisfactions and needs are closely linked to our basic instinctual drives. Our contentment and our distress is not a matter of running up a positive balance in the summation of little pleasures, distributed over the screen on to which our stream of consciousness is projected, as on a kind of skin we extend towards reality; in fact they come, on the contrary, in big brutal blows, linked not to our skin, but our innards.

2. *Situationality.* These satisfactions are situational, not atomized. What satisfies and what disturbs us is not the pleasure- and pain-flavoured little specks on the screen or skin (adding up the pleasures and subtracting the pains); it is a three-dimensional and persisting *situation*. Our concern is with such total situations, and not with a pleasure/pain balance sheet.

3. *Reality is Other People.* The type of situation which satisfies or disturbs us is primarily one involving other people, and, above all, people with whom we have persistent, intimate and emotionally charged relationships – members of our family, or generally fellow-members of the persisting immediate elementary community. What matters above all are relationships of power and of submission.

4. *Trauma and Gestalt.* Our perception of the situations in

this intimate and immediate realm of our deepest and genuine concern, and the manner in which we form attitudes and assessments within it, do not in the least follow the atomic, slowly and cautiously cumulative, accountant-like procedure postulated by empiricist philosophers. Perception, formation of permanent pictures and attitudes, is by *trauma*. Single crucial events act like switches which deeply modify our vision and valuations, irrespective of whether that single strategic event is, by some external standards, either 'objective' or important.

5. *Covertness.* The manner in which these kinds of crystallizations of vision and attitude occur is such that it is not generally conscious or accessible to the consciousness, or to the deliberate control, of the person concerned.

6. *Infancy.* Many, perhaps all, of these crucial crystallizations occur very early in life. In any case they persist in the same person over long periods. (This doctrine is prominent in Freud, whereas in Nietzsche it is just a plausible corollary of other ideas. But nothing really hinges on whether this point is explicitly worked out in Nietzsche.)

7. *Surrealism.* The 'logical' principles, if they can be dignified by such a term, which govern these crystallizations, are strangers both to the principles of perspective, and to all the normal rules of time, space, logic and causality, which more or less govern (or are meant to govern) our conscious thought. They are devoid of perspective or sense of proportion: 'objectively' important ones may be ignored, 'objectively' insignificant ones may be crucial. Logic and the known laws of causation are ignored: logically incompatible convictions or aspirations can coexist, causal impossibilities are ignored, distances in time and space disregarded, and so on.

8. *Cunning.* While low on logic and sense of reality and real possibility, these inner reactions are not random, but most cunningly functional, and at the service of our persistent instinctual drives, and linked to the objects which those drives selected in the trauma-governed ways indicated above. So, these activities display a curious combination of great cunning and, by waking-hours conscious standards,

equally outstanding stupidity, in their insensitivity to fact and logic.

9. *Fraud*. These attributes – cunning, camouflage and inaccessibility to consciousness, enslavement to instinctual needs, stupidity in the face of reality – apply not merely to the aspects of our personality generally considered to be a bit beastly, but also, and equally – *at least* as much – to the activities traditionally considered to be furthest removed from our beastliness: conscience, reason, pursuit of ideals, etc. These are as much at the service of the cunning and disguised agents of instinct, as are our more blatantly animal concerns; but they suffer from the added disadvantage of being more twisted, dishonest and linked to weakness and illness. They are more repulsive aesthetically, and more harmful.

10. *Pathology*. These deceitful, hidden and instinct-linked phenomena are often linked to disease, by being the cause of symptoms which traditional medicine, and in modern times common sense also, had attributed to physical, physiological causes.

It need hardly be stressed how much these ten principles are contrary to the psychological assumptions of the Bundleman.

It is part of our argument that the NM has been taken over by Freud from Nietzsche. What was it that Freud added to the NM which helped it conquer the world? The NM on its own had *not* conquered the world.

But even within the actual content of the ten principles, as formulated, there are no doubt some differences, notably in stress, between Nietzsche and Freud. For instance, Nietzsche was not particularly interested in the role of infancy in character-formation; Freud, on the other hand, was not so preoccupied with the aesthetic or political demerits of over-conscientious civilizations. (On the whole he stuck to the Public Health aspect of the matter.) In brief, minor differences in the Nietzschean and Freudian versions of the NM are not denied: but they do not matter much. What does matter a very great deal is the difference in the external use of the NM by the two men (external to the meaning of the ten principles themselves). Summing it up from Nietzsche's (but not so much Freud's) viewpoint, what those ideas all amount to is:

1. *The self-devouringness of morality.* The more demanding, self-torturing moralities spring from the very same inner force which is also responsible for our more openly this-worldly, animal desire; but they are distinguished by their inner dishonesty and tortuousness, a tendency to engender inner malaise which does not haunt their more candidly animal partners. It is not the case that a Higher Voice is speaking, only that one of the low earthly drives has turned in upon itself, or has acquired the cunning to disguise itself as its own denial, or strives to destroy its rivals from the rear. (This is one of the points where Nietzsche's consistency may be doubted: if all drives are alike, with what right do we aesthetically condemn the tortuous, dishonest ones – given that, on his own admission and to his regret, they do often succeed thanks, precisely, to their deviousness?) Is not the condemnation of dishonesty itself a survival of that self- tormenting conscience which is being damned? In the name of what value or ideal can we damn cunning and the moralistic self-torturers if they prevail? Was it not they themselves who invented the ideal of an abstract truth? So do we not damn them in the name of a pseudo-standard which they themselves deceitfully invented, and in disregard of the more terrestrial norm of success which we ought really to reinstate? Nietzsche was fully aware of this regress and of the tendency of his own ideas to devour themselves.

2. *Excellence is Parasitic on Aggression.* The humanitarian, dishonest, aggression-denying moralities do not merely commend something which does not correspond to our real psychic constitution; the way of life they recommend is incompatible with the kind of excellence which we still partly recognize and which was preached by an early, healthier, aristocratic morality. Excellence will not survive the victory of the resentful, compassionate, humanitarian pseudo-morality.

3. *Social Darwinism.* The supposedly harmonious, con-
flict-free, universalistic and humane ethic, apart from being
in conflict with our true natures and inimical to excellence,
is also incompatible with the real possibilities of life on
earth. Here Nietzsche's thought converges with the implications others have found in the work of Malthus and
Darwin. Whether realism, honesty, survival, psychic health
or excellence is our consideration – we had better have
another good look at our values.

So the humanistic and humanitarian view of man,
preached by the Enlightenment in secular terms, is incompatible with the true nature of our satisfactions, with our
real ways of choosing our beliefs, with our old standards of
excellence and with the realistic possibilities of life. Though
it had been presented as the antithesis and overcoming of
the religious view of man, it was in fact merely its perpetuation in secular terms, the perpetuation of an ethic of
resentment by other means. Under the new packaging, the
old priestly venom, the resentment and self-hatred of the
weak, the attempt to set up their weakness as the norm and
to stigmatize vigour as evil, are all lurking, more insidiously
than ever before.

One of my central arguments is that the psychoanalytic
revolution, the impact of Freudian ideas, is intimately
connected with the recognition of the *pays reel* of the mind.
But if the main characteristics of that *pays reel* were already
discerned by Nietzsche, albeit with a different political
stress, why did they need to wait for Freud to make their full
impact? (One must admit that Nietzsche included certain
ethical and political conclusions which Freud did not share
or endorse.)

This question is fundamental. Hence, a list of the differences between Nietzsche and Freud or rather, perhaps,
between their presentation of these ideas, becomes supremely important. What are they?

1. The NM is sketched out by Nietzsche in a loose,
general and unspecific way. He seems to be saying: this is
the general way in which the human mind and heart work,

and here are some historic and concrete examples – but between the rather general NM and individual cases there is no corpus of apparently precise generalizations or laws. By contrast, Freudian and psychoanalytic theory seems to be full of them.

2. Furthermore, one finds in Nietzsche's work a rather general entity, the Will to Power, whereas Freudian theory is preoccupied with sexuality. It is not entirely clear whether the Nietzschean Will to Power is simply a generic name for all striving, like Schopenhauer's Will, or whether it is a little more specific. Admittedly, Freudian sexuality also often looks like something much broader than sexuality in any normal sense. The libido seems fairly free-floating. It lusts after What it May Concern, rather than some circumscribed object. Nevertheless, there seems to be a contrast between the two thinkers at this point, and Freud does at least seem to be much more specific.

3. The sombre recognition of the *pays reel* and its bitter, harsh realities, is not in Nietzsche accompanied by any promise or genuine recipe for personal salvation. The Transvaluation of Values, which he commended, is questionably coherent, highly nebulous, sounds as if it might be arduous and perilous, and, let's not beat about the bush, is a bit above the heads of ordinary people. A highbrow classicist-philosopher is shrieking against long-term historical trends which are hardly involved in the daily concerns of most people. One knew what he was rejecting: no one has ever been sure of the exact nature of the alternative he was proposing, though some have claimed it for their own values, or attributed it to their enemies. It is for this reason that the endemic debate about whether or not he was a proto-Nazi is pointless. His proposed alternative was not coherent or determinate enough to enable one to answer this question with any finality.

By contrast, Freud does offer a position, concrete and identifiable, and a technique for attaining *individual* salvation in the face of problems only too real for ordinary people. In fact, his theory attained fame only as the accompaniment of that technique of salvation. Soteriology came before doctrine, as perhaps it should.

4. Nietzsche neither did, nor could, engender any organization to sustain his doctrine. He was simply a professor and writer, who had to rely on his published word for whatever impact he was to make. The contrast with psychoanalysis, whose ideas have a well organized guild/church to sustain them, and which has a definite role within medicine and thus is incorporated in science, is obvious.

5. Nietzsche was a professor of classics who wrote brilliantly though somewhat wildly, and went mad in his old age. The aphoristic brilliance and frequent ambiguity of his writings made him a permanent favourite with those who have a taste for literary philosophizing, but they conferred no authority whatsoever on his pronouncements. By contrast, Freud was a doctor, a psychiatrist, and thus occupied a place in that unutterably crucial, strategic area in the present intellectual life of mankind, where science, known to be true, but painfully distant and indifferent to the sufferings of individuals, meets therapy and care for the ailing, notably for the psychically ailing – in brief, where guaranteed truth meets the crying need for salvation. He also endowed the NM with a terminology which appears to link it to medicine and to science.

One might sum this up by saying that Freud added specificity where there had been only a general outline; sexuality where there had been a semi-metaphysical, semi-biological abstraction, the Will to Power; a reasonably specific recipe for personal salvation and therapy, where there had been only a most ambiguous indication of a collective transvaluation of values; an organization where there had been none; an ostensibly scientific terminology where there had been only literature; and an insertion of these ideas into the context of medicine, when they had previously lived only in the doubtfully prestigious ambience of philosophy. All these transformations, severally and jointly, were of the utmost importance.

THE BATTERING-RAM

In the end, the Will to Power is a far, far more disturbing, more corrosive idea for humanist optimism than is the domination of the human psyche by sexuality. The optimistic vision of the Enlightenment – whether in its liberal, Marxist or any other form – which envisages a social order without oppression or dogmatism, egalitarian, cooperative and consensual, is deeply threatened, if it turns out to be true that *domination*, the imposition of our will on others, is the only thing which truly turns us on, and that all else is but façade and self-deception. If this be the ultimate truth about us, well then the sad prospect for humanity is either the perennial frustration of our deepest needs, or a social order in which some may fulfil themselves – but only at the cost of the oppression and humiliation of others. It is for this reason that Nietzsche is a profoundly disturbing thinker, a corrosive acid poured over the various forms of humanist optimism.

By contrast, the thesis of the dominance of sexuality in our psyches is, at any rate by now, far less worrying. If, throughout our youth and until the sad decline of later middle age, we are unutterably randy, and really think of nothing else, whatever we may pretend to ourselves on the surface – what of it? Society and the optimistic vision of mankind, in an age of contraception and effective medicine, can as far as I can see accommodate themselves to any amount of randiness on the part of its members, at any rate once we get used to the idea (a state of affairs which seems to be well on the way). If in truth we are all sex-mad apes, this may sadden those who hope that some pure and abstract values mean most to us: but people who cling to that belief must by now be in a minority. The naturalized idea of mankind has, on the whole, taken over.

So, from an objective viewpoint, or from the viewpoint of the current climate of opinion in 'developed' countries, sexuality and the acceptance of its vigour and its early arrival on the scene, present no terrible, unmanageable threat to our ideological peace of mind. But it is as well to

27

remind ourselves that this was not always so, and that at the time of the emergence of psychoanalysis, its stress on the importance and pervasiveness of sexuality was felt to be its most notorious and scandalous doctrine.

There are various obvious reasons why sexual puritanism should have been rampant in nineteenth-century Western Europe. The early stage of industrialism throws up an appallingly impoverished and uprooted urban proletariat, whose precarious condition inevitably drives a large proportion of its womenfolk into prostitution. *The Communist Manifesto* was very explicit: 'Our bourgeois, not content with having the wives and daughters of their proletarians at their disposal, not to speak of common prostitutes . . .'

The consequence of this situation, of a kind of enormous economic/moral sump at the bottom of society, of a constant threat to all as a consequence of the ever-present possibility of destitution, is that the large sections of society immediately above the sump, signal their 'respectability' in the only way available to them. When brothels are as numerous as they were in Victorian London, girls are unlikely to wish to signal their liberation from sexual taboos: that was to come only much later. Another obvious factor making for prudery was of course that the sections of the population who did well out of the new industrial order, and who set its tone, were, for reasons well explored by sociology, recruited disproportionately from groups already given to puritanism, and they were unlikely to abandon very quickly the values which had helped them rise in the world.

These reasons, and perhaps others, were the historically specific factors which helped to make the world into which psychoanalysis burst somewhat touchy about sexuality. But, even if (in my view) it is not particularly disturbing for developed society in the long run, sexuality nevertheless does constitute a problem for most, and perhaps for all societies. There is probably no aspect of life where the *pays reel* of the mind and the *pays legal* are so endemically at variance. There can hardly be any point where their divergence is so forcefully brought home to the individual mind.

The sexual stirrings of a person are unpredictable and

erratic. They are no respectors of the system of personal relations sanctioned in a given community, or indeed of its customs and proprieties, or of its practical needs. This is almost as true in an 'enlightened', liberal, permissive society as it is in a repressive and puritanical one. Even in the most liberal and promiscuous commune, it simply is not feasible to practise the sexual equivalent of demand feeding. Whatever may be possible in the course of occasional orgies, it would totally disrupt daily life, its activities and relations. Sexual activity also involves the use of bodily parts which in the Western (and most other) traditions normally remain hidden, held to be unclean, and are physiologically connected with excretion.

> But Love has pitched his mansion in
> The place of excrement
>
> W. B. Yeats, 'Crazy Jane Talks with the Bishop'

It is true that William Blake, an eccentric and mystical spirit, found genitals beautiful: 'The head Sublime, the heart Pathos, the genitals Beauty, the hands and feet Proportion.' (*Proverbs of Hell*)

There is little point here in entering on a discussion of aesthetics, but it is obvious that, if allowed to be beautiful, the aesthetic considerations which make genitals so are highly discontinuous from those which otherwise operate in assessing human physical beauty. Generally speaking, parts of the human body are considered beautiful if round, firm, smooth, dry, unsmelly and clean. Wrinkles are normally associated with age. Bodily smells are not usually deemed attractive and the repulsion they inspire attaches by association to any part liable to produce them. Primary sexual organs have a number of features which, in any other context, would be deemed anything but attractive. Moreover, the entire early education of children in most Western traditions predisposes them against an overt or avowed preoccupation with these parts.

Hence, the fact that, in sexual activity, they suddenly acquire an enormous affective charge, signals in the most dramatic way imaginable the discontinuity between sex and the rest of life – a discontinuity which inevitably persists in some measure even in a permissive society, but which had been very much accentuated during the period when Freud made his impact. Anthropologists have noted how the shock of the inversion of normal conventions is used as a kind of social punctuation, as a means of highlighting a *special* occasion. As a distinguished anthropologist observed: 'Why should it seem natural to wear top hats at funerals, and false noses on birthdays and New Year's eve?'[7]

Leach's answer is that both heightened and inverted or abandoned formality of dress and/or role, mark out special occasions and endow otherwise shapeless time with its structure. Sex is a role-reversal given us by nature. It brings its own discontinuity and intensity which fortify, and sometimes subvert, the relations sanctioned by society. It seems as if nature, through sexuality, had made humanity a present of a kind of proto-ritual, ready to be turned into a ritual proper by culture. It is tempting to speculate about the origins of ritual in pre-social patterns of courtship and mating.

The next step is now ready: even though, in the long run, the addiction of the human heart to violence or domination (if it obtains) is far more disturbing than our sexuality, nevertheless, for reasons pertaining both to the permanent condition of complex society, and to the special accentuation of puritanism in the nineteenth century, sexuality was the ideal battering-ram for bringing home, in the guise of a great new discovery, the disparity between the *pays reel* and the *pays legal* of the mind. In the nineteenth century, the age of belief in progress and the perfectibility of man and the human condition, that disparity was specially acute; and at the same time, sexual puritanism, the collective conspiracy making for a kind of social invisibility of sex, remained very strong or even grew stronger. Before 1914, the bourgeoisie of Europe might well worry about sex. What else was there to worry about? So it was no accident that it was used to hammer home an awareness of the dark side of man.

II

THE PLAGUE

GIVE US THIS DAY

The coming of affluent industrial society has totally transformed the human condition. In all other ages, men had cause to fear hunger: 'give us this day our daily bread' was no empty or trivial request. It has now become such. To an astonishing degree, fear of famine or even of premature death no longer haunts the developed world. People do of course perish in accidents, and some die of disease: but these things are apparently known always to happen to *other* people. People do not positively anticipate such tragedies for themselves, and do not live their lives in dread on that account.

There is of course the incalculable threat of a nuclear holocaust for us all: but like the existence of God, this seems a unique and *sui generis* supposition, and consequently the allocation of numerical probabilities to it, or a personal anticipation of it, has an unreal and unconvincing feel. Whether justified or not, man in the rather extensive secure strata of developed societies goes about his business with a reasonable confidence in living out his full span, of being sustained by the productive potential of his society, and of being protected by its medical science.

It was not always so. Writing about belief in magic in sixteenth- and seventeenth-century England, Keith Thomas says:

. . . one of [the] central features [of these beliefs] was a preoccupation with the explanation and relief of human misfortune. There can be no doubt that this concern reflected the hazards of an intensely insecure environment . . . Of these the first was the expectation of life . . . it is beyond dispute that Tudor and Stuart Englishmen

31

were, by our standards, exceedingly liable to pain, sickness, premature death. Even among the nobility, whose chances are likely to have been better than those of other classes, the life expectation at birth of boys born in the third quarter of the seventeenth century was 29.6 years. Today it would be around 70. . . . The food supply was always precarious and throughout the period the fate of the annual harvest remained crucial . . . Rich and poor alike were victims of the infections . . . Epidemics accounted for thirty per cent of reported deaths in seventeenth-century London.[1]

This type of situation had its consequences in the sphere of belief: David Hume summed them up well:

In proportion as any man's course of life is governed by accident, we always find, that he increases in superstition; as may particularly be observed of gamesters and sailors, who, though, of all mankind, the least capable of serious reflection, abound most in frivolous and superstitious apprehensions . . . All human life, especially before the institution of order and good government, being subject to fortuitous accidents; it is natural, that superstition should prevail every where in barbarous ages, and put men on the most earnest enquiry concerning those invisible powers, who dispose of their happiness or misery.[2]

Hume already noticed that the institution of good government and order significantly diminished the extent to which human life is subject to 'fortuitous accidents'. David Hume and Adam Smith both saw the nexus between the new growth of wealth and good government. Today, in developed liberal countries, we do in the main have such government, but we also enjoy a degree of affluence unimaginable in the eighteenth century, and effective and relatively accessible medical services. The material aspect of individual life has become immeasurably less precarious than it has ever been in the past.

The relative sense of security (whether or not it will eventually prove to be illusory) which the citizen of modern affluent society enjoys, is no doubt a major factor in the diminution of his religious ardour. Sure of his daily bread, and of a good deal else besides, he will not, as 'the vulgar' did in Hume's day, '. . . tell you of the sudden and unexpected death of such a one: The fall and the bruise of such another: The excessive drought of this season: The cold and rains of another.'[3]

Such things seem to have lost their terror, and hence their capacity to inspire faith. Drought does not interest contemporary man. Rain only disturbs his holiday. Sudden death is something that happens to others and that one reads about in the papers. Does that mean that modern man is free of fear?

He is not. Perhaps every liberation only brings a new servitude. Terror has not vanished from the earth, but has merely assumed a new form. Modern life in affluent societies, though accompanied by a sense of secure material well-being, is notoriously riddled with other anxieties – anxieties which were not wholly absent in the past, but which those who lived in physically less comfortable ages could not afford to place at the very centre of their attention. These new anxieties now force themselves on us, and not merely because we have been freed from our earlier fears. They have also become more pressing for good objective reasons.

Modern society is or tends to be mobile, fluid, egalitarian and liberal, incomparably more so than most large and complex societies in the past. The price of this liberation from forcibly and/or ideologically ascribed identities, statuses, rituals, practices, employments and family links, is, notoriously, a sense of disorientation and insecurity, for which a variety of thinkers has coined a wide range of terms: *alienation, disenchantment,* and *anomie* are perhaps the most celebrated. The disorientation contains, among other things, at least three important elements: first, the material environment has been largely replaced by a social environment, consisting not of things but of people; second, this crucial social or human environment has no stable or reliable structure, and everything in it is uncertain and up for grabs; and third, there is no widely shared and seriously accepted ideology or vision, which could decree how things should properly be arranged.

Man now lives in a local community which is optional, and the same holds true of the school which trains him, the work institutions which pay him, and of any association, formal or informal, which he cares to join. It is *people* who constitute his environment, and make or unmake his life, but exactly *which* people, and how they are to comport themselves and how he should view and treat them, is not prescribed, and often not greatly regulated. Consequence: though he is no longer at the mercy of natural forces and accidents (or at any rate, he feels that he no longer is), he is, more perhaps than he ever was before, at the mercy of people.

This servitude or precariousness is particularly marked for what might be called the paradigmatic citizen of a developed affluent society, who is in clerical, bureaucratic or professional employment, and whose home life is spent in the bosom of a nuclear family. Though no longer at the mercy of the forces of nature, this *homme moyen sensuel* is not particularly rich or powerful. His fulfilment and contentment, and his self-respect, are at the mercy of other people: of his spouse, other close kin, and work colleagues and superiors. And when it comes to their comportment, he may well feel some equivalent of Hume's 'vulgar' sentiment, a pervasive and compelling sense of precariousness, of a crucial pattern which is indeed there, but cannot be comprehended and controlled by purely rational means, but which one may only hope and endeavour to appease.

Our environment is now made up basically of relationships with others.

Hell is other people. (Jean-Paul Sartre)

Once upon a time, nature too made its contribution to our hell, but it is now redundant: you can't stop progress. We are now alone with each other. People, unaided by nature, suffice to make a hell.

There may be some among us who are so well placed, or so brilliant, so indispensable, or on the contrary so self-sufficient, that the attitudes of other people hold no terrors for them. But such persons must be rare. Most of us are, inevitably, mediocre. Our success or failure, our acceptance or rejection, are not predetermined by the certainty of brilliant or of deplorable performance. In the nature of things, the performance is, in the overwhelming majority of cases, middling. This being so, everything depends on the people who make up our home and social and work environments. It depends, as the phrase goes, on how we get on with them.

There is every indication that this realm of human relationships has taken over that overwhelming load of anxiety and sense of precariousness which had once attached to the natural world. This realm now has a peculiar quality which once characterized the natural world (but apparently does so no longer): a sense of *tight pattern*, of lurking danger and fatality, which at the same time cannot be apprehended or controlled by rational and intelligible methods. The realm of nature had once been endowed with this compelling feel, for most or all of our ancestors in the agrarian age; but nature has been tamed, and we now really see that it is subject to intelligible and impersonal laws, whether or not each of us individually knows just what they are and how they are to be applied.

By contrast, the realm of personal relations, which has now become the area of our most pressing concern, the sphere in which we stand to lose and fear most, does have *just* this particular feel about it: it seems anything but random, and the pattern of experiences which befall various people generally has an air of some kind of hidden and ineluctable logic about it – yet at the same time, attempts to seize, capture and utilize this logic for our ends, are totally unavailing. The popular psychology self-help magazines and manuals, which do a good trade by promising to fill this gap and to allay these anxieties, do not contain any genuine knowledge or information not already available to common sense; and the generalizations offered, by them or common sense or academic psychology, are riddled with evasion, exceptions, ambiguity, and have little real value. Yet a vacuum must be filled. People find it impossible to remain passive in the face of acute and recurrent anxiety. What is to be done?

ORIGINAL SIN

Before a cluster of ideas can rapidly take control of people, there must perhaps be a plague upon the land. Everyone, or at least very many people, must have good cause to be afraid. Secure and justifiably complacent populations will not spontaneously turn to ardent faith. But fear of God, or more simply, *fear*, will concentrate the mind wonderfully, and incline it to give assent to some doctrine or practice which offers hope of relief.

The human condition is sad, and the Plague often descends upon the land, though the form it takes varies a good deal. In the agrarian phase of human history, the joint threat of famine, disease, spoliation and oppression was generally sufficient to ensure that most people had good cause to be afraid. Ingenious religious devices were available which made doubly sure that no one remained complacent. The fact of death, which awaits us all, is much invoked by clerics fearful lest there be too much cheerfulness among men: both our eventual extinction, and our alleged non-extinction, can be invoked to spread fear and trembling. Nietzsche noted that Pascal had tried to see to it that no one should escape despair. The splendid doctrine of Original Sin ensures that no one may shelter behind a consciousness of virtue. It is a spiritual equivalent of universal peasant indebtedness. Such universal and *starting-point* moral indebtedness makes certain that no one can even begin life with a clear ledger. Everyone then has ever-renewable and self-perpetuating debts to pay right from the very start, and must work arduously to pay them off, if he is to be granted even the hope of salvation. The Unconscious is a new version of Original Sin.

The plagues which have haunted the past of mankind have now abated, at any rate temporarily. Nature is tamed, and though there is some little dispute among theologians about the death of God, there is virtually none whatever about the dismantling of Hell. But a new plague is upon us. Hell is other people. Optional human relations in fluid sub-communities have become – at any rate for members of the white-collar classes and upward in affluent liberal societies – the very centre of life, the area where happiness or misery is decided; and they are menacing, incomprehensible and uncontrollable. To face them without support or solace is unthinkable. Yet where can one turn?

PASTORAL CARE

It is obvious that any solace and support must consist of pastoral care.

But sheer availability is not enough. Pastoral care, to be effective, even temporarily, must inspire confidence. Above all, the practices and promises of the person offering relief, aid and care must make sense in terms of the widely accepted background beliefs of the age.

A person in our time who finds himself in an intolerably stressful situation can theoretically turn for help to at least three different kinds of specialist:

1. He can turn to the surviving clerics of pre-industrial, pre-scientific belief systems, who normally count pastoral care among their duties. Unfortunately, the background doctrine with which these clerics are associated enjoys so little genuine intellectual respect in the wider society that a person in distress, who is not interested in straws but hopes for some solid support, is unlikely to turn that way. Characteristically, these clerics can perform their pastoral duties only if they also train so as to perform them in quite a different idiom, notably that of psychotherapy itself.

2. He can turn to the seriously respected knowledge of his society, i.e. natural science, and its applied branches. The abstract, individual-disregarding, conjectural, etc., nature of science, makes it quite outstandingly unsuitable as a solace for a person in acute and immediate distress. The anaemic quality of the psychological doctrines inspired by the empiricist theory of knowledge, greatly reinforces all this.

3. He can turn to one of the modern, secular religions which are articulated in an idiom which is not immediately

and manifestly archaic and absurd, and which at the same time, unlike 'science', are (as their propagandists so insistently urge) *relevant* – i.e. they have a fleshy, non-anaemic doctrine of man and of his destination and salvation. The best known, and by far the most popular, of these secular faiths is of course Marxism, and it will serve as an example for them all.

Though very highly 'relevant' (i.e. blessed with an elaborate and central soteriology, and an ethic and a willingness to offer authoritative guidance on life's problems), Marxism is curiously ill-equipped to offer any kind of pastoral care or solace for individual anguish. (It is not easy, for instance, to give any Marxist content to life-stage rituals in the Soviet Union, though of course such rituals remain indispensable.) Perhaps this is so in the nature of the case: it may be of the essence of Marxist eschatology that it is inescapably collective. Until our liberation and the termination of pre-history, our sorrows cannot really be alleviated; and after our liberation, they will no longer – what? – grieve us? It can hardly be suggested that they will no longer occur, that death or broken hearts will be abolished under communism. Anyway, whether inherent in the overall position or merely accidental, Marxism lacks much potential, doctrinal or organizational, for pastoral care.

But how would it be if a system were available which shared in the overwhelming prestige of the currently most respected form of science, and which at the same time not merely contained the potential for individual pastoral care, but actually emerged from, and was very much centred on clinical/pastoral care? And if such a system were also a recognized part of medicine, which in turn is a generally accepted part of applied science, what then? Such a system would not suffer from any of the quite crippling disabilities which evidently adhere to the other potential sources of pastoral care in our society.

THE CLICK

The general precondition of a compelling, aura-endowed belief system is that, at some one point at least, it should carry overwhelming, dramatic conviction. In other words, it is not enough that there should be a plague in the land, that many should be in acute distress and in fear and trembling, and that some practitioners be available who offer cure and solace, linked plausibly to the background beliefs of the society in question. All that may be necessary, but it is not sufficient. Over and above the need, and over and above mere background plausibility (minimal conceptual eligibility), there must also be something that *clicks*, something which throws light on a pervasive and insistent and disturbing experience, something which at long last gives it a local habitation and a name, which turns a sense of malaise into an insight: something which recognizes and places an experience or awareness, and which other belief systems seem to have passed by.

This condition is very conspicuously satisfied by the belief system which concerns us. It is endowed with an excellent and suggestive idiom for that disturbing, menacing, anxiety-engendering *pays reel* of the mind, which the old traditional image of man had perhaps recognized but treated without sympathy and severely reprobated, and which the new secular naturalist and empiricist vision had tolerated, but neither recognized nor understood.

So the powerful click, the overt recognition-at-long-last, the conceptual orchestration of something everyone knew and almost no one knew how to speak about, was achieved by psychoanalysis, using the scandal, the Offence (to use Kierkegaard's crucial term for this aspect of a belief system) of Universal Sexuality as its battering-ram; the location of psychoanalysis within the edifice of science (being part of the medicine wing) ensured its cognitive legitimation; and its deep clinical involvement was the means of turning it into a pastoral technique and a soteriology, and thus making it humanly, and not just cognitively, relevant. All these tremendous advantages had been totally denied to the

39

philosophers who had also noted the discrepancy between the *pays reel* of the mind and the *pays legal*: poor dears, all they could do was write books about it. Philosophers have only tried to understand the world; the point is to endow one's understanding with a ritual and a promise of salvation.

THE WAGER

A compelling, charismatic belief system must also possess something over and above promising succour in a plague, possessing links to the background convictions of the age, and stunning the potential proselyte with what he more than half knew, but never knew how to put into words. There is a further condition.

The belief must engender a *tension* in the neophyte or potential convert. It must tease and worry him, and not leave him alone. It must be able to worry and tease him with both its promise *and* its threat, and be able to invoke his inner anxiety as evidence of its own authenticity. Thou wouldst not seek Me, if thou hadst not already found Me in thy heart!

Though belief systems need to be anchored in the background assumptions, in the pervasive obviousness of an intellectual climate, yet they cannot consist entirely of obvious, uncontentious elements. There are many ideas which are plainly true, or which appear to be such to those who have soaked up a given intellectual atmosphere: but their very cogency, obviousness, acceptability, makes them ineligible for serving as the distinguishing mark of membership of a charismatic community of believers. Demonstrable or obvious truths do not distinguish the believer from the infidel, and they do not excite the faithful. Only difficult belief can do that. And what makes a belief difficult?

There must be an element both of menace and of risk. The belief must present itself in such a way that the person encountering, weighing the claim that is being made on him, can neither ignore it nor hedge his bets. His situation is such that, encountering the claim, he cannot but make a decision, and it will be a weighty one, whichever way he decides. He is obliged, by the very nature of the claim, to commit himself, one way or the other. Advanced (though perhaps not traditional) religions often present themselves in this manner.

Consider a political prisoner incarcerated with doubtful prospects of fair trial or eventual liberation or even survival. He is approached by a fellow-prisoner who claims to be a member of a powerful underground organization which can help them both to escape. It may be true; but, equally, the man may be an *agent provocateur*, under instructions to help create a situation in which the first prisoner can be shot while trying to escape. In the very nature of the situation, the prisoner cannot investigate and test the fellow-prisoner's claim prior to taking the desperate chance. And there is no strategy corresponding to the rational supposition that it is about 50:50 whether the fellow-prisoner is genuine or a stool-pigeon. The only courses of action available are either continued passivity, or participation in the attempt to escape.

This too is part of what Kierkegaard meant by Offence: he considered it inherent in Christianity. But the point can be generalized. It is very commonly, perhaps always, found in the kind of belief system that has a powerful hold over people. Uncontentious beliefs, however plausible, demonstrable or certain, have no such power. The point is admirably expressed in Nigel Balchin's *Mine Own Executioner*:[1]3

I feel about this stuff . . . rather as I do about religion. If it is of any importance at all, it must be far more important than anything else. If people really believe what they say they believe about God, I don't see how they can waste their time on anything else. In the same way, if one really believes that the methods of abnormal psychology can solve people's psychological problems, I don't see that there is any alternative but to devote one's life to solving them.[4]

In fact, with age, *logically* powerful wager-engendering faiths often lose their potency. But this has not happened to a very great extent to psychoanalysis. Its techniques (expense in time and money) help to postpone routinization.

How is this fatal wager-engendering power initially acquired?

1. The doctrine to be embraced must contain the promise of a salvation that is ardently desired.

2. There must be some good reasons for believing its claims.

3. There must also be some good reasons for doubting it, or for fearing its truth.

4. The middle ground between acceptance and rejection, a mixed strategy which covers itself against both alternatives, must be denied to the person facing the issue.

5. A quick and conclusive test of whether or not the wager-engendering supposition is or is not true, must simply be unavailable. This can be achieved in a variety of ways. As Kierkegaard bluntly made plain, Christianity ensures this by making its terrifying and attractive claims trans-empirical and untestable. In the case of our hypothetical prisoner, any sustained inquiry on his part would automatically destroy his chances of escape.

Frequently and characteristically, the carriers of the wager-engendering belief system demand assent with menaces: dire consequences will follow if the belief is not adopted. (The person facing the dilemma knows of course that dire consequences may indeed also follow if he *does* embrace the proffered doctrine.) And if it be false, though to express this supposition is blasphemous in the presence of those who press him to accept the belief, acceptance also carries a risk, albeit sometimes a lesser one. Acceptance is demanded by means of a confident, uncompromising, so to speak non-negotiating, non-negotiable assertion. The gipsy at the fair offers to tell your fortune, and does so, but will not discuss her sources or methods. Any anxious appeals that they be disclosed will be dismissed with calm contempt: she *knows* and you doubt her at your peril.

Sheer confident assertion, in a plague-menaced world in

which no one of any sense has any grounds to be confident of either certainty or doubt, makes a certain impact.

> The best lack all conviction, while the worst
> Are full of passionate intensity.

W. B. Yeats, 'The Second Coming'

Provocative, calm, arrogantly disdainful certainty, does possess, if not authority – and it often does claim to have that – at the very least a certain disturbing quality. Those who are openly haunted by doubt cannot but doubt their own doubt as well, and wonder whether the enviable certitude of others may not have some powerful and valid secret foundation. The fact that the confidence is devoid of visible means of support hardly seems to diminish its authority. In fact, were its means of support visible, they could be subject to evaluation; and the assertion would have given hostages to fortune, and also conceded its own ordinary, human status – making its own contentions arguable, negotiable, imitable, publicly available rather than tied to a single source. But bare, brazen, unnegotiated assertion, if skilfully presented, can have a kind of stark authority. That is how the gipsy makes her pronouncements.

But what if the authority and the silence, the refusal to negotiate (or support, substantiate) the claims are further supported by a background theory for other reasons also not susceptible to doubt, and which positively demands, validates such a stance? – and which as it were makes an honest woman of the gipsy? If the theory may not be discussed in the course of receiving succour, but may be discussed only *after* its successful implementation had validated it? If the theory possesses both a powerful element of plausibility, *and* an in-built exclusion of doubt about itself, an exclusion which neatly follows from some of its own central, most cherished and plausible premises?

THE PIRANDELLO EFFECT

FREE-FALL

Psychoanalysis is not only, perhaps not even primarily, a *doctrine*. It is also an institution, a technique, an organization, an ethic, a theory of knowledge, an idiom and a climate of opinion. Implicitly it contains theories of politics, history and aesthetics. The Founder himself had worked out his (or *a*) theory of religion. Some of these aspects may be more important than the doctrine; and it is certain that some of them are *as* important.

Let us summarize very briefly, in general outline, the course of a psychoanalytic treatment. A would-be patient approaches an analyst, or is referred to him by a doctor. His inwardly and outwardly avowed motives may be various. He may be suffering from an ailment which, it is suspected, has a psychosomatic component. He may be suffering from no relevant physical ailment, but feel unhappy about aspects of his personal or professional life, and be persistently unsuccessful in his dealings with colleagues or family, and hope that these may be helped by a course of analysis. Or he may hope that analysis will help him in his professional work – notably if he is a doctor or social worker or social scientist. He may even live in a social milieu within which psychoanalysis has virtually become the norm. He may feel that he needs it to cope with the strains of his life. Any combination of these or similar motives may lead him to enter analysis: or rather, any combination of these or similar motives may be invoked, with or without sincerity, with or without conviction or doubt, as he is about to enter on this course of action.

Now take a last look at our patient as he is, so to speak, in the outer or public, ordinary world. He has an ailment or problem, specific or diffuse, acute or tolerable; he knows that a theory, technique and agency exist, which claim that they may be able to help him. There is a certain cost, in time, money and commitment; and there is a certain risk, for what in this world is not fallible? So, in the light of his assessment of the risk, the intensity of the need, and the means at his disposal and their value for him, he decides whether or not to enter on this course of action. (Or so he says, but all he says will in due course be treated as suspect, as inconclusive, as susceptible to interpretation and for inversion.)

In other words, he still acts in accordance with the established conventions of the outer world: or rather, his conduct can still be interpreted by those conventions. Those conventions asume that theories are fallible, and techniques based on these theories are likewise fallible (either because the theory is false, or because the application may be faulty); and a therapy is therefore a risk, in which cost, probability of success, and need of cure are weighted against each other, as rationally as possible in the light of available evidence. (But another set of conventions for interpreting his subjective intentions and ideas is available, and the therapy consists of submitting at least *pro tem* to those other conventions; and someone other than himself will be authorized to decide which conventions are to apply. Someone else will control this switch.)

The description of his conduct in the preceding paragraph (outside parentheses) is carefully formulated in what might be called public, neutral, unprejudicial language; or rather, it is unprejudicial, open-minded about the claims of the doctrine and technique in question. On the other hand – and this is going to be of supreme importance – the description in question still assumes that he is reasonably well informed about his own motives, needs and priorities. It gives him the benefit of the doubt, and assumes, as indeed in daily life we normally do, that he knows more or less what he is up to, and is not wholly devoid of self-knowledge.

The description, or something very much like it, would

apply equally if he were contemplating taking the waters, undergoing a physical operation or enrolling himself for a course of instruction. The entire conduct can be characterized in terms developed by economists or 'praxeologists': an aim is pursued, at a certain cost, on a given assessment of the efficacy of certain means, and of the veridicity of the theories in the light of which those means are to be selected and deployed. As in other social situations, a certain perfectly reasonable amount of argument from authority, trust and reputation enters into it all: the patient cannot possibly check for himself all the background information which has gone into the selection and elaboration of the means, of the technique, which is about to be employed; any more than an ordinary medical patient can conceivably retest the entire corpus of medical knowledge every time he visits his GP with a pain in his stomach.

He places some (though of course not absolute) trust in the consideration that the doctor has been examined, and is implicitly supervised, by a reputable professional guild, whose leading lights in turn have the respect of the leading scientists of the society and age in question. So, in accepting the recommended cure for stomach-ache, without personally setting out to do research on it, he is in some measure relying on the entire stratified hierarchy of cognitive authority in his own society (though he does not formulate it to himself in these terms). He assumes that the training and guild supervision of medical practitioners is such that, all in all, what they recommend for stomach-ache is more likely to do good than not, and moreover is more likely to do him good than any alternative remedy and, finally, is very unlikely to do him positive harm. Reassured by the tacit operation of all these background assumptions (which I for one piously hope are valid), he eagerly swallows the stomach-ache pills.

So far, and seen from the outside, in neutral language which for the time being they both employ, the patient waiting in the analyst's ante-room is no different from the humble stomach-ache sufferer. He too is simply trying out something, for a given end, at an anticipated cost, in the light of background belief, including an unspecific and less than total faith in the all-in-all efficiency and integrity of the entire cognitive apparatus of his society. He is not or not yet choosing a vision which, if true, devalues all rival visions: nor opting for one which is so constructed as to be incommensurate with all the others, so that a choice between it and them can only be a *leap*, and never a reasoned argument.

But now the situation changes. Our stomach-ache sufferer knew he came because he wanted to be rid of the pain in his tum, and whatever happens – whether the pills cure him brilliantly or fail miserably – he is really rather unlikely to say later that the stomach-ache was really irrelevant, a pretext, that what had impelled him to seek medical aid had been some far deeper need, which had masqueraded as stomach-ache, or had simply used the stomach-ache as a code-word for something far more deeply interfused with all the hidden layers of his self. Most stomach-ache sufferers stubbornly stick to their story for years to come, if they recollect the episode at all. They persist in the conviction that their subjective state of mind as they experienced it when they went to see their doctor – they had a pain in the stomach, *and* wished to be rid of it – was entirely veridical. Worse still, they don't think anything else was greatly relevant to their visit to the doctor.

Not so our analytic patient – for this is where the differences begin. The objective language – the opportunity–cost assessment, and all that goes with it – he leaves in the ante-room with his coat, hat and umbrella, not necessarily at the first visit, but not too long after. That he should do so is recognized as an integral part of the treatment. As he goes 'into analysis', he enters a different world. Its basic, crucial features have already been highlighted in connection with the doctrine, but they deserve brief recapitulation. The basic assumption of analysis is that virtually everything that is really decisive in his life and psyche takes place in the Unconscious; that he has no immediate access to it at all; and that his hope of gaining some access to it in due course depends on the analysis, and

47

its successful pursuit – and this cannot be a quick and brief process.

The motives he had invoked consciously for coming at all are out in the waiting-room, with his hat and coat. They are suspended, in a state of complete *sursis*; that is of the very essence of analysis. What he has also left behind in the ante-room is that tentative, experimental, cost–benefit evaluating attitude: the only reality that really matters is within himself, and knowing it, knowing himself, is a good which is totally incommensurate with all others; in fact, it is a precondition of truly enjoying any other good. It is far beyond all calculation of opportunity–cost: rather, its accomplishment is the absolute precondition of all other rational calculations. He is in the presence of liberation from a merely superficial dream. When he had been assessing his own motives and evaluation of treatment prior to its commencement, he had still been at the mercy of his own, powerful and very cunning, Unconscious.

One can perhaps best describe all this as a kind of 'free-fall' condition. All foundations have been removed from underneath the analysand's feet, *by the very terms of reference of the therapy which he has freely consented to undergo*. The terms of reference of that therapy are – the unmasking of all the deceptions which the all-cunning, nearly all-powerful Unconscious has imposed on him. But that Unconscious knows no bounds, it has also not respected the framework within which the therapy is taking place. The concept of the Unconscious is a means of devaluing all previous certainties, above all his assessment of himself. It is not so much a hypothesis as a suspension of all other hypotheses. The more secure they seemed, the more suspect they are. All moral guide-rails are thus removed or made loose. The suspension of intuitive logical certainties (of what would normally be called reason) is obtained in virtue of an idea which is in no way religious, but on the contrary utterly, indeed paradigmatically naturalistic: the Unconscious.

The Unconscious may lurk – it almost certainly does lurk – *precisely* there, in his own views of the motives, symptoms, expectations which have brought the patient to the therapist, in his anticipated criteria of cure, in his aspiration for a post-therapeutic condition. Just these things must be explored, 'worked through', suspended, treated with suspicion, probably revalued, perhaps wholly inverted. Does he think the therapy is no good? Is he failing to get good value out of the analysis? Does he find the proffered interpretations far-fetched? Why, just that must be worked through . . .

The obligation to 'work through' his own reactions and his attitude to the analyst, supports the persistent impression that psychoanalysis is largely *about itself*, that, in Karl Kraus's celebrated words, it is itself the illness which it claims to cure. The analysand 'works through' his attitude to analyst and analysis.

Everything must be worked through, including (above all) those initial framework terms of reference of the analysis itself, which he had left behind with coat and umbrella, in terms of which he had initially discussed the feasibility or desirability of analysis. This universal *sursis* is made necessary by the fact that after all the Unconscious itself *ex hypothesi* respects no boundaries, and hence it must be legitimate to pursue it into any lair. There simply is no external court of appeal, no check, by means of which the patient could steady himself . . . If indeed we are in thrall to a powerful and devious Unconscious (most plausible), and if *this* is the only way out (well, it seemed worth trying), there is now no longer any way of challenging the authority of the therapist and his doctrine. The consequence, however, is that the patient is and must be deprived, if he is cooperating with the therapy, of retaining some stance from which he could attempt a critical evaluation of it. The internal terms of reference preclude it; the external ones are superficial and devalued by the very concept of the Unconscious. If he does not cooperate, plainly he can't blame the therapy for failing to work; but if he does cooperate it is even plainer, for it is built into its theory and practice, that he can't blame the therapy either. Criticism at this level of mere consciousness proves and establishes nothing. No bona fide can be invoked, for no one can know himself to be in good faith. That much is entailed by the very concept of the Unconscious. The concept of the Unconscious exorcises all bona fide.

INSIDE AND OUT

The above account of the metamorphosis of the analytic patient is only a first approximation. It isn't really quite as simple as that. When he was still in the ante-room, not yet separated from hat and coat, or from his instrumental, cost–benefit, calculating tentative ordinary spirit, he was nevertheless *already* distinguishable from the stomach-ache martyr in the GP's waiting-room. For one thing, the worries which brought him there were almost certainly less specific, more diffuse, more deep and disturbing. For another, he knew enough about psychoanalysis to know that he was not coming for some pills or their equivalent. And, on the other hand, when he crossed the threshold into the consulting-room proper, he did not really and totally leave the cost–benefit-addicted pragmatic gentleman behind. This gentleman will often continue to haunt him with his doubts.

The coexistence, conscious or latent, of the two persons, the insider within an absolutely defined situation, and the outsider for whom all is conjectural, is an essential part of the situation. It contributes to the tension which is part of the motive force of it all. I believe that this particular kind of dualism is characteristic of many ideologies: they are bilingual, they simultaneously operate within a language in which they alone absolutely define the facts and norms, and another more public and neutral language within which they adopt a more modest stance and can be called to account.

But note – and this is supremely important – there is no *logical* path from the one vision to the other, and from the gentleman in the ante-room to the one in the consulting-room. They inhabit one body, and in a legal sense they are one person, but . . . as the phrase goes, their visions are incommensurate. Only a qualitative leap can lead from one to the other. They inhabit discontinuous worlds.

If indeed everything of importance is decided in a realm called the Unconscious, and if indeed there is but one way only of gaining access to and influence within it – well then, pursuing that one way clearly takes priority over everything else. Everything can and must wait till this is done. The other gent, who says that all this is questionable, like everything else, and in any case must be weighed against other priorities – *is he not, by the very nature of the situation, the manipulated dupe of that Unconscious which is 'resisting'?* Don't listen to him: he is frightened of the things he fears he will find out as the analysis proceeds and really gets somewhere . . . From *his* viewpoint, in turn, all this is credulity: but from the inside, the scepticism is but the voice of our *agent provocateur*, planted by the enemy inside. Psychic and emotional reality is in one place; legal and financial reality is in another. Under one law born, to another bound . . .

All one can say neutrally is that two utterly complete and incommensurate circles of ideas face each other, and compel the unfortunate, legally single person, haunted by the two souls within his breast, to make a wager one way or the other. Whichever way he bets, he can explain away the alternative option as a snare and a delusion. Just this confrontation of two complete orders of ideas logically *forces* a wager on him. This also, as already indicated, is an important general trait of powerful ideologies: they are so constructed that the potential believer is compelled to 'leap', to bet one way or the other. Tentative occupancy of a middle ground, bet-hedging area, is precluded by the very way it is all set up. Propositions which permit the occupancy of a middle ground, are not the stuff of which charismatic ideologies are made.

The fact that, from the inside vision, the circle is complete, is of course very important. But it is not a sufficient explanation of the phenomenon which concerns us. Some other conditions must be invoked to explain that. There are in fact two such additional factors.

First, there is the fact, already mentioned, that the circle is not merely self-maintaining, but that some of the elements in it have quite independently a very powerful appeal. In some sense or other, there clearly *is* such a thing as an Unconscious (though whether it can indeed be explored and influenced in the way in which the movement claims, is quite another matter).

Secondly, there is the fact of *Transference*. The gentleman who has left his hat, coat, sceptical spirit and cost–benefit analysis in the ante-room, is not prevented from escaping the new situation in the consulting-room simply by a logical circle. Logic has never had such power over men. Stone walls and bars *do* a prison make: but logic, never. For better or for worse, we are not so easily constrained. Reason alone does not constrain. Whether or not man is a slave of his passions, one thing is sure: he is *not* a slave of his reason.

TRANSFERENCE (Greater Love Has No Man)

Transference is a crisp fact. I use this term in opposition to sloppy facts. The term can be extended to explanations as well as facts, and in any case the boundary between 'facts' and 'explanations' is context-relative: what is a fact *vis-à-vis* some more general explanation, may itself be an explanation for something more specific.

Most or all of the micro-theories contained within psychoanalysis are notoriously sloppy. Take the most famous of those theories, the claim that children have strong unconscious sexual feelings for the parent of the opposite sex. It sounds plausible. No doubt many people do have some feelings of this kind. But is it really certain that diagonal feelings in a nuclear family are more intense than parallel ones, between parents and children of the same sex? Does the term 'sexual' have any very precise meaning, other than that it is intense, can in some circumstances lead to sexual manifestations in a more narrow and conventional sense, and that in some way these feelings resemble those which take place between people who experience manifestly sexual passions for each other?

In brief, this doctrine has a certain nebulous plausibility: and being deeply familiarized with it, as indeed we are in our Freud-permeated culture, means that we are on the lookout for the less obvious patterns of diagonal parent-child relations and their possible manifestations. The value, it seems to me, of seemingly precise and general doctrines such as those of the Oedipus relationship, is that they sensitize us to the kind of deviousness and intensity of personal relationships, in all the polymorphous variety in which they occur in real life.[2] In other words, these doctrines are not really abstract explanatory schemata related to concrete life as generalizations relate to instances: rather, they are pseudo-concrete specimens of the NM, reminding us roughly of what *kind* of pattern we should expect.

We might, had we been clever, have learned just as much from the abstract principles of the NM. But most of us find it hard to take in abstractions, and we much prefer to learn from concrete, sexy examples. So the real role of the various specific doctrines found within psychoanalysis is to guide us to think in a Nietzschean way ... Their specificity, however, is spurious. They are but code words for a sense of the deviousness, covertness, self-devouringness, surrealist lack of proportion, of the way we really feel deep down about ourselves and each other. Their apparent specificity has no bite: the seemingly precise and specific generalizations are formulated with the help of concepts whose operational anchorage in actual conduct is so unutterably loose, that reality can always be made to conform with them.

But there is at any rate one striking and shining exception to this, and that is the doctrine of transference. Here, there is a striking generalization which could *not* have easily been anticipated, whose truth seems genuinely evident (rather than being poised, as the others are, between equally heavy weights of positive and negative examples), and whose meaning seems reasonably precise. There is an almost comic contrast between the overwhelming and genuine evidence for this one phenomenon and the sketchy, dubious evidence for most other psychoanalytic ideas, notably the claim of therapeutic effectiveness. The phenomena which this generalization covers are not (as is the case with the other theories) in effect brought into being as artefacts or shadows of the very terms occurring in it, nor are the terms so constructed that all counter-examples can be, *ex post*, spirited outside the purview of the generalization. No: the terms occurring within it have fairly precise meanings whose range of application can be .determined before the event; it is known in advance whether the example is a confirming or disconfirming one, not afterwards (as is otherwise the pretty custom of psychoanalytic interpretation).

What this marvel of a generalization says is: when a person, self-identified as a patient, comes in repeated and sustained contact with a person whom he recognizes as a doctor or therapist, and the latter listens to the deliberately unstructured confessions of the former, and only occasionally and tentatively offers interpretations of them – in brief, if the two comport themselves as the therapeutic technique recommends – then the latter will develop very strong, and in the main, initially and on the surface, positive feelings towards the therapist, accept his authority, and so on.

First of all, this has the merit of being novel, surprising. Secondly, unlike for instance the promise of cure and adjustment, it seems overwhelmingly true. Thirdly, the manner in which the terms occurring in the generalization pick out the phenomena which illustrate and corroborate it, is plainly quite independent of the theory itself. The terms are not applied in a manner calculated to ensure that the theory always comes out right. They possess a descriptive content which is not a by-product of the theory, but exists independently of it.

Why is this so very important?

We have seen that the entry into the psychoanalytic world passes through a kind of 'conceptual valve', permitting entry but blocking an exit. (Any self-respecting belief-system must be well-equipped with these.) The tentative, uncommitted man-in-the-ante-room must, in order to try out this technique, assume certain doctrines about the

Unconscious which, when adopted, then no longer logically allow him to return to his coat and hat and doubt in the ante-room. But the pulleys and levers of the trap-door, which ensure that the passage is one way only, are made of frail materials: they are only logical, conceptual. An intelligent and forceful man, when he notices the creaking machinery, the pulleys moving and the doors shutting, could and would kick them down without difficulty and return to his normal coat and hat. Some of course do so. But many do not. *Transference* is the key. Only transference can prevent the entrant from breaking though the ingenious, but utterly flimsy, logical contraptions of the valve. To put all this another way, psychoanalysis is powerfully addictive, and 'transference' is the name, though not in any serious sense the explanation, of this phenomenon (though Freud was rather easily satisfied when it came to its explanation). Without transference, the entire system simply could not work.

Transference is the covenant, the bond, the social cement, the social contract of this movement. The movement as a whole clearly constitutes a charismatic community, but though united by a common doctrine and experience and also by some humdrum organizational sanctions (which it shares with any association that is allowed to have a bank account), the real central emotional bond holding the system together is a striking network of intense binary relations of analysand to analyst. It is both sad and astonishing that little research has yet gone into establishing a full map of these networks. Such a map should be fairly easy to establish – given cooperation.

So transference fulfils a crucial function in both the conceptual and the organizational systems. Binding, loyalty-requiring organizations normally possess entry-valve-reinforcing rituals, solemn *rites de passage*, oaths, initiation ordeals, which ensure that the entrant henceforth has a psychic investment in membership and does not easily or carelessly relinquish it. Transference does this for the psychoanalytic system, and does it supremely well. There are of course other factors making for loyalty – hope of cure, professional prospects, investment of time – but the main initial valve-sanction in this case plainly is transference. Its lasting after-effects, however, also endow the entire community with its structure of basic binary relations.

CONCEPTUAL DEPRIVATION

Why or how does transference work?

The simple and correct answer to this question is that no one knows. Freud thought he knew, and that the answer was simple:

All the libido, as well as everything opposing it, is made to converge solely on the relation with the doctor. In this process the symptoms are inevitably divested of libido. In the place of his patient's true illness there appears the artificially constructed transference illness ... Since a fresh repression is avoided, the alienation between ego and libido is brought to an end and the subject's mental unity is restored. When the libido is released once more from its temporary object in the person of the doctor, it cannot return to its earlier objects, but is at the disposal of the ego.[3]

If you are satisfied with this kind of explanation, you'll be satisfied with anything. This level of sophistication and fastidiousness in explanation-seeking is alas entirely characteristic. At this level of generality, Freud was easily satisfied.

What his explanation amounts to is that force or psychic plasma called libido temporarily homes in on the therapist. The whole account is a strange mixture of intuitive psycho-hydraulics, associationism (strangely enough), and an unexplained attribution of eventual curative power to consciousness, which is not further defined or explained. (Consciousness cannot be equated with what we normally mean by it, for it is a central part of the doctrine that mere intellectual consciousness is therapeutically unavailing. An unkind observer might suggest that 'real' consciousness is operationally defined as consumer satisfaction with the therapy plus acceptance of the doctrine.)

While, until the appropriate research is done, it is

impossible to answer with any confidence the question concerning why transference occurs, it is in the meantime well worth while to explore some plausible candidate-explanations. There is a number of them and they deserve our attention:

1. The patient's duty is to 'free-associate' in the presence and hearing of the therapist, withholding nothing. 'Withholding' is the prime sin.[4] In normal life, we spend all our time presenting a reasonably coherent and favourable, well-selected image of ourselves to others. The imperative of free association is in effect an obligation to do the very opposite: to refrain from both order and selectiveness. Though in one way it may be a great relief to abandon the strenuous efforts to maintain the normal façade, to let go the sphincters of the mind, on the other hand it cannot but inspire shame and guilt to present a mass of material, inevitably disreputable and undignified both logically and morally. The normal presentation of self *must* be selective: it isn't just the improper parts that are hidden, but so is, perhaps primarily, that total chaos which pervades our stream of consciousness. To free-associate genuinely in the presence of another is like undressing on a day on which one is wearing badly soiled underwear: or like receiving someone in a bed-sitter which one hasn't tidied up for weeks. To do it deliberately is to indulge in an extreme case of that role-reversal which signals the presence of the Exceptional, an initiation to the sacred.

The manifest, official or internal view of free association, is that it eventually by-passes by stealth the defence mechanisms of the Unconscious, and thus in the end penetrates its secrets and leads to liberation from its compulsions, to an apprehension of previously hidden reality. A set of defences quite impervious to frontal assault, may nevertheless be open to slow infiltration by a large mass of undirected, unstructured, unplanned probes, supervised by the qualified expert whose main qualification consists of having previously had his own Unconscious similarly penetrated. Once penetration is achieved, the skilled analyst knows how to expand the bridgehead . . .

But the real, operational function of free association probably is that it furthers transference, by first placing the patient in a situation of unselective nakedness *vis-à-vis* the therapist (thus heavily underscoring the special, dramatically life-discontinuous status of the whole situation), and then making him feel at the mercy of the willingness of the listener to condone these indulgences in both logical and moral abandon.

2. Closely connected with the shame of logical and moral abandon are the joy and pleasure to be found in it. Is it not nice to escape from the unending task of presenting a façade, into a state of suspension, *sursis*, a bolt-hole in which pretences are at long last, and at least for a relaxing interval, cast aside? We are most of us given to feeling that *tout comprendre c'est tout pardonner*: here at last there is a chance to give all the information and in due course receive, one hopes, total comprehension and total forgiveness, absolution.

3. Simple hope of cure, in the case of those impelled to enter analysis by some genuine anguish; the hope fed by the background authority of science and medicine endorsing the authority of analyst, and protected from disenchantment by the analyst's silence, allowing all optimistic expectations and therapeutic powers to be projected on to him, while protecting him from uttering disappointing assertions.

4. The judo technique. Certain Japanese techniques of physical self-defence seem to hinge in part on not resisting the opponent's thrusts but, on the contrary, skilfully evading or 'going with' them, thereby enlisting the opponent's own energy and force for one's own end, to his detriment. In ordinary encounters between two egos, the two individuals concerned make explicit and implicit claims on their own behalf, and try to torpedo those of the other, in the kind of verbal duel which constitutes conversation. In the analytic situation, the therapist neither contests nor, of course, endorses the claims, poses and challenges of the patient. The latter, habituated to opposition in ordinary life, has put a certain amount of psychic force behind each claim – and

finds himself falling forward and bewildered when his habitual expectation of opposition fails to be fulfilled. Eventually brought quite off-balance by all this, he must lean on something, somebody – and who else, who but the therapist? The doctrine itself is presented somewhat in the manner: whatever objection he raises tends to be accepted. The analyst doesn't normally *argue*. He asks the patient to *work through* the allegations.

5. Delayed pattern completion. The need to complete patterns, to have some kind of pattern in what he perceives, in one's environment – all this is, I suspect, one of our strongest, most insistent tendencies. It may not be as immediately vociferous inwardly as our sexuality, but in its quiet and persistent way, it may well be as important, or more so. Certainly such work as has been done on 'brainwashing' techniques, on breaking down prisoners by sustained isolation, disorientation and 'sensory deprivation', suggests that this need is a very strong one indeed, and that dramatic consequences follow if it is not satisfied. 'Conceptual pattern deprivation' is at least as important as sensory deprivation.

The analyst's silence does indeed constitute or engender, not so much sensory, as conceptual deprivation. The patient is not allowed to erect and maintain patterns of his own (that would not be free association), and he is initially denied any patterns by his prestigious therapist. Seeing is *not* believing. We believe only what others confirm. The thirst for pattern may become very, very powerful. And eventually, after the lapse of some time, the analyst does slowly begin to offer some partial 'interpretations', patterns. The patient is now positively ravenous for them, but they only come slowly in very measured and often further and carefully delayed doses. His need for them, the gratitude he cannot but feel for what he gets, the anxiety for more, his dependence on a carefully controlled supply – are all these factors not likely to engender powerful 'transference'?

6. Revaluation of patient's environment and identity. When interpretations finally come to be made, and are more or less accepted by mutual consent by the two

participants in the situation, they are, so to speak, negotiated by them. One or the other suggests them and, eventually, acceptance is conditional on joint agreement – each has a kind of *liberum veto* on interpretations, though the weaker partner, the analysand, needs a lot of tenacity if he is to stick to any ideas stigmatized as 'resistance'. This eventual consensuality is joined to another implicit rule of the game, namely that the interpretations must in a reasonable proportion of cases contradict, invert, what the patient had initially supposed and feared. After all, unless the Unconscious has some surprises to offer, what point would there be in establishing a private line to it, and paying through the nose for it? An Unconscious which merely reproduced our conscious ideas would hardly be worth having.

The requirement of surprise – by the well-known logic of the Unconscious, a certain number of things must be the very opposite of what they appear at the conscious surface – jointly with the consensuality which is also a condition, has this consequence: in the end, the patient is presented with something which, on the one hand, has the authority of long exploration and all the weight of therapeutic endorsement, and, on the other, is agreed by him *and* yet differs on some fundamental particular or particulars from the picture with which he had started.

But remember, he had started with a picture which made him feel uneasy and inadequate, if not worse. The patient lives in a competitive world and feels inadequate in it. The analytic *sursis* suspends his low rating in the public world, gives him top rating in a private one, and finally restores him to the public world at a higher point. He now has a picture which is different (that is part of the rules of the game), but which he has agreed (and would he agree something which is too unpalatable?). He has found himself in a preferable environment. The new picture can be assumed to be more acceptable, less wounding to his self-esteem, than the starting-point. Must he not be grateful, will he not be dependent on the source and condition of such a welcome metamorphosis?

7. The price and value of attention. Modern man (at any rate when living in the social regions which provide the normal catchment area of psychoanalysis) does not live in fear of hunger, nor of being the object of constant physical aggression. But, all the same, he does live in fear and trembling. What scares him is other people. Life is not a struggle for bread, but for attention and acceptance. He is terrified of being disliked and ignored – above all, perhaps, of being ignored. *Give us this day our daily attention!*

Moreover, he lives in a formally egalitarian society not well-endowed with rank badges, so that there are few contexts in which most people can demand attention from their fellows as of right. Officers can make soldiers stand to attention while they talk to them, but that is quite untypical of most of modern life, even in relations between unequals. Attention is granted only informally, as a relatively unconstrained, volatile, informal recognition of an informal, unstable, precarious ranking. The consequence of all this is that, while in some overtly hierarchical traditional societies people *knew their place*, which meant at least that they had one, in this one people suffer the insecurity and the pangs and humiliations of *continuous assessment*. Almost no one can be sure that when he starts telling a story, someone else won't spoil his punch-line by conspicuous inattention at the crucial moment.

And what is by far the most important sign of being assessed favourably? That others really listen when you speak. We are social animals. The essence of our lives is not that we pursue aims dictated to us directly by our biological condition but, on the contrary, that we enact *roles*, which mediate between biology and society. Our contentment depends on being allowed to enact the roles we yearn to assume. We rather fancy our roles, and we act out our roles to a Generalized Other when no one else is about. We fear for our existence, like the tree in the quad, if our role is not perceived and accepted. But most of the time *no one listens*. We are not allowed to deliver our message, to play out our role . . .

If something is ardently desired but in short supply, the

inevitable consequence is that some people will purchase that passionately sought commodity. In the case of sex, the result 'is prostitution. One of the latent but supremely important aspects of psychoanalysis, is that it provides the possibility of purchasing a regular supply of sustained, careful *attention*. (If you can't quite afford it, you may have to make do with the gang-bang of group therapy.) But there is an interesting difference between this aspect of the technique and prostitution: both in the case of sex and of attention, some shame attaches to buying that which attractive and prestigious people get for free. But the person who purchases the regular hour's attention of a therapist does not need to concede, to himself or others, that it is attention he is buying, and that he is incapable of securing it by more conventional means. After all, the whole technique contains as part of its associated ideology, a plausible account of why the technique itself is used – and that account does not include an acknowledgement of the role of attention-starvation.

In the analytic situation, two things happen. For once (the only time ever, perhaps) attention is complete. (A man I knew once caught his analyst fast asleep while he, the patient, was free-associatively baring his psyche. However, such *demonstrable* cases of analytic inattention must be rare.) But the attention-swamped patient is at the same time forbidden and denied a role! At least, until much later on, when the therapist deigns to endorse a self-interpretation. The pleasure of receiving attention is enormous, but the thirst for role-resumption is at the same time overwhelming. Could there be a greater pleasure than having both attention *and* a role? Only the therapist can grant this second boon – having already so generously, copiously, uniquely and professionally, *ex officio*, granted the first – by finally endorsing an 'interpretation', i.e. a role, and giving it that stamp of acceptance by the Other, without which it altogether lacks the feel of reality. He is, after all, the Authorized or Officiating Other.

Can one have anything other than overwhelmingly strong feelings about someone who has this tremendous power, who has so great a benefit in his gift, but is for the time being legitimately withholding it? A plausible theory of romantic love affirms that it originated in the mediaeval work situation of an apprentice knight, serving the master's wife, the 'mistress' in the original sense, and thus combining closeness with unattainability. The origin of transference love – and hate – is probably the same.

Attention-deprivation is a very common condition. Psychoanalysis is an exceptionally, indeed uniquely, efficacious way of remedying it, and the analyst's silence ensures that good value is given for money: but, at the same time, it withholds role recognition. He endorses a role only much, much later, which of course enhances the eventual pleasure.

8. A foolproof relation. The analytic relation may not be the only intense relation in a person's life (though it probably is the most intense one), but it differs from the others in one supremely important way: the loyalty and the qualities of the 'cathected' person cannot be put to the test. An ordinary relationship which becomes important is very soon put to searching tests, which is of course why intense relationships tend to be turbulent and unstable: the beloved is asked for advice, more time, support in disputes, a loan, exclusiveness, and heaven knows what else. He or she may grant these requests and thereby show the required love and devotion, but, objectively or subjectively, a point will inevitably be reached when the lover proves *false*, by failing to deliver the required tokens of love.

Not so the analyst. He is institutionally, professionally, protected from such testing, by the recognized rules of the therapeutic situation. When the hour is over, it is over, and cannot be prolonged by appeals to the intensity of the feelings, as a lovers' meeting inevitably would be. You cannot touch your analyst for a short-term loan because you are temporarily embarrassed. The analyst makes few if any *explicit* promises or predictions (the ones implicit in the situation call for separate discussion). So, one way and another, he is fully protected from the danger of disappointing the person fixated on him.

This test-proofing of the therapist could on its own go a long way towards the explanation of transference.

9. The patient is under the strain of contradictory expectations and demands. Softlee Softlee Catchee Unconscious is the official principle: the crucial secrets cannot, *ex hypothesi*, be wrested by frontal assault, and the quarry can be approached only by a stealthy, gentle, downwind approach: in other words, he must relax and abandon himself to free association, otherwise the required penetration of the unconscious defences will never ever occur. At the same time, however, it is well known that analyses 'go well' or (more often perhaps) 'go badly', and it is somehow up to the analysand to help make it go well. Under these contradictory rules, it can always be ensured and insinuated, tacitly conveyed, that it is *his* fault. Perhaps he is not trying hard enough? Or equally, and with even greater cogency, is it not failing because he is *trying*, exercising his will, when he should be surrendering himself?

The Double Bind is introduced in a variety of ways. Extreme hope is encouraged by the very logic of the situation – what could be greater than the attainment of liberation from unconscious forces which had been so destructive? – and, in any case, it is a recognized part of transference and the attribution of great power to the therapist. At the same time, the patient also knows that the cure will mean no longer having any unrealistic and excessive expectations. Now what is he to do? He can't win. Transference is a legitimate part of the process and involves attribution of great powers of relieving distress to the therapist: but the cure involves an 'acceptance of reality' and the abandonment of unrealistic hopes.

There is also the ambiguous suspension of morality. It is understood of course that in free association everything is permitted. Everything? Morality makes its sudden and disconcerting reappearance in the otherwise ethically suspended psychoanalytic world. The patient is not freed from all obligation, he is under a kind of contract (Freud's term). 'In psychoanalysis every neurosis is considered a failure of moral control.' There you have it, straight from the shoulder. This affirmation comes as part of a vigorous defence of psychoanalysis by Else Frankel-Brunswick.[5] How is the patient to know when morality is relevant and when it is an intrusion?

The double bind situation of any patient may also make its significant contribution to the transference. It is not easy to feel neutral about someone who has us in his power. Political prisoners love their interrogators, recruits love their drill sergeants. The analyst has all conceptual exits covered: and even total surrender does not ensure success. In the nature of the case, of the situation, no extraneous appeal is possible, such as exists in ordinary relations – in terms of which the therapist could be called to account. The outside world has been absorbed into the analytic situation. Yet so much is at stake – one's access to that crucial inner reality which alone may allow one to live and function effectively . . . When so much is at stake, yet one doesn't know what one can do to influence the outcome (or rather, the instructions about what one can do are both contradictory and elusive), would one not develop strong feelings about the one agent who seems to have the power to make it go right, who alone has the power to declare it to have gone right, and who according to the theory has access, denied to oneself, to that realm within which it is all decided?

This is the checklist of admittedly overlapping and intertwined factors which may help explain that indisputably crucial and genuine phenomenon, Transference. No doubt the list is less than complete. It is quite impossible to tell which of these factors, in what proportion, are really operative; and until they are linked into some plausible background psychological theory, they still would not amount, perhaps, to a satisfactory explanation, even if one knew them to be true. But it would be really interesting to see some serious, sustained and objective research on this topic. It is not too difficult to design the strategy for such research.

The obvious questions which could be asked are these: to what extent is transference conditional on belief in the background theory of the therapeutic technique? It would not be difficult to assemble otherwise comparable groups of people, differing only in this particular, that members of one group would, and of the other would not, initially have the required faith. Similarly, it would not be difficult to assemble otherwise similar groups, members of one of which would all be in some kind of stressful emotional situation, and others not. It would also be very interesting to find out the extent to which transference occurs only among members of the so to speak bourgeois populations – i.e. people whose work is non-manual and consists of manipulating people and meanings rather than things, presupposes education, verbal sophistication, the habit of persistent inner monologue, the expectation of coherence which is offended by free association, and status-anxiety due to a formally egalitarian, fluid, yet prestige-seeking and status-conscious milieu.

Psychoanalysis simultaneously swamps the patient with more attention than he has ever known before, thus enormously raising his sense of his own status; and at the very same time, wholly deprives him of any role, by ordering him to associate 'freely', i.e. to refrain from presenting *any* coherent façade. He is given the expectation, however, that a role will eventually be restored to him – but only if for the time being he cooperates in temporarily shedding any and every role. The exquisite pleasure of being (at long last) listened to by someone, and the eager hope of acquiring a role (and a better one to boot) in due course, keep him shackled inside the system. The attention saturation, coupled with total role-deprivation, and the slow, very slow role-granting, is probably the main key to the understanding of transference.

THE TERMINAL VALVE

Our discussion of the crucial phenomenon of transference occurred in the context of following the patient who passes through psychoanalysis.

Let us assume that our hero, having passed through the

entrance valve, has eventually negotiated suitable and acceptable interpretations with the therapist, and found a certain amount of relief from his ills. In the later stages, it is part of the process that the transference be as it were run down and diminished. The termination of analysis is an obscure, cloudy subject, and it is not clear that those deeply involved in the psychoanalytic culture ever terminate their analyses. There is a fair amount of evidence that suggests that many do not. The termination of analysis is not an event in life. Analysis has no limit, as the visual field has no bounds.

But, in principle, the concept of termination clearly is part of the system. Here one must ask the crucial question: what are the criteria of a termination? – or of a successful termination, if indeed that is not a pleonasm? I shall here use the term 'successful' in a way such that it is *not* a pleonasm: it is assumed that everything in the procedure has been correctly carried out, without prejudging, however, whether the patient accepts the efficacy of the technique and the correctness of the theory.

It is an obvious part of the present inquiry that the general procedures and ideas of the movement are described, with as much objectivity and accuracy as space allows and as the author can muster, *but not in the language of the movement itself*, i.e. not in 'internal' terminology. In 'internal' language, an analysis is ready for termination when the patient has come fully to perceive, understand and come to terms with those internal factors or forces which had initially operated in hiding and been inaccessible, and when he has 'worked through' his relation with the therapist, having passed through a powerful transference, through both positive and negative feelings (which help him acquire self-knowledge, by exemplifying his emotional patterns, or in other ways); and having done all these things, he is ready, at least for a while, to face the hardships of life unsustained by analysis. As the analyst in the *New Yorker* cartoon observes patronizingly to the astonished-looking patient – the time will really come, Mr Blenkinsop, when you will be able to live without me. One should add that there are no precise criteria of termination as agreed within the movement, and no agreed formula seems to exist. But what we have offered is, I trust, a reasonable and unprejudicial approximation to the 'internal' views of the matter.

A certain crucial question imposes itself at this point. Can a situation even arise which could be described by the following set of grammatical, intuitively intelligible English sentences: Mr X has passed through a properly conducted analysis carried out by the entirely competent analyst, Dr Y. At the end of his analysis, Mr X came to the firm and secure conclusion that the ideas of psychoanalysis are invalid, that they do not apply to his, Mr X's, psychic processes, and that the analysis, though possibly an interesting experience, had been of no positive benefit to him whatever?

If there is a case of this kind, it seems to have been left out of any record. On the other hand, there appear to be numerous cases which (shortening the story to essentials) run roughly as follows: Mr X terminated the analysis before it was properly completed, because he became frightened of what he would find out about himself if it continued. There are of course numerous variants on this account of the possible motives of Mr X, but this is the much-favoured paradigm. A significant alternative story is available: Mr X prematurely terminated his analysis, because unfortunately Dr Y is less than competent, is himself disturbed, or had become so, etc.

In brief: within the conceptual structure of the system, there is a certain number of possibilities: that the analysis be completed *successfully* (though there seems a good deal of doubt, not about the success, which is guaranteed *ex hypothesi*, but about genuine completion occurring frequently); that it goes on indefinitely; or that it is terminated and unsuccessful, not because of a deficiency in the basic corpus of ideas and techniques, but through some deficiency of either analysand or analyst, or of course both. But a sentence which conjoins correct and proper completion of the process with the repudiation of the system by the patient (or of course by the therapist), appears itself to have no possible employment within the system itself. Apparently it cannot correctly describe any actual state of affairs. The English language has it seems been too liberal in permitting an expression for which there can be no possible valid employment. In other words, the exit valve ensures the maintenance of the system.

THE IMPLICIT PROMISE

There is of course an intimate connection between the Entrance Valve and the Exit Valve. They are linked by that pervasive dependence of the entire system on a Naïve Realist theory of knowledge, and its associated Stoic ethic.

The link is as follows. The question is sometimes raised whether psychoanalysis does really make promises, extravagant or other, as inducements to prospective patients.[6] That tempting and explicit promises have in fact been made is hardly in doubt, but the interesting and important thing is that they are not really necessary. It is said that a good con-man says relatively little, that his skill consists of letting the victim's hopes and fears work for him. The promise is issued by the patient himself, to himself. Not, however, without some skilful background encouragement.

Let us, once again, recapitulate the situation of the prospective patient. He is often in some measure of distress. The theory unambiguously asserts that the roots of psychic conflict are in the Unconscious, a realm about which at any rate this much is known with absolute and axiomatic certainty – it is not accessible to the unaided intelligence of the individual, least of all to one who is in distress the roots of which, confessedly, he does not properly understand. However, fear not: rescue is nigh. For happily, there *is* a technique which can, does and will, if properly employed, give him such access and, eventually, the means for coping with the source of distress, as effectively as the situation objectively allows.

What exactly will the technique achieve, what can it

promise? No miracles, certainly. It can only, by helping him to see and understand how things truly stand, help him accommodate himself to them. Stoic ethics in general promise no miracles, but only the recognition of necessity; and the Freudian version of the Stoic ethic modifies it in one respect by teaching that the emotional accommodation can be attained only with the aid of a certain technique. Stoic acceptance *cannot* be attained by the unaided efforts of the individual: Freudianism is anti-Pelagian.

Now let us assume our hero is in anguish for a relatively specific immediate cause: say he has lost the affections of a person without whom life seems meaningless to him. However, let's be realistic: the *kind* of anguish which leads people to seek therapeutic aid is not occasioned by being crossed in love *once* (however acute the feelings which that may provoke). People seek such aid because they are possessed by the suspicion that this is all part of a recurring pattern, which, in some way which they do not properly understand, they bring upon themselves. Such a suspicion is all too often well founded.

So the technique or its mediator promise him or her no miracles, certainly not the remedying of the anguish-triggering tragic situation. But it *does* promise to teach him to recognize and live with 'reality'. Now for a person suffering the pangs of unrequited love, the promise that he may learn how to live with reality means, in concrete terms, the hope that he will no longer mind losing that which he cannot have. Now that of course is not nearly as good as having what you want, but in a certain way is almost as good (by Stoic standards, it is identical, for it too establishes that sought-after congruence of fact and desire); and anyway, it is as good a substitute as you can hope to have, in those sad circumstances. And that already is quite a lot.

But there is more to come. Any honest account of the matter must concede the following: there is a certain implied contrast implicit, and often explicit, in that entire diagnosis of how people are unable to live with their situation – because they frustrate their own aspirations by obscure, frequently self-punishing unconscious mechan-

isms. That contrast is with an 'un-neurotic' person whose
Unconscious does not deliberately and masochistically trip
him up all the time. The un-neurotic person pursues only
what he can reasonably hope to get, but then he usually
secures it, for once the inner self-imposed obstacles and
blinkers are gone, a man will be as effective in his pursuit of
his ends as objective, external circumstances allow. And
that, one is given to understand, is pretty effective. The real
obstacles and impediments in life are generally *inside*.
Perhaps the truly tragic ones are *only* inside. The whole
system is pervaded by the assumption that tragic predica-
ments are indeed self-imposed. Presumably by definition,
neurotic unhappiness can originate only inside the psyche.
Of course, 'ordinary' unhappiness may have external
causes: but one is somehow given to understand that
'ordinary' unhappiness is not so terrible, and in any case
does not inhibit effectiveness in the pursuit of realistic ends.

So nothing in the theory promises miraculous manipulation of external reality – a promise that would of course be
absurd. Unlike Stoicism, psychoanalysis does not promise
the good man that he will be happy even on the rack: but
only that his unhappiness on the rack will be ordinary, and
not neurotic. He will no longer be tormented by the
unconscious meanings which the rack has for him.

The un-neurotic man knows how to manage the outer
world; or if he fails, you can trust him to live with that
occasional failure without neurotic, but merely with ordinary (hence tolerable), unhappiness. But most probably,
once he has got himself sorted out, he won't need to face
that situation too often. In any case, given the overall
situation (being at the mercy of the Unconscious we do not
understand), the only sensible strategy is to get oneself
sorted out first, and *then* deal with the outer world on
optimal terms.

Note that all this must sound like the promise of bliss to
our hero. He can't cope very well with the external world;
he has failed more than once, and plausibly suspects that
the fault is in himself not in his stars; and he most certainly
isn't capable of accommodating himself to his failures with

merely 'ordinary', un-neurotic, tolerable unhappiness. (In brief, he exemplifies the human condition.) He suspects that his failure to manipulate the outside world to his own satisfaction, and his failure to come to terms with his own lack of success without acute, 'neurotic' unhappiness, spring from the same source. He is certainly encouraged in this supposition. He is explicitly promised the ability to face reality, and implicitly he is more than half-promised a greater efficaciousness in attaining his ends. So is he not, in effect, promised a very great deal? No wonder he is liable to go through the entry valve.

Psychoanalysis presents a picture of the human condition which is both original and enormously persuasive. Think of yourself bicycling through the streets of a city full of ferocious, careless and brutal traffic, and note that you are blindfolded, and absolutely incapable of removing the blindfold yourself. The situation really is too terrible to contemplate. Yet you must cycle on, for life leaves you no alternative. And you cannot, *cannot* remove the blindfold: the more you try, the firmer it is set over your head. In fact, it is more like some kind of dreadful, stifling, *cagoule*.

The sheer perception of the reality of this situation would be enough, for any rational person, to try and seek help. And indeed, many clear-sighted persons do seek help, without even waiting for any serious mishap to drive them to it. But imagine, as is only too likely, that you have already come up painfully a number of times against lamp-posts, traffic, other cyclists. Blindfolded by the *cagoule* as you are, you are not really to blame – but not only are you sore and bleeding, you have been roundly and vigorously abused for your inept and careless cycling, and several serious threats of prosecution are hanging over your head.

But despair not. Since about the turn of the century (how lucky one is to have been born so late!) a powerful *cagoule*-removing agency is available. It owns the patent and near monopoly of *cagoule*-removal, and is only moderately expensive (at any rate if you consider the value and importance of the boon offered), though acutely jealous of anyone wishing to poach on its monopoly, but what of that? The *cagoule*-

removing operation is not only mildly expensive, it is also somewhat protracted and energy-absorbing, and some nasty sceptical people have suggested that its efficacy is questionable, and indeed its practitioners themselves seem a bit shifty and evasive when making definite promises about the timing of cagoulotomy, but what of all that? Anyone profusely bleeding, with broken nose and countless bruises, and wearied of the interminable and virulent abuse from other hooded cyclists, is only too likely to turn to the agency.

What all this amounts to is this. Psychoanalysis does not need to make any explicit promises (though, in fact, it quite often does so). A truly tremendous promise is immediately, visibly, and dramatically implicit in its entire presentation of the human condition, and that vision in turn has enormous plausibility. There *is* an Unconscious; we clearly are, all of us, permanently hooded. We do suffer, and our suffering does seem to have a pattern to it, though we cannot properly understand it, which suggests that if only the hood were lifted, we could avoid future painful collisions. Psycho-analysis does firmly claim that it can (and a little more ambiguously, but none the less audibly, that *only* it can) lift those horrendous, stifling and sticky hoods. About the first of the two premises – that we live hooded – there can be no serious doubt whatever. About the second – that a good de-hooding technique has been discovered – there can alas be doubt, only too well founded. Psychoanalysis has con-flated the true doctrine of the hood, with the questionable claim that it possesses a technique of de-hooding. Psychoanalysis does claim firmly that it does know how to de-hood, that the Founder had actually and heroically de-hooded himself, that no other sound techniques for doing so are available, and that it is quite good at doing so. All this the movement claims vociferously, and it does so in an idiom which is not implausible.

But, of course, if he reads the small print, the only promise formally made to the cagoulotomy-seeker will in retrospect turn out to have been the promise to teach him how to recognize and accept reality. This promise, moreover, is made without any delivery deadline, or only with the loosest indication of what it *might* be. There is *no* date at which he could ever claim that the promised delivery has not been made. All he can legitimately claim, according to the terms of the implicit contract, is that by some unspecified date he will no longer be *neurotically* unhappy. But what is the test for successful termination? That the patient no longer be neurotically unhappy, though of course ordinary unhappiness is allowed. Neurotic unhappiness is indicated by unacceptability of his condition to himself. So an unsuccessful termination becomes a contradiction in terms. Conversely, the promise of success is tautological. He who complains of failure has failed to fulfil the conditions of therapy.

IV

ON THE RACK

LICENSED TO CURE

The key doctrines of the Psychoanalytic Movement may be summed up as follows:

There is a realm known as the Unconscious, which is reasonably similar in much of its *contents* to the conscious mind and continuous with it – it contains ideas, feelings, fears, aspirations, memories, but differs from it in the crucial particular of not being accessible to consciousness. Though it constituted a novelty and seemed most exotic at the time it was discovered, the striking thing now is that, all in all, except for being *un*conscious, the Unconscious is astonishingly like the Conscious. Its activities seem to resemble those of the conscious mind, except that they evidently lack any sense of proportion and order, and are of course inaccessible to consciousness. The Unconscious seems rather like a mind plunged into darkness *and* deprived of orderly categories and of the negation sign . . .

Many, perhaps most, or perhaps all, important turning-points in a person's life – which determine his basic attitudes, emotions, orientation – occur within this realm.

Many of these crucial decisions – or predetermining events – occur very early in a person's life. (The precise cut-off point is a subject of dispute between various sub-schools, and it does not concern us here.) If important decisions are taken later, they are in some way determined or at any rate limited by those early ones. By a fairly early date in a person's life, *les jeux sont fait.*

Though this realm is not accessible to consciousness or common sense, its general laws are the subject of an autonomous science, namely psychoanalysis. Though books containing the doctrines of this science are publicly sold and eagerly read, the propositional knowledge contained in them does *not* give access to the specific content of any one person's Unconscious (least of all to the person himself). Possession of even perfectly valid but merely propositional and general knowledge about the Unconscious does not confer any power to manipulate it. Hence, such knowledge is *not* power. (As only *real* knowledge is effective, the suspicion arises that the alleged effectiveness of real insight is tautological. Who will endow ineffectual insight with the honorific epithet 'real'?)

So merely propositional knowledge provides no real access to any deep level. This is not due merely to the usual gap between an abstract proposition and a concrete instance, such as may occur in any field. It is due to a more fundamental reason, namely, that the Unconscious is not merely hidden from consciousness, but actively seeks to remain so, and has great powers which enable it to impose its own private Unconscious Secrets Act. The Unconscious is purposive and intelligent (in these particulars as in others resembling the conscious mind), and possesses ample, and devastatingly effective, devices which protect it from direct conscious inquiry or control. Neither intelligence nor conscious honesty nor theoretical learning in any way increase the prospects of by-passing and surmounting the counter-intelligence ploys of the Unconscious.

Though not accessible to direct observation or ordinary inquiry, nevertheless this crucial realm *is* accessible, and even manipulable and appeasable. There is one technique, and one technique only, which can grant such access to it, and the hope of at least some control or accommodation with the forces contained within it. That technique is psychoanalysis. It can gain access to the contents of the Unconscious, and thereby cure such ailments as have their origin there.

That technique was discovered, jointly with the ideas on which it is based, by Sigmund Freud. He also successfully applied it to himself, when practising self-analysis.

Other people can also practise it, but only provided they are properly qualified. Proper qualification is formally confirmed by the sole body authorized to issue such qualification, which distinguishes psychoanalysts from mere psychotherapists. 'Psychotherapist' is a generic description of a person indulging in a certain kind of activity, and does not, as such, prejudge that person's competence, success, authorization or qualification. 'Psychoanalyst' however is a guild-controlled ascription.

Formal authorization by the guild is granted on the successful completion of two preconditions: the person should have received proper theoretical training (which includes teaching seminars and the carrying out of one or more 'analyses' under supervision); and second, that he should be himself successfully analysed by a person already qualified, this constituting by far the more crucial of the two preconditions.

The following are properly qualified to perform the technique (provided they also satisfy the requirement of 'theoretical' training).

1. Sigmund Freud.

2. Anyone successfully analysed by Sigmund Freud or endorsed by him as an analyst.

3. Anyone successfully analysed by anyone qualifying under 2.

4. Anyone successfully analysed by anyone qualified under rules 1, 2 or 3, and 4, allowing for the recursive (repetitive) applications of rule 4.

It must be stressed that successful analysis is now a necessary though not a sufficient condition for competence to transmit further the legitimate practice of analysis, though this apparently was not so at the beginning of the movement. (As far as I know, this most significant historic cut-off point has not been pin-pointed. Who was the last unanalysed analyst, and just when was he fully ordained by Freud?)

The interesting question as to whether the entire

psychoanalytic church has a neat structure, emanating from a single apex, Freud, reaching any member in a straight line or chain with a finite number of links, does not seem to have a simple affirmative answer. During the early years, cooperation and assent to doctrine seems to have been held sufficient for inclusion in the movement. It seems difficult, at any rate for Ernest Jones, the docile and deferential My Dear Watson to the Sherlock Holmes of the Unconscious, to distinguish scholarly discussion or analysis from personal initiation/training analysis at this stage. Thus, for instance, speaking of Max Eitingon's initiation, he says: 'Eitingon . . . passed three or four evenings with Freud and they were spent on personal analytic work during long walks in the city. Such was the first training analysis!'[1] Evidently, it was, in this enterprise as in so many others, well worth while being in at the start. To qualify in four evenings! Jones proceeds to reminisce: 'I remember the swift pace and rapid spate of speech on such walks. Walking fast used to stimulate the flow of Freud's thought, but it was at times breathtaking for a companion who would have preferred to pause and digest them.'

So it seems that it was Freud himself who did a great deal of the talking. Can this count as an analysis of Eitingon and Jones? There is nothing to suggest that the *Parade-Goyim* of Zurich either were ever, in any serious sense, subjected to what was later to become the ineluctable and awesome *rite de passage* of entry. In the same year (1907) Freud also met Karl Abraham, destined, as Jones observes, to become a 'more permanent' friend. Abraham seems to have bequeathed to his analytic progeny the distinction – boast or complaint? – that *his* lineage too, like Freud's, was self-starting, by a kind of depth-psychological parthenogenesis. One of the analysts discussed in Janet Malcolm's *Psychoanalysis: the Impossible Profession* observes: 'My analyst's analyst was Menninger, whose analyst was analyzed by Abraham, whose analyst was no one. Which makes me an orphan . . .'[2]

What it all amounts to is that during the early crystallization of the movement, incorporation was informal though, even then, it was impossible without contact with, and acceptance by, Sigmund Freud. So, although the initial links in this spreading family tree do not have the same sharp and unambiguous outline as they acquire later on, nevertheless there *is* a single apex, consisting of a loose group whose members were variously related to each other, and who were dominated by Freud. But notwithstanding this small element of fuzziness at the start, *thereafter* no independent initiation of descent lines is permitted. The heroism of the Founder's *ex nihilo* self-analysis, though greatly admired, may not be emulated, at any rate to the extent of allowing the generation of *new* pyramids of analysts.

The important implication of this is that the guild possesses a monopoly of the technique. Everyone in it must be linked, by a finite number of steps-analyses, to Sigmund Freud, rather in the way in which every Christian bishop is linked by a finite series of steps to Jesus Christ.

Psychoanalysis is not overtly formulated in religious terms, and formally contains no doctrine to the effect that final truth entered the world only once – no official doctrine of the Incarnation or Subsumption. Hence, theoretically, there could be no logical objection to someone else performing Freud's feat, analysing himself successfully, and then setting up as the *fons et origo* of another proliferating population of qualified analysts. There is however obviously a latent tension between the monopolistic-apostolic implications of the above tacitly used definitions, and the common-sense assumption, natural in the modern world, that any effective technique is open to emulation, and cannot be kept for ever as part of the arcana of a single guild. In practice, this tension seems to be kept within certain bounds by the distinction between psychoanalysis proper, which remains the monopoly of the guild and works apostolically, and psychotherapy, a term used in a fairly generic, neutral manner.

A STATE OF GRACE

The nature of psychoanalytic training or initiation is one of its most important, highly distinctive and indeed idiosyncratic characteristics. Brain surgeons are not required to undergo brain surgery as part of their training; still less, if they happen to have undergone it, does it constitute a part of their training which overshadows all other parts of the preparation for their careers. Nor is it the case that, before they can qualify, the crucial assessment of their competence to do so comes from the brain surgeon who had operated on them. Only the examiners, theoretical and practical, can have a say in that matter.

Psychoanalysis is altogether different. It is curious that this idiosyncrasy has been so little challenged, if challenged at all. In so far as psychoanalysis is *an* important method, among others, in the medical treatment of a class of illnesses, it would have been natural, and in line with normal practice, that some external scrutiny into the thoroughness and objectivity of the tests applied by the guild, in the course of licensing practitioners, would have been imposed. In fact, there seems to be no such external checking. Psychoanalysts who are also psychiatrists have of course undergone the public examinations which allow them to use their *medical* titles, and lay, non-medical analysts are controlled in so far as and to the extent that their acceptance of patients is linked to a medical practitioner. But the idiosyncratic training and selection methods of psychoanalysis seem to have been accepted at face value, and as legitimately inherent in the technique and its theory.

James Strachey comments on the curious early situation in the movement as it persisted in a milder form into the 1920s. He describes himself as possessing

... the barest of BA degrees, no medical qualifications, no knowledge of the physical sciences, no experience of anything except third-rate journalism. The only thing in my favour was that at the age of thirty I wrote a letter out of the blue to Freud, asking him if he would take me on as a student.

For some reason, he replied, almost by return of post, that he would, and I spent a couple of years in Vienna . . . I got back to London in the summer of 1922. And in October, without any further ado, I was elected an associate member of the Society. I can only suppose that Ernest Jones had received instructions from an even higher authority, and that he had passed them on to the unfortunate Council. A year later, I was made a full member. So there I was, launched on the treatment of patients, with no experience, with no supervision, *with nothing to help me but some two years of analysis with Freud.* [Italics added][3]

The entry fee in terms of time and effort had grown considerably between 1907 and 1922, between Eitingon and Strachey, but it was still fairly exiguous. Training analysis has since become more strenuous, and above all much more prolonged; but it is still *the* key qualification. The initiation-training, the *analyse de passage*, seems to have a tendency to become even more protracted as the movement grows older.[4]

The situation is odd, and highly eccentric. The perfectly customary and normal employment of psychoanalysis within medicine means that the technique and the corpus of ideas associated with it receive the indirect stamp of authorization from the *general* medical guild. This markedly distinguishes it from the many practices known as fringe medicine. Historically, the fact that psychoanalysis was born within medicine and not outside it, that Freud was a properly qualified and reputable medical practitioner, is no doubt crucial in explaining this anomaly. Yet the consequence is very odd: it means that a person can receive and treat patients, with the support of the prestige and authority of modern medicine as a whole, even though his or her own training for this task has been of a kind which inherently and confessedly eludes any possible examination, by any reasonably public criteria such as prevail in other fields.

When I commented on the oddity of psychoanalytic qualification to Dr M. Balint, then training secretary of the British Institute of Psychoanalysis, he replied that he could not see how any kind of public examination *could* be applied in this field. He went on to expatiate on the difference between theoretical subjects such as sociology (where it was possible to examine people), and a practical one such as

81

psychoanalysis, where direct involvement with psychic reality rendered formal examination irrelevant and unnecessary. The implications of such an absence of extraneous checks did not seem to worry him. But he was right in suggesting that such checks were inherently incompatible with the basic theory itself.

How is this possible? The answer is, of course, that psychoanalysis has succeeded in persuading the world to accept a certain background theory of knowledge, which is presupposed by the entire technique, and which may indeed seem uncontentious. I shall call this theory Conditional Realism. An additional difficulty we encounter at this point in our exposition is that we are dealing with what might be called the *logical* unconscious of psychoanalysis itself: psychoanalysts, including Freud himself, are or were not very clear that they hold this theory, and generally lack the philosophical sophistication which would tell them what it implies, and what problems it raises. The term is mine. Nevertheless, Conditional Realism is clearly presupposed by the entire approach, and plays an absolutely essential part in the working of the system.

A REALIST THEORY OF KNOWLEDGE

By realism I mean in this context the doctrine which asserts that knowledge consists of a kind of contact between the mind and its object, so that the mind, thanks to this contact, apprehends the object as it actually is. The mind knows the object either because it is in direct contact with it, or because it can reproduce within itself a copy of the object, thanks to being in some kind of communication with the original. Realism in this sense is widely taken for granted by people in a kind of unreflecting way. It is a very pervasive, tacitly assumed theory of knowledge. It may seem quite uncontentious, even obvious.

Psychoanalysis holds, or rather presupposes, a variant of it which may best be called Conditional Realism. It holds that the mind *can* know objects it is concerned with, by means of contact with them, but that it does not necessarily or always succeed in doing so. It fails to do so, because it chooses (unconsciously) to deceive itself. The Unconscious is a kind of systematic interference, which hampers full and proper contact between the mind and its object, and thereby prevents effective knowledge. If, however, the barrier/obstacle is removed, contact is re-established, and knowledge becomes possible and indeed easy. (It is *error* which becomes hard to understand, once the barrier is gone. Contact-knowledge makes error hard to conceive. This is a point of great importance in the internal economy of psychoanalytical ideas, and helps to account for the absolutist and dogmatic quality of the putative insights of psychoanalysts. If no interference, then, *ex hypothesi*, valid perceptions. But a competent analyst *has* overcome the inner interference within himself. Ergo, all his perceptions are valid.)

The removal of the barrier, of the inner veil of unknowing, is the condition which must be satisfied before untrammelled, full knowledge can occur. But once the veil is off, knowledge becomes unproblematical. It is for this reason, that the position is best described as *Conditional* Realism. It is of the very essence of psychoanalysis, of course, that it constitutes the removal of inner obstacles to perception. It *is* the hindrance of hindrances to clear insight.

Psychoanalysis is not terribly interested in knowledge in general; its concern is with our knowledge of ourselves, of our inner states. But it is worth noting that its doctrine of Conditional Realism easily can be, and sometimes is, applied to the perception of external objects as well. It is easy to demonstrate that our perception of external objects is also subject to interference by the Unconscious: under the effect of hypnotic suggestion, for instance, some people can fairly easily be brought to 'see' things which are not there, or to fail to see things which objectively *are* there, and which can be assumed to be making the normal impact on their sense organs. So, even with respect to external reality, our perceptions normally operate only by grace and favour of our Unconscious. Unless it grants its *nihil obstat*, we have eyes but we see not. But of course the most significant application of the principle is to our inner states, our real motives and concerns, etc.

It is now possible to spell out the tacit theory which underlies, and which alone can explain and justify, the wild eccentricity of psychoanalytical training and the habitual dogmatism of analysts. The training analysis is the central and essential part of the training of an analyst, *because* (so the theory runs) in the course of it, the trainee learns to penetrate and neutralize the internal obstacles to his own vision. To do so is the very essence of an analysis. Hence, if the analysis is successful and the inner barriers are down, objects are clearly and easily visible to the mind. Veil-removal is a sufficient condition of knowledge. There is no further problem.

Moreover, the theory assumes somehow that a man who sees clearly into himself (because properly analysed) is qualified – and only he is qualified – to lead others to do the same. That is why only (or at most) erstwhile or indeed current analysands can analyse. The logical inference from seeing clearly into oneself, to being able to help others to see into themselves, is not self-evidently cogent, unless one reapplies and generalizes Conditional Realism once again: the only things which obstruct vision are inner barriers, and the barriers are *ex hypothesi* removed by successful analysis, so the successful analysand can see *anything* clearly, including other people. Analysts are not credited with telepathy, even when they have surmounted all inner barriers; so it can be assumed, on this argument, that free association has a double role: not only is it meant to outflank the defensive measures of the patient's Unconscious, but it is also meant to present raw material for the analyst who, though clear-sighted and inner-obstacle-free, still needs something on which his unhampered gaze can alight for, as we have agreed, even he is not telepathic.

Note now that the whole psychoanalytic theory is liable to scrutiny and criticism from (at least) two quite distinct points: 1. Does the technique in fact succeed in by-passing the cunning of the Unconscious, and score therapeutic successes in the process? And 2. Can knowledge in fact *ever* be of the kind that the realist theory assumes, i.e. consist of an unproblematic contact of mind and object, hampered only by obstacles which, if removed, leave the whole matter unproblematic? Are those who are pure of heart granted automatic clear sight? Is there an unambiguous reality out there, in the Unconscious or anywhere else, which can be automatically seized by anyone, provided only one has mastered and neutralized one's own inner self-deceptions? Does not knowledge require more – for instance, the possession of sound theory, which can never simply be the fruit of any kind of inner purification?

Neither of these paths of criticism challenge the contention that there is indeed something like an Unconscious, and that it is very cunning.

HIRE-PURCHASE STOICISM

Psychoanalysis presupposes, or rather constitutes, a very contentious theory of knowledge, though this is not at all clear to its own practitioners. They are generally unaware of the eccentric theory of knowledge which they presuppose. Similarly, it does not just presuppose an ethic, it *is* an ethic. Its ethic dovetails very closely and neatly with its presupposed realist theory of knowledge. Generically, its ethic can be described as Stoic in type.

By Stoicism, I mean a certain attitude or doctrine which has periodically cropped up in the history of human thought. It takes its starting-point from the idea that contentment consists of the congruence between a man's desires and reality. This is only the starting-point. The crucial step comes next. Reality is extraneous to us, seldom very much under our control, and often not under our control at all, and never *reliably* under our control. Our desires, on the other hand, are *within* us. Therefore (a most questionable step, this) we should be able to change them, thereby attaining the required congruence.

Things within us should be more accessible to us and

more under our control than things outside; so, the congruence between desire and fact can best be attained not by endeavouring to modify external fact, as is the habit of most men, but by modifying and mastering inner desire, as is the way of the Stoic sage. Once inner desire is mastered, the good man can be happy even on the rack (for, presumably, he has mastered his own aversion to the rack). There is the celebrated reply of the undergraduate to Dr Jowett's question as to whether a good man really can be happy on the rack: 'Perhaps, sir, a very good man, on a very bad rack.'

Stoicism does not work. Its crucial error is psychological. It assumes that because desires are within us, therefore they can be mastered easily, or at any rate, that they *can* be mastered. Nothing could be further from the truth. As Schopenhauer pertinently observed, man can do as he will, but he cannot will as he will. Nothing is less under our control than the real direction of our desires. In a way, the entire tradition of thought to which psychoanalysis belongs starts from the clear perception of the erroneousness of this version of Stoicism. We cannot easily tamper with our deepest desires. In fact, we cannot really tamper with them at all.

But just this enables psychoanalysis to put forward a new and highly appealing version of Stoicism. Our discontents, or rather the anguished neurotic part of them, sprang precisely from our failure to make our peace with *inner* reality. Where the old Mark One Stoicism preached acceptance of external reality by means of bending inner reality, Freudianism (relatively indifferent to external reality) preaches acceptance of inner reality, by providing us with a technique for identifying it, telling us that it is not to be changed fundamentally, and by unmasking the compulsions which led us to suppose that it could be changed, and that it should be changed. Above all, this technique promises to enable us to accept as well as identify that inner reality, and thereafter to live with it, and perhaps modify it a little and adjust to it.

The Stoicism which is implicitly built into psychoanalytic theory and practice is quite distinctive. It differs from other kinds in at least two very important ways. For one thing, it makes quite plain that the recognition of inner reality cannot be attained without aid: this is an un-Pelagian Stoicism. (Freud himself and his companions, however, are possible exceptions to this.) It is no use trying to go it alone. Secondly, it is delayed, so to speak Hire-purchase, Stoicism. (Strictly speaking, it is inverse hire purchase: in ordinary HP, you get the goods and pay over time. In psychoanalysis, you pay over time and hope to receive the goods only at the unspecified end.)

Conditional Realism and HP Stoicism dovetail and complement each other to perfection. Neither could really manage without the other. Conditional Realism helps to account for the fact that past stoicisms failed to work so lamentably, and that no immediate relief may be expected from 'recognizing reality': the obstacles to identifying reality and accepting it are hidden, cunning and deceitful, and can be unmasked only by a process taking a very long time. So it is obvious that you must wait. There are no short cuts to recognition of necessity.

The Stoicism, on the other hand, ensures that every proper analysis is successful. The Stoic theory of contentment or adjustment is that peace is to be had if you accept reality. If you are dissatisfied, *you* are at fault: reality is not accountable, but in a strange way, you are. You have failed to recognize the unrealistic aspirations, and of course their hidden springs, which impel you towards dissatisfaction. Your dissatisfaction proves that your analysis has not been properly completed. (Proper analysis never fails, for if it fails it will not be called proper.) The Conditional Realism makes delay mandatory, the HP Stoicism defines the successful completion of the delay in a way such that the theory is safe.

FROM ADJUSTMENT TO IDENTITY

In the interests of historical completeness and accuracy, it must be said that the movement as a whole did not remain exclusively wedded to this Stoic-type ethic of adjustment or acceptance. This is indeed the central and most elegant moral idea contained within this belief system, and it plays an essential and indispensable role within it. It manages to account for and underscore and prove the contention that nothing unrealistic, nothing magical is being offered – no mysterious transformation of reality. All that is being offered is a way of coming to recognize, and live with, a reality which itself may well remain quite untractable. This sounds and in a sense is indeed modest, and when modesty is required (notably when implied or explicit promises are not fulfilled), this modesty is becomingly stressed.

But even in this formulation, the claim is not really modest at all. If a technique really existed which would enable us to recognize reality – *recognize* in both the crucial senses, 'identify' and 'accept' – and no longer to fret over anything which cannot be otherwise, that would indeed constitute a total and revolutionary transformation of the human condition.

It is in this form that the Freudian ethic has truly penetrated and conquered ordinary speech and thought. The idiom of 'adjustment' and 'maladjustment' has largely replaced the old moral terminology. To castigate something as wicked sounds archaic, and immediately provokes a challenge to justify the criteria which are being invoked – a question to which answer comes there none. By contrast, the castigation of a personality as maladjusted carries virtually the same injunctive force, or at any rate as much force as can be mustered nowadays, but at the same time seems to be based on an objective and hence authoritative reality, whereas, to modern minds, the old moral imperatives now simply, and rather embarrassingly, hang in thin air.

Nevertheless, despite these enormous advantages, the Ethic of Adjustment faces grave problems. In the simplest terms, the question is – *adjustment to what?*

By the 1930s and during and after the Second World War, it was impossible not to reflect on the question – is

adaptation, adjustment to *any* regime, including a tyranni-
cal one, a sign of mental health? The earlier, simpliste-Stoic
position was that the world is as it is, and the rational or
sane person takes it as he finds it, and adjusts to it when he
cannot change it (which in the overwhelming majority of
cases he cannot). But this view has a disagreeable corollary:
a person who accepted and made his inner peace with the
Nazi regime, was mentally, morally sounder, than one who
found it emotionally unacceptable. This problem continues
to be acute: is the tiny minority of Soviet dissidents, who
insist on taking on the overwhelming might of the Soviet
state, which the great majority of their fellow-citizens
outwardly accept mainly because they feel it cannot be
resisted, sane or insane? If acceptance of the inevitable is a
touchstone of mental health, then there is indeed some kind
of a case for consigning the dissidents to psychiatric
treatment.

In brief, it is very awkward to define mental (in effect:
moral) health in terms of adjustment, without qualification.
This and other considerations led some people within the
system to reformulate its ethical theory. The device they
turned to is also one with a long, venerable philosophical
history: the notion of identity, of the 'true self', etc. The idea
is that health is not to be defined simply in terms of
recognition of necessity and adaptation to external constraints, but of the identification, release, fulfilment of a
person's 'true self'. This has the additional advantage of
seeming to offer something more meaty, in contrast with the
rather anaemic ideal of mere 'adjustment'.

The problem this approach faces, or ought to face (and
which in practice it only evades) is this: how on earth is that
'true self' identified? Is it given by God, by nature, or self-
chosen? The last of these alternatives is most in keeping
with current background beliefs, and constitutes a kind of
confluence of the psychoanalytical and existentialist traditions of thought. It involves the absurdity of assuming that
the self must somehow choose or invent itself before it exists
(who guards the guardians, and which self chooses the self-
choosing self?), and presupposes a curious and in practice

arbitrary capacity to distinguish between ephemeral, capricious acts of choice or commitment, and those that are for real.

THE ERRORS OF REALISM

The 'identity' or 'true self' ethic is a kind of accretion to the system, added partly to avoid the embarrassment of endorsing (through 'adjustment') unpalatable regimes, and partly to satisfy the craving of some for a more positive, uplifting ethic than can be extracted from a mere recognition of reality. None the less, the elegantly sparse idea – learn to recognize the realities within thyself or, more briefly, know thyself – continues to be the core of the guidance which the movement in effect offers to mankind.

This stoic ethic is in turn dependent on the realist theory of knowledge. Thou canst know thyself, if and only if the appropriate kind of knowledge is indeed possible. Is it?

The realist theory of knowledge consists essentially of the contention that when the mind is confronted with an object, it can and will apprehend that object correctly and without further ado, unless there happens to be some impediment within itself which prevents it from doing so. Psychoanalysis builds on to that model, by possessing further, original and striking theories concerning precisely what those impediments, those inner obstacles are, and possessing techniques by means of which it claims to be able to identify and neutralize them.

If realism is a totally false theory of knowledge (which alas it is), what is the correct one? The co-presence of mind and object simply is not sufficient for an apprehension or comprehension of any object. Before one can seize an object, one must be equipped with a whole mass of sensitivities, concepts, expectations, background assumptions. A layman looking at a car engine just sees a jumble of metal objects and wires; a person who knows about car engines can immediately identify the parts and see their interconnection. Countless similar examples can be invoked: the capacity to perceive depends on the possession of the appropriate concepts. As Nobel Prize winner James D. Watson once observed, it is very difficult to describe the behaviour of something unless you know what it is.

And here's the rub: the concepts, the anticipatory classifications and interpretations, contain theories which a) had to be discovered and built up by a long process, and b) may yet in the future turn out to be false. So even the purest of hearts, free of inner deception, will not perceive and understand an object unless endowed with proper *intellectual* equipment. Perception is never, so to speak, the innocent encounter of a pure mind with a naked object, and therefore capable of serving as an untainted foundation for an edifice of knowledge; perception is the encounter with some given element, which cannot be seized or isolated in its purity, but depends on a corpus of knowledge acquired up to that time, but open to revision in the future. We are in the curious position of using cognitive raw materials, but never seeing them in their raw state: by the time we are capable of seeing them, they are no longer raw. We can only assume that the raw material must have arrived somehow, for we most emphatically do not invent our experience; but we only see it as and when processed.

This, stated in the briefest possible form, is the crucial truth contained in the theory of knowledge, or what I hold to be such. If accepted, however, it has very important consequences. It destroys the naïve realist theory of knowledge, a special variant of which in turn is presupposed by psychoanalysis, and which is wholly essential to its internal conceptual economy.

Freud insisted, roughly speaking, that to be eligible for analysis one had to be of sound character and a reasonable educational standard. (A curious restriction, come to think of it, for something that purports to be a universal psychological theory, and moreover one which brings us back to our elemental animal realities, but let that pass.) But he said nothing about patients needing to be endowed with a certain conceptual or theoretical equipment. It would have been most odd for him to have required this, and indeed psychoanalytic practice tends to insist on the separation of theory from therapy.

But the whole idea of knowledge, even, *or especially*, of oneself and one's own inner states, attained by direct contact and not dependent on theoretical and conceptual assumptions, is absurd. Yet this kind of knowledge *must* be assumed by psychoanalysis – for without it, the centrality of the training analysis in the formation of an analysis, and the relative unimportance of the accompanying seminars and theory, simply do not make sense.

The truth about the theory of knowledge of course helps to explain the well known, uncontested, and somewhat comic fact that Freudian analysts tend to uncover Freudian material, Jungian analysts Jungian material, and so on,

depending upon the point of view of the analyst, the patients of each school seem to bring up precisely the kinds of phenomenological data which confirm the theories and interpretations of their analysts! . . . Freudians elicit material about the Oedipus complex . . . Jungians about archetypes, Rankians about separations anxiety, Adlerians about inferiority, Horneyites about idealized images, Sullivanians about disturbed . . . relationships, etc.

So wrote Judd Marmor, erstwhile president of the American Academy of Psychoanalysis.[5]

In this connection, it is customary to talk about 'suggestion'. I do not find this very helpful, partly because 'suggestion' is not much of an explanation (though it tends to masquerade as one), and partly because it misleadingly suggests a kind of forceful, Svengali-like interference with material. But introspected material is terribly inchoate and labile, and we have no good or natural language for it; Freudian and similar theory doesn't so much transform it – rather it is a net which enables us to seize it all, to give it a local habitation and a name. The assumption of a fully determinate Unconscious seems to me odd and unwarranted. If it is highly ambiguous, these theories do not so much force themselves on it, as give it shapes it previously lacked.

The dependency of perception (including inner perception, or perception of one's own character, attitudes, and so on) on theory-saturated concepts, and of the precariousness of those theories and the concepts which they pervade, in the face of future and as yet undiscovered facts, quite demolishes the distinctive psychoanalytical model of self-knowledge, according to which a man who has been helped to understand and neutralize his inner impediments, thereafter sees the world, or at any rate himself, truly. What he sees depends on his theoretical assumptions; whether they in turn are true depends on facts, most of them as yet not available. (Future generations of facts always outnumber those already in our possession.) This original sin or weakness of knowledge is not something specially attached to psychology or self-understanding: it applies to all knowledge without exception.

But this destroys that curious purity-cognition tie-up which is so characteristic of psychoanalysis and essential to it. In a curious way (about which a good deal remains to be said), Freudianism is profoundly akin to Platonism, according to which also those who were Good saw the Truth, and those who saw the Truth were Good. Given the world as it is, and above all given knowledge as it is and must be, this alas is entirely incorrect. He who possesses a reasonable, sound theoretical equipment will perceive correctly, however neurotic or wicked he may be personally; he who lacks it or possesses an unsound one, will perceive incorrectly, however pure of neurotic tensions or compulsions *he* may be. Truth and Goodness (or Beauty) are *not* one, Plato, Keats and Freud notwithstanding. On the contrary, perception of truth and goodness of heart are alas largely independent, an idea correctly mirrored by the philosophical doctrines of the inherent separation of fact and value.

The tacit, pervasive and indispensable assumption that a form of knowledge exists – namely that induced by psychoanalysis – which is theory-independent and direct, (though conditional on a kind of inner purification), seems to me one of the crucial and conclusive weaknesses of the whole psychoanalytic edifice. It is also an essential precondition of the dogmatism for which the movement is famous. Essentially, it does not propound theories open to further

93

testing, for it is in direct contact with concrete reality: and this must be so, if its training and therapeutic techniques are to make sense. A kind of 'cognitive licence' is conferred on those whom the technique has made pure of heart.

The fact that the reality to be uncovered in this case is the Unconscious which controls our destinies, gives it all its importance and urgency. The fact that this direct contact is not immediate but conditional, presupposing a monopolistically controlled and very protracted technique, gives those who are licensed to use it their exclusive authority. As it appears to be the only technique effectively adapted to this most important of ends, no external check on its effectiveness would seem to be possible. The very nature of the situation precludes it. As the only path to knowledge is the removal of the inner veil, rather than acquisition of difficult information (with the inner veil off, it is all plain to see), and as the only available helpers in veil-removal are those who have already had their own inner veil antecedently lifted, external testing really is quite inappropriate. All those critics who have been appalled by the lack of inclination, to put it mildly, of the movement to have its ideas checked, have on the whole failed to see that this disinclination is not simply a human weakness, but a perfectly logical corollary of the central ideas of the vision.

Naïve realism is the natural belief of mankind, alas. When applied to the mind, it generates a further natural error, which I shall call Naïve Mentalism. Freud is popularly associated with the discovery that the human mind is more complex and harder to understand than had previously been supposed. But in an important sense, his message is the very opposite. The imposition, and occasional removal, of the inner veil is indeed a complex matter: but Freudianism assumes that, *once the veil is off*, all is plain. It implicitly attributes to the post-veil-removal mind that very transparency which had once been credited to *any* mind. But is there any reason to accept this assumption?

Most of us do not know or understand the grammar of the language(s) we speak, not because we have repressed this information as too hot to handle, but because we never had it in the first place, because we are not clever enough, or have failed to go through the requisite linguistic training. The grammar of our conduct and motivation is presumably at least as complex as that of our language; in so far as the capacity to articulate ideas in a way brings them into being, the grammar of conduct must have all the complexity of the phrases which express it, plus the complexity of any conduct, constraint or consideration which we 'cannot put into words', and I believe there are many such.

Freudianism speaks as if this kind of complexity either did not exist or did not matter. This is combined with the fact that when underlying physicalist models are added, these in turn are simple metaphors, push-pull parables, and not at all operational models. The competence of our consciousness – how can it initiate or inhibit action, and how, according to Freud, can it release us from the thrall of previously unconscious attachments, etc. – all this is profoundly mysterious and problematic. Consciousness is in a way much more mysterious than the Unconscious. Freudianism takes the naïve self-explanatoriness assumptions of daily life, treats them as a kind of residue or baseline, which remains over and is self-sufficient once unconscious interference has been eliminated. Alternatively, conduct is linked by psycho-hydraulics to a schematized account of the biological foundations of our being. Human competence and conduct are treated as either self-explanatory or explained by a pseudo-neurological, make-believe material model. The curious fact is that psychoanalysis is a *homunculus* theory. (By this is meant a psychological theory which 'explains' some human competence or capacity by an inner self, which is supplied by the outer, physiological self with its data. For instance, our capacity to *see* objects can be explained in homunculus terms by assuming that some Little Man is watching the retina.) Further selves are assumed to lurk within us, which are then anthropomorphically credited with human competence(s).

The circularity and unsatisfactoriness of this kind of explanation is obvious and well known. (Does that inner man have an eye and retina of his own, in turn?)

The homunculus quality of psychoanalytic explanation, noted by B. F. Skinner at least as early as 1953, the tendency to credit the Unconscious with the same competences and capacities as we normally and unthinkingly attribute to ourselves (only somewhat modified by a lower logical and other orderliness and restraint), is obscured by the fact that this particular homunculus is rather special. Because he is so primitive, elemental, dark, brutal, biological, it *seems* as if he were a rather suitable element in a scientific explanation of our conduct. He looks like a very primary inhabitant, a founder member of nature. Moreover, there is good evidence to suggest that he *exists*. The truth of the matter seems to me to be that he does exist, but explains little – certainly not any of our intellectual capacities.

The notorious habit of analysts of explaining away disagreement rather than considering the critical arguments, also hinges on this. They virtually know no other mode of discovery other than (putative) veil-removal (aided only by a little common-sense observation). Hence they can help others, when they are under the sway of error, only by trying to pin-point and highlight the inner veil which is responsible for the error. Notoriously, motives not reasons are what matter. Analysts don't really know any method other than inducing illumination by bringing motives to the surface; moreover, to admit that the issue is really *sub judice* and to be decided by some external independent judge (e.g. 'facts') would be to admit by implication that they themselves might be mistaken, subject to interference by inner veils, and hence not properly analysed and ill-qualified for their own posts and professions. Everything about their work situation and conceptual milieu, and the way both have been constructed, impels them towards an *ad hominem* rather than bona-fide-conceding reply to critics.

Anthony Quinton, in his contribution to *Freud: the Man, His World, His Influence*[6] claims that 'the doctrine of resistance is not a central and crucial part of psychoanalytic theory', and therefore that this 'polemical strategem', characterized in Quinton's view by 'a certain intellectual vulgarity', can be excised from Freudian theory without significant loss. Not so. It is really the complement and obverse of the veil-removal theory of knowledge, which in turn is essential to the entire system. Vulgar or not, *ad hominem* arguments are not mere polemical support for empirical evidence, a kind of irregular flanking force: it is the other way round. In a sense, the system allows only *ad hominem* arguments. If human veil removal is crucial to knowledge, then the only cogent argument really is: I am freer of inner veils than thou. Empirical evidence, in this system, is only and at best a kind of inconclusive, tangential support for *ad hominem* appeals, to a validation by inner health, or disqualification by inner disturbance. Justification by Inner Grace alone is what counts.

V

THE CUNNING BROKER

THE CONCEPT OF THE UNCONSCIOUS

This is evidently *the* central concept of psychoanalysis. It is its central notion and forms its core, jointly perhaps with its aetiology of the neuroses, its stress on sexuality and on the early formation of personality. In a way it embraces all these, for they make their impact through it: it mediates between them and human conduct. What is it? Does it exist? – or should we say, in what senses does it exist?

When originally introduced, it constituted part of that *scandal*, that *offence*, that resistance-engendering trauma, through which the movement made its impact, by means of which it obliged men to take their stand, to be counted for it or against it, to face the wager. Early and incestuous sexuality, enslavement to the episodes of mental constellations of youth, the mental determination of physical symptoms – these items constitute further shocking pieces of substantive information, and no doubt they were very important: the shock element was essential, and it is difficult for mankind, on the whole, to be shocked by abstractions. None the less, a sustained general or abstract idea was probably also required to endow the excitement engendered by relatively specific ideas, such as infantile sexuality or persistent incestuous longings, with coherence, with a logical backbone. The idea of the Unconscious provided it.

And although the possession of an Unconscious as such is not inherently shocking in any kind of appealingly salacious way – after all, the contents of that Unconscious *might* have been entirely proper and respectable – nevertheless, at its

98

own abstract level, the idea also administered a shock to previous conceptions. Perhaps the distinctively Freudian Unconscious *could not* have been prim and proper, in so far as it sometimes seems as if its contents were recruited exclusively by repression. Freud on occasions appears to hold a kind of Inner Enforced Exile theory of the Unconscious; if this is the correct interpretation, the Unconscious postulated by him does not simply embrace all primal forces in us, including such as have never reached consciousness, but merely those which as it were bounced off consciousness, back into the deep – a kind of psychic government-in-exile. An impulse or idea must have been *expelled* from the conscious Garden of Eden, on this interpretation, before it enters the dread realm.[1] This would lead to the view that there is nothing in the Unconscious which wasn't previously in consciousness – parallel to the pseudo-Aristotelian dictum that there is nothing in the mind which wasn't previously in the senses.

Nowadays the idea is so common and familiar and is (no doubt rightly) accepted, that a certain amount of historical imagination may be needed before one can sense how, when it was first presented and widely canvassed, the idea could appear bizarre, repellent and even contradictory. An Oxford don 'refuted' Freud by pointing out that mind was defined in terms of consciousness, so that 'unconscious mind' was simply a contradiction, and that was that.

My own belief is that the weakness of psychoanalysis, at this point so central to its theory, is not that the notion of the Unconscious is intolerably daring, but quite the reverse: that the Freudian concept of the Unconscious is, first of all, *far* too parasitic on the ordinary, unsophisticated idea of the conscious mind (that, in other words, it is guilty of naïve mentalism), and second, that this notion of the conscious mind and its powers is treated far too uncritically and naïvely. The trouble with psychoanalysis is not, as was initially supposed, its excessively daring revision of our ideas of mind, but rather, on the contrary, its uncritical and rather naïve conservatism in this sphere. It was our conception of *consciousness* and its role in conduct which needed revision: what Freud in effect did was to supplement and fortify a naive mentalist model of conscious human behaviour, by endowing the conscious mind with a kind of strange *doppelgänger* who, however, all in all, rather resembled his partner. This defect lies not in the attribution to him of unconsciousness, once relatively novel, but, on the contrary, in the fact that in all other respects he remained far, far too close to his prototype, to the conscious human mind as it unreflectively sees itself, or believes itself to be, in daily life. The flaw of the Freudian Unconscious is not that it constitutes a scandalous inversion of conscious proprieties, but that it remains far, far too close to them. Freudianism is a kind of animism. It projects (rightly or wrongly), on to forces outside our consciousness, the kind of trait or attribute which our culture had habitually attributed to our conscious activity. As in other forms of animism, this is combined with the claim that these spirits of the deep can be understood, conjured up, appeased and rendered harmless only by certain practitioners of mysteries, members of a restrictive guild with specialized initiation rites.

There can be no serious doubt about the 'existence of an Unconscious', in some sense, probably in quite a number of senses. On the contrary, all too obviously, there is not one, but many, many kinds of 'Unconscious', and the best approach to this topic may well be to begin by listing some of them.

1. The physiological, neurological infrastructure of our capacity to act simply is not accessible to our conscious introspection. These mechanisms either control, or constitute a condition of, 'our' mental processes. Yet if accessible at all, they are accessible only to 'external' investigation by neurologists and others. Their role in our daily functioning, which must be assumed to be crucial, will remain absolutely hidden from the individual until such time as neurological research has progressed far enough to lay them bare. In this sense, these processes are part of us, but remain 'unconscious'. If one adopts a 'materialist' interpretation of Freud, this sense of 'unconscious' is not wholly unrelated to the one which is central to psychoanalysis.

2. It is conceivable, or at any rate it has been suggested, among others by Noam Chomsky, a thinker second only to Freud in his impact on our views on the mind,[2] that it is possible that our basic conceptual equipment is such that our psychic processes may remain for ever inaccessible to our comprehension, and that this explains the poor performance of psychology. The ineffability or incomprehensibility thesis is frequently encountered in religious thought, and patently serves as a blanket cover, an unanswerable Joker card, an omnibus reply to any criticisms pointing out incoherences in a system. If some important truth is inherently beyond our comprehension (though none the less part of the dogma of a given Revelation), then of course we may not criticize it by the canons of our reason, to which, *ex hypothesi*, it is not subject. If this is the situation, there is nothing we can do about it, and such a Joker card trumps everything. The fact the card is so very convenient for those who use it, and that they use it just when it is so convenient for them, must make us somewhat suspicious. Chomsky, of course, invokes the idea only as a possible explanation for the sorry state of psychology and perhaps of the social sciences in general, and not as a protective cover for any positive view of his own.

This sense of the Unconscious, as that which is *inconceivable* for those with either our intellectual equipment or with our neurological infrastructure, in other words inherently inaccessible to our consciousness, is extremely important and intriguing, but does not seem to bear any significant relation to the Freudian Unconscious. Freud's thought seems pervaded by a kind of tacit, naïve realist or 'echo' theory of mind and knowledge, as discussed in the previous chapter, and he did not seem to be much given to supposing that there was anything much beyond his own conceptual reach. The contents of his kind of Unconscious are not *generically* unthinkable: they are *specifically* excluded from conscious thought.

3. Sociology clearly needs the notion of what might be called *relative* conceptual inaccessibility. It is plausible to suppose that there are ideas and mental operations, which

can be articulated only in some, but not in all, conceptual/ linguistic/cultural systems. An obvious example are complex physical theories which make sense only in the context of mathematical systems, which in turn can be operated only by those who have been trained in them, where the training in turn presupposes a conceptual and institutional background which can be located only in some societies.

But the kind of technical complexity found in advanced science may well not be the only specimen of this type of socially relative conceptual inaccessibility. The supposition must at least be entertained that some societies or languages succeed in blocking conceptual alternatives which would be contrary to their interests, and so at least approximate to the situation sketched by George Orwell in *1984*, where Newspeak is so constructed as to make political heresies unthinkable and unsayable.

The Freudian Unconscious does presumably in some measure depend on moral reprobation for the selection of items destined for repression from consciousness. In so far as morality is a collective, social phenomenon, this kind of Unconscious obviously is of some relevance, which might repay more investigation than it has hitherto received. Social anthropologists sometimes speak of 'structural amnesia', by which they mean facts eliminated from a community's consciousness not by individual psychic repression, but by social mechanisms. Nevertheless, the collective and *conceptual* devices for excluding disturbing elements from consciousness do not seem to have been at the centre of Freud's attention, notwithstanding his concern with collective phenomena in his theory of religion.

4. An assemblage of items which *are* accessible, in principle and as far as the conceptual equipment of the relevant community is concerned, but which are nevertheless firmly excluded from a *particular* consciousness, for reasons relevant to the internal psychic economy of that person (though allowing for the fact that the selection of an element for repression into the Unconscious may be influenced by the negative moral loading of the item, by the standards of the given community in question).

In brief, the content of this Unconscious appears to be made up of elements which, as such, *could be* perfectly accessible to consciousness – but for the fact that in some other sense they *can't* be, that they are barred. This seemingly contradictory characterization is of course perfectly consistent. The barring is individual, even if encouraged by collective moral prohibitions. The barred elements are conceptually and socially accessible, but barred for private reasons. Whether or not there are private ideas, the black-balling of ideas can for Freud be private. Even if, as another Viennese guru taught, there are no private meanings, there can, it appears, be private repressions. Generically, these repressed elements belong to classes of things which our consciousness habitually can and often does handle, without batting an eyelid; but specifically, they belong to individual clusters which, owing to the particular psychic constellation of this or that person, happen to be too hot for him to handle.

This is one of the most important general features of the Unconscious as conceived by Freud and the entire tradition of thought stemming from him. An alien realm with alien laws, but its denizens are utterly familiar – occasionally bigger and smaller perhaps than their neighbours in the realm of the Conscious, wearing all kinds of fancy dress, habitually and compulsively given to all kinds of transvestism and role-swapping, disobeying all the habitual rules of space and of time sequence, of addition, subtraction, plus and minus signs, proportion and perspective, and every other kind of regularity – but, when all is said and done, closely resembling their familiar neighbours from the good old conscious world: not only are all the normal inhabitants to be found there, but no one else much seems to have swelled their ranks. The Unconscious is like some low hostelry just across the border, where all the thieves and smugglers indulge themselves with abandon, free of the need for camouflage and disguise which they prudently adopt, for fear of the authorities, when they are *this* side of the frontier. At the same time, they allow themselves any fantasy they like while they indulge in their revelries. But under all that, they are still the same persons as we knew this side of the border, where they present themselves with deceitful sobriety.

In brief, it is like meeting all one's friends, enemies and acquaintances, but at the carnival and in fancy dress: one may be a bit surprised at what they get up to, but there are few, if indeed *any* surprises as to personnel. At carnival time, the townsfolk dress and behave strangely: but the population of the town seems to be exactly the same on working days as during the great fiesta. They invert their roles and alignments; ranking goes topsy-turvy; but the *kind* of thing that they do still seems to make perfectly good sense in terms of ordinary weekday language.

But there is even more to it than this. The conservatism and, in the end, the staidness of that allegedly exotic realm, the Freudian Unconscious, is even more remarkable. The mechanisms which animate this carnival population seem to be roughly the same, or at least to be of the same general kind, as those which move the burghers of the daytime town. The personnel reappear, in strange apparel, swollen or shrunk in size, fancifully transformed in the night version of the same town. The *psyche by night* is wilder, more colourful, much, much more disregardful of proportions and propriety than what we are used to in the cold grey light of day: but when all is said and done, it is not really all that different . . .

In daily life, we tend to assume, or at least work and talk in terms of, naïve mentalism. Naïve *realism* assumes that things are as we think they are, that by some miracle the properties which they really have, have migrated into our consciousness, and are mirrored there with reasonable, tolerable accuracy (give or take a bit of perspective, and the addition of harmless colouring and other permitted 'secondary' additives and of course, in the case of *conditional* realism, subject to the removal of hindrances).

Naïve mentalism assumes something parallel about our *inner* world: in daily life, we take for granted our inner habits and motivation, our susceptibilities and competences. We use them, as old, reliable and above all as *self-explanatory* friends. Our talk about ourselves and others constitutes a psychology of kinds. What is really striking about this 'psychology' is that it takes our amazing range of competence, and all kinds of connections we establish between thoughts, feelings, things, actions and institutions, for granted. It builds on these seemingly self-evident connections, by working out the consequences of their superimposition on each other, or their conflict, in a kind of rough and ready way, and it invokes special extraneous explanations if these connections or powers, capabilities, fail to work. But it doesn't query them. A system of such seemingly self-evident connections is known as a culture, and presumably that which all such cultures have in common is what is known as 'human nature'. But inside each culture, human nature is conceived as the totality of these assumed connections or competences.

Now the truth of the matter is, of course, that our range of competences and connections is *anything but* self-evident or self-explanatory. Though many thinkers have noticed it – consider for instance Lichtenberg's observation that we ought not to say 'I think' but 'it thinks' – nevertheless it seems to me Chomsky's great achievement was that he has at long last really rammed this point home. This enormous achievement is quite independent of whether his particular strategy for reconstructing the generative core of given languages, which is based on this insight, has or has not been successful in detail, or successful at all. Chomsky has managed to hammer this point home for a number of reasons: partly because he applied it to a single field, namely linguistics, where the range of competence can be mapped far more easily than elsewhere, because the 'output' consists of relatively insolable units (there really are, more or less, things identifiable as 'sentences' – but are there insolable units of conduct?), and partly because the discovery was linked to concrete techniques (and here there is a certain parallel with Freud).

On the other hand, Freud's model for the behaviour of the human mind, both the daytime visible bit and its subterranean, carnival, surrealist, domineering *Doppelgänger*, is a strange and unstable, vacillating mixture of naïve mentalism, and the crudest, basically metaphorical materialism of drives, forces, blockages, expressed in terms of what one might call pseudo-psycho-hydraulics. Forces blocked in one way find outlets elsewhere, forces balance each other, etc. This kind of intuitive, metaphorical, and quite untestable psycho-hydraulics or, if you like, hydro-hermeneutics, is somehow married to the naïve acceptance of our habitual introspective characterization of human motivation, feeling and association. Freud may have taught us to be utterly distrustful of the face value of introspective evidence, on points of content and detail: but, ironically, the whole psychoanalytic jargon is not in the least distrustful of the ordinary conceptual machinery of our introspection taken as a whole, generically, which reappears, admittedly in garish carnival colours, in the new idiom it employs for our psychic life.

My own suspicion is that the advancement of psychology depends rather more on scepticism concerning the idiom as a whole, including these sexed-up variants of it, than on the alleged unmasking of detailed affirmations made within the idiom. The Unconscious may or may not be simply a wilder, randier, more brutal and undisciplined savage brother of the Conscious, devoid only of any sense of proportion, disregardful of all logical as well as moral proprieties: all this may be true, and probably *is* true. But it does *not* follow that its conduct or influence is explicable by applying to it the naïve mentalism, the acceptance of culturally standard meanings and their theoretical load, which passes for 'understanding' in daily life. This may well be the crucial methodological error of psychoanalysis. Ordinary language accompanies conduct, but lacks the power to explain it.

Two assumptions pervade the Freudian treatment of the mind. One is that, once the unconscious hindrances are removed, the working of the mind, the connections between circumstance, motive, aspiration and act, are really rather self-evident and self-explanatory, and that (unconscious hindrances once again being absent) introspection is to be trusted. It had only lied on points of detail, so to speak; the general idiom was sound, or becomes sound, once recognition of its wild, randy, unhousetrained *Doppelgänger* is added. In fact, all this seems to me overwhelmingly doubtful – for all the reasons which Chomsky has adduced against the self-evident nature of our linguistic competence. The range of conceivable actions is as rich as the range of intelligible sentences, and our competence is as mysterious, and as devoid of automatic self-intelligibility, in the one case as in the other. The fact that some possible acts and motives and constellations are 'repressed' does indeed add an interesting complication; but the highlighting of this little complication, assuming for a moment that Freud has explored it adequately, does not resolve the far bigger problem of understanding our overall psychological competence, and in no way obviates the point that this competence cannot be accounted for in terms borrowed from our naïve intuitive way of thinking about our mind.

The second assumption which pervades the model is, in itself, overwhelmingly plausible. It is that 'hydraulic' element, the idea that the driving force behind the agitation of our mind is related to powerful instinctual forces, with a deep physiological basis, and related to the biological needs of survival and procreation. There is no need to doubt this assumption: its plausibility is overwhelmingly great. What one may doubt, however, is whether the sketchily constructed model of sluices and channels and chambers and locks and water-wheels, which translate these forces into concrete and specific directions of conduct and feeling, is in any way scientifically serious, as opposed to being mere metaphor. It is loose, sloppy, merely verbal, and explains any conduct only in retrospect. The point which Chomsky made in his celebrated critique of behaviourism – that the stimulus-response model, when applied to linguistic competence, works only if one retrospectively invents the stimuli required to account for the given response – applies with at least as great a force to this aspect of Freudianism.[3]

There is in existence a hydraulic Keynes machine, in which a flowing liquid simulates the movement of the economy according to the Keynesian model. There is no Freud machine, in which a fluid libido courses through the available channels and in which diverse constellations of Super-Ego, Oedipal reaction, etc., could be set so as to simulate the appropriate psychopathological consequences, and predict them in advance of the event. All we do have so far is a facile hydro-hermeneutic jargon which accommodates the facts, all facts, any facts, after the event. There is of course a problem: Freud insisted that the libido cathects, attaches itself to, diverse objects, and that once so cathected, is very difficult to detach. So the libido in the Freud machine will have to be represented by an extremely viscous liquid, which is then liable, as you might say, to gum up the works. However, a good engineer should be able to solve this problem.

Nevertheless, sloppy and inadequate and *ex post* as the model may be, what is of supreme importance for the understanding of the ideological impact of the whole system, is that the model does indeed fuse these two elements, the libidino-hydraulic and the semantic. It seems clearly true that we are instinct-driven animals, and it is equally clear that we respond to very complex patterns of meaning. Any theory of man which neglects either of these two aspects can hardly be very useful. But it is not easy to bring these two aspects into relation with each other. One reason for the importance of the Freudian concept of the Unconscious is that it seems to provide a realm within which the dark gods can communicate with the baroque complexities of our semantic structures. To do so, our meanings evidently have to lose all that categorial orderliness, sense of proportion and perspective, that sense of logic and conceptual hierarchy, that fastidiousness about placing all events into a single spatio-temporal order, which, according to Kant, our reason and understanding so painstakingly impose on us.

When our concepts are let loose in that dark cellar, they leave all that behind, and indulge in a liberating or frightening Saturnalia. But for all that, they remain recognizable and identifiable, and we can still address them, or

108

speak of them, especially if provided with a good interpreter guide who has been instructed in the conventions of this subterranean and perennial Walpurgisnacht.

The Unconscious speaks with a slurred voice, but it does speak English. So communication is not lost. To change the simile, the Unconscious is a kind of gearbox, in which the tremendous force of the elemental drives within us can mesh into the complex, intricate and fragile meanings in terms of which we live; though this is possible only if those meanings are first adjusted and loosened up in accordance with the requirements of this gear machinery.

This Janus-like or broker nature of the Freudian Unconscious is something of very great importance. But for this bio-hermeneutic fusion, the system would not lend itself to assuaging the distress of sufferers, or to buttressing the authority of the healing pastors who succour them. Access to the 'meanings' which guide our conduct, on its own, confers no authority, no power, no promise of cure, no aura on the practitioner. For one thing, we can do it for ourselves. For another, we know that meanings are fragile things and we stand in no awe of them. Theories about dark biological forces, likewise, have no appeal on their own: who wants to be reduced to a bundle of animal drives?

But inherently secret meanings which at the same time mesh in with the dark bio-forces – now that is an altogether different matter. Their links to the deep confer authority and inspire awe. But their links with *our* meanings help us to retain our human dignity. We are understood as people, as ourselves, not as things or machines or beasts. So bio-hermeneutics is simultaneously reductive (thereby giving control) and restorative (dignity-preserving). And note at the same time that the Unconscious, just like the Transcendent (and for parallel reasons), is not only a concept but also a social programme. Blended into a theory of how the powerful Unconscious can be approached and appeased, it automatically points the way to a unique salvation and thereby establishes a hierarchy. He who can guide the sufferer along the path, is automatically vindicated in his authority and standing.

PSYCHO-HYDRAULICS

The mélange of this somewhat uncritically imposed, and
sloppily articulated model of the psyche, is made up of two
main elements – naïve mentalism and metaphorical
psycho-hydraulics. *Which* of these two elements is fundamental, depends on your exegesis of Freud. Philosophers
offering interpretations of Freud tend, at this crucial point,
to fall into two rival schools, which might be called the
Materialist and the Hermeneutic. The former will treat the
'scientific' aspiration to link psychoanalytic theory to biology and to a theory of drive and to the physiological bases of
our mental life, as central. The latter, by contrast, will
concentrate on the closeness of psychoanalytic theory and
practice to life as actually lived. It is important for them
that the theory remains close to the realm of *meanings*
experienced by individuals.

This fundamental dilemma in the interpretation of Freud
is of course essentially linked to the crucial strategic position occupied by Freudianism in one of the great intellectual issues of our time, the struggle between those who
aspire to naturalize man once and for all and for good,
making him part of nature and treating him as such, and
those who, on the contrary, wish to *save* man from science,
or from what they call 'scientism', from 'reductionism', and
allow man to go on seeing himself in human terms, which
means, in practice, in terms continuous with those which he
employs, intuitively and with ease, in daily life.

What is the truth of the matter? Can Freud be more
correctly and justifiably enlisted on the side of science or on
the side of anti-scientific 'humanism'? Where does the
centre of gravity of the system *really* lie?

Anyone who hopes for a definitive answer to this crucial
question is bound, I fear, to be disappointed. It isn't so
much that the system just happens to be ambivalent and
located on an important conceptual boundary: rather, it is
of its very essence, *and above all of the essence of its appeal*, that
it should be inherently and permanently ambiguous at this
point. Asking for a definitive answer here is exactly like

asking, with respect to the Hegelian system, whether or not the Absolute Spirit is, or is not, to be identified with the Christian God. The whole point of Hegelianism was to articulate a doctrine which could be (and was) read *either* way, as on the one hand the reaffirmation of the God of Abraham in a scientific or historicizing age, and on the other as a new vision, breathing a bit of acceptable meaning into a unitary and levelled-out world. What Hegel had achieved, so to speak, for the mentalism or anthropomorphism applied to the universe at large, Freud had in his curious way achieved for mentalism or anthropomorphism of *man*. (Hegel had taught, though not quite in these words, that history is psychosomatic.) Whether you are tough-minded and wish to see man as part of biological nature, or whether you are one of those beautiful spirits who insist on seeing man as *man*, either way, satisfaction is guaranteed. This of course is a central fact in the comprehension of the success and impact of psychoanalysis: it manages to be located astride one of the really big divides of our age, and to give satisfaction in *both* directions. And this is not the only big divide it straddles.

An interpretation of Freud which would eliminate either of these two crucial elements, in the interest of consistency or coherence, would thereby largely emasculate and indeed paralyse the system. The purely 'hermeneutic' interpretations give us a truly anaemic Unconscious, and cannot do justice to the overwhelming power of our lust, aggression, resentment. The purely biological interpretations miss out just as badly on the astonishing intricacy, cunning, deviousness, semantic sophistication of the actual outward manifestations of the dark gods. But a bio-hermeneutic system confers great powers on its shamans-pastors: the *bio* bit ensures that they communicate with the dark elemental forces which threaten to devour us, the hermeneutic part ensures that it is done in human and reassuring terms. Pure science would be too abstract and distant, pure hermeneutics would not have any mysteries and inspire no awe. Bio-hermeneutics contains just the right mixture of threat and familiarity. The dark gods remain, but with a human face.

The ambiguous location of the system, astride this septic and disturbing boundary, is also valuable socially. A literary-semantic exercise is attractive and accessible but, not partaking of the magic of hard science, inspires little therapeutic confidence. A biological science might inspire confidence, but is hardly a suitable pastime for the idle rich. A technique which ambiguously blends both these aspects, which delves into biological secrets, yet speaks the intuitively accessible language of unspecialized educated Western man, is ideal.

A CUNNING BASTARD

The Unconscious is cunning. But ·that isn't quite an adequate, quite a strong enough way of putting it. If one says it like that, it sounds as if the Unconscious happens to be cunning — but it might also, had we been built differently, have been straightforward, guileless, simple.

Cunning is not just an attribute of the Unconscious. Cunning is its very essence. Were it not cunning, it would be trivial. There is no doubt, and never has been any, but that there are various physiologically rooted processes, with psychic consequences, of which we are not conscious. An 'Unconscious' which might have been exhausted by contents of that kind would not have constituted a discovery of any importance, let alone any kind of intellectual trauma. What made it interesting and shocking was precisely its great deviousness, its ruthless purposiveness in the pursuit of aims unsanctioned or damned by consciousness, its protean ability to assume any disguise, its matchless intelligence service which rapidly and effortlessly penetrates the secrets of its opponent, the hapless conscious Ego, and as effectively and effortlessly places any desired 'disinformation' therein . . .

Its cunning is as limitless as is its force. Let us once again reconsider the human condition, as it is so very plausibly portrayed by the entire psychoanalytic system.

112

The conscious Ego is engaged·in a kind of chess game with the Unconscious. But what an unequal contest!

The Unconscious, it is true, lacks logic and sense of order. It is quite insensitive to any contradictions within its own set of beliefs, it does not respect the rules of causation or of the time series in establishing connections, it cannot tell a large object from a small one, or a distant one from a close one. But what of that? Richard Wollheim observes: 'Freud gives us . . . "the special characteristics of the system *UCS*" Freud lists . . . "exemption from mutual contradiction, . . . timelessness . . ." Freud, it must be emphasized, held not merely that contradictory elements . . . can co-exist in the unconscious, but that they exist there without contradiction.'[4]

Wollheim thinks that some modification of this may have been required but, except perhaps at the very end of his life, Freud would seem to have continued in his denial of unconscious logical conflict.

But if there is no logical constraint at all in that realm, why need the Unconscious be devious? After all, *everything* is allowed down there. Frank Cioffi notes this contradiction in Freud and the need to allow the Unconscious at least some sense of logic, just enough to make it choose between interpretations.[5] If contradictory interpretations can be valid, why should *some* interpretations be therapeutically valid and effective?

These disadvantages of the Unconscious – if such they be – are puny compared with its assets. While its opponent is virtually in complete ignorance (not to mention the deliberate disinformation) about the Unconscious, the Unconscious itself is in possession of every piece of information that is available to the Conscious. None of its data or codes are hidden from it . . . But this total superiority in the sphere of Intelligence is not all. When you look at the relative fire-power, the situation is just as disparate. The Conscious can appeal to various ideals, values, overall policies, which the person in question overtly endorses, but whose hold over the real human personality is notoriously frail. The Unconscious, by contrast, can release the wild hordes of the Id, ferocious and irresistible savages who easily sweep all before them, who can slice through the puny defences of our official façade like a hot knife through butter . . .

Given that this is how things stand – and this is how things do indeed stand, both in fact and according to psychoanalytical theory – the only astonishing thing is that there should be any game, any conflict at all. The Unconscious could, could it not, use either its superiority in the field of Intelligence and win while deploying only minimal force, or equally, it could use its overwhelming superiority in brute force, and not even stoop to use its total Intelligence penetration of the enemy. It is strange that neither of these should happen completely; I suppose the explanation lies in the fact that the Unconscious had, bizarrely, deployed its great force on both sides, acting both through and for the Id *and* for the Super-Ego . . . The turning of the dark Will upon itself is of course a phenomenon already much noted and commented on by Freud's intellectual ancestors Schopenhauer and Nietzsche. So the Unconscious does not simply dominate and sweep all before it: instead, it fights on both sides, and creates a tense and unhappy situation for man: *Under one law born, to another bound* . . .

There is hope, just a little hope, in this unequal contest, since the turn of the century: an agency and a technique now exist which can restore the balance, at least in the Intelligence field, and make the contest a little more equal.

Naturally, of course, the Unconscious resents this recent tilting of the balance against itself, the loss of its previous privileged position. Strangely, it can identify the new enemy who has done it this harm (so, for once, apparently overcoming its old a-logical habits, for it can now identify complex rival *theories* articulated in intricate arguments in books and learned journals). It can unleash resistance, it seems, even against abstract doctrines. It naturally tries to use its old tricks against the new enemy, and to subvert him by inspiring cunningly camouflaged doubts about his scientific validity, his scientific testability, etc. But be not deceived! The New Science can see through all that.

Note that if this is indeed the situation – and it is a plausible picture, the only element lacking plausibility in it, alas, being the promise of succour – then the premises of this belief-system are very strong indeed. A little stronger even, perhaps, than is altogether comfortable for its adherents and missionaries. This, in fact, is not an uncommon situation with respect to belief-systems. To browbeat opposition, they strengthen their doctrines to a point at which the implications are a little more extreme than is convenient for the true believers themselves. If a God exists who attends to all details of His creation and allocates its members to eternal bliss or the opposite, it seems somewhat absurd for anyone to attend to any business other than placating Him. In fact, the Church does not wish the faithful to neglect this world altogether, puny though it be on the above assumptions. Similarly, if the role of the Unconscious in our life is what the model claims, it is somewhat absurd to be interested in any other topic. If the balance of forces is as indicated, any unanalysed person who lives anything like a tolerable life, must be doing it by pure accident.

In brief, if all this were true, at least two consequences follow which normally it is not convenient to implement, articulate or stress:

1. Everyone ought to be analysed. What kind of life is it, which is satisfactory only by a purely fortuitous accident? There are milieux – such as that of psychoanalysts themselves, *ex hypothesi*, and, less tautologically, among some groups of social scientists, notably in America – where this ideal is approximated. But this is untypical.

2. The whole of history should be rewritten in terms of Before and After Freud. The difference between a humanity wholly enslaved to forces of which it knows nothing, and one which at least contains some members endowed with psychological understanding, is more fundamental than any other conceivable barrier line. At least one psychoanalytical thinker, Money-Kyrle, has indeed tried to

work out something along these lines: '[if] the Communist autocracy had been allowed to dominate the world, most of the psychological knowledge we have painfully organized would have been lost, and might take centuries to rediscover.'[6]

Indeed: if Freud is right, most of the previous intellectual and political history of mankind was nothing but tragic shadow-boxing, sound and fury signifying nothing. Men fought and suffered, but knew not what they did. Consciousness and the possibility of liberation came only after the Incarnation of 1897, After Freud. An anti-Freudian dictatorship would be the equivalent of a new dark age.

All this *does* logically follow. Few of those within the fold of this faith spell this out fully or stress it. In the main, the ambience of psychoanalysis is rather unhistorical (though so-called psycho-history now does exist). When explicitly formulated, the Freudian vision of history constitutes somewhat too shattering and fundamental a revision. As in other faiths, the basic ideas are a little *too* powerful, and believers prefer to operate with a somewhat watered-down, weaker version, ignoring some excessively strong corollaries of the central ideas.

REDUCTION AT THE SERVICE OF MAN
(or, a Plethora of Omens)

The fairly coherent cluster of related ideas which came together as psychoanalysis is indeed strategically located at a number of stress-points on the changing map of the intellectual and social life of mankind. We have seen how empiricism – the essence of which is the setting up of *evidence* as the supreme judge over all cognitive claims – led by fallacious reasoning to its supposed corollary, the anaemic Bundleman, the sensualist accountant who however is quite free of guile or of any deep destructive inclinations towards either others or himself. Psychoanalysis owes its overwhelming sense of plausibility to the powerful backlash against that all-at-once sickly and yet unjustifiably complacent vision of man.

But the Bundleman is not the only problem in our collective self-interpretation. The cold, disenchanted vision does not enter only through empiricism, through the subjection of all cognitive claims to the Last Judgement of experience. It also has another source, and one as powerful, disturbing and corrosive for the traditional view of man. There is another aspect of naturalism, of the firm inclusion, without retention of any special rights and privileges, of man within nature. Where empiricism achieves this by making man subject to the tender mercies of evidence, the other path leads through the subjection of man to universal, impersonal, causal explanation. If the first problem is best seen in terms of David Hume, the second one was best articulated by Immanuel Kant.

The problem is basically simple. We normally attribute a kind of autonomy to ourselves, and to our thoughts and feelings, or at least to those with which we identify properly. We assume that we deem *this* to be true, and *that* to be morally repugnant, not because we were somehow wound up by some extraneous causal mechanism to think or feel in that way, but because *we* chose to come to such a conclusion in the light of our valid appreciation of the facts and principles relevant to the case. At least, we fondly hope that this is how the matter stands. We know that there seem to be disturbing exceptions to such autonomy – when, for instance, we are under drugs or the effects of hypnotic suggestion. But we hope those cases are exceptional, and that when we are truly ourselves, we are free, and perhaps vice versa.

Unfortunately, this belief is in conflict with something that seems to be a presupposition of the scientific intelligibility of the world, to which in turn we are also deeply attached – namely, the assumption that events, including those we call human actions and choices and decisions, are parts of nature and subject to its laws, whether or not we are fully acquainted with those laws. Kant was acutely aware of the problem. Ironically, his theory of science was concerned with establishing the universal applicability, within nature (*including* observable man), of notions such as causality; while his theory of ethics was concerned with *saving* human autonomy and morality from what he considered the successful demonstration of the applicability of causation (and certain other related notions) to the whole of this observable world and hence to us, its inhabitants.

In outline, his solution was simple. It can be called the 'theory of double citizenship'. Each and every one of us, as objects within nature, is subject to its laws; and at the same time, as moral and responsible agents, we are exempt from them and subject to a different set of self-imposed laws. Kant knew that the two visions were mutually incompatible, and thought that we were simply doomed to live with this bi-focal vision. All we could do was to understand its sources and learn to live with the resulting conceptual astigmatism. We could learn to live with this (once we understood the situation and its inescapability by reading his books): to expect to be positively comfortable with it would be asking too much.

In a way, this was also one of the last great formulations of the beast/angel view of man, but formulated against the background of a naturalistic vision of the entire observable world, so that this world could contain only beasts (or machines, which in this context came to the same thing). The angel remained and was driven to the very edge of the world, or just beyond, and was made responsible for cognition and for our sense of morality. The angel could never be directly observed, but could be inferred from the fact that certain beasts, namely ourselves, possess the twin (and, for him, closely related) capacities for attaining knowledge and for feeling moral obligation. The angel was the necessary presupposition of knowledge and morality in the world. As such, he was allowed to remain, but only on condition that he was never visible in the world. We know him by his fruits, and *only* by his fruits. We can never meet him face to face. The world-machine leaves us no room for either knowledge or value. The fact that we recognize and respect both of these, shows that the ghost-angel is operating within us.

Kant's astigmatic or double-status theory is extremely uncomfortable, mainly because within each single man, there simply doesn't seem to be room for two such contrary beings. This is not the place to discuss the merits of Kant's theory. What is highly relevant is that Kant has merely elaborated in formal terms a terribly awkward view which is widely held, as a tacit presupposition, by very many people in the contemporary world. We assume both that we are explicable, like other natural phenomena, and that our key thoughts and values are somehow exempt, extraterritorial. When something – for example, accounts of experiments with drugs, or brain-washing – reminds us of the strain between the two ways of looking at ourselves, we feel uncomfortable, as well we may.

Kant's position was highly coherent and quite outstandingly uncomfortable, more so than the common-sense variants of it. He saw that it was no use supposing that sometimes we were free and at other times we were machines: it had to be both of them together, all the time. Common sense is less coherent and less uncomfortable: instead of insisting on double citizenship all the time, it likes to think that we hop from one side of the boundary to the other. Superficially, this *seems* to put less of a strain on our credulity.

Every thinking person in the modern world has to face this problem, tacitly if not overtly. The problem doesn't arise simply for those who have a taste for philosophic conundrums: it arises from two absolutely pervasive features of our world, that is, first, we believe the world we live in susceptible to causal explanation, and second, we believe ourselves to be responsible, at least some of the time, for our thoughts and actions. Many people tacitly resolve this by some sloppy and semiconscious version of Kantian dualism. Instead of perpetual bi-focalism, they suppose that some of their actions and thoughts are what may best be called *reducible* – to the antecedents or causal frameworks which engender or generate them; and that others are not so reducible and are what may be called *authentic* or, in Kant's terminology, autonomous.

Generally speaking, pre-scientific societies take a naïve realist view concerning the beliefs they favour, and a reductionist one about those they oppose. Truth is manifest for the approved members of the society, and the question of its validation is not posed, or posed in a blatantly circular manner (the theory itself singles out the fount of authority, which then blesses the theory). Those who deviate, on the other hand, are *possessed* by evil forces, and they need to be exorcized rather than refuted.

It is only in our technological/industrial society, the only society ever to be based on sustained cognitive growth, that this kind of procedure has become unacceptable. A theory of knowledge has developed, as a kind of stimulus and ratification of genuine science, which is symmetrical, and asks for the same kind of validation-by-evidence for any kind of assertion, rather than allowing *a priori* and circular damnation of some, and a similar ratification of others.

But we face a double predicament. Because we no longer claim to know the true and the false *a priori*, and to link them to Good and Bad people, *all* beliefs are now ideally required to be authentic, rationally justified by publicly available evidence. But at the very same time, because we no longer exempt man from nature, but insist on seeing him as part of it and subject to its laws, all beliefs are also seen as consequences of causal processes within us, and thus inauthentic, 'reducible'. The Kantian 'dual-man' theory is a desperate solution for this very genuine problem.

Some writers sometimes speak as if 'reduction' were simply a bad habit, like picking one's nose in public, which ought to be discouraged and which well-mannered thinkers avoid. This is not so. 'Reduction' of beliefs to their causal antecedents, 'explaining-away' why someone believes something because he is what he is, is a logical, wholly appropriate corollary of seeing man as part of nature.

The Kantian double-self theory, though honest, is so strained and uncomfortable as to be in practice unacceptable. I cannot live with two selves, one sensitive to reason, evidence and the voice of duty, and the other a slave to the laws of nature. This is like putting two men into one tight suit; what happens if one of them wants to go somewhere?

Psychoanalysis possesses a solution which is incomparably more acceptable. It could appropriately be called Selective or Controlled Reductionism. It doesn't put two men into one suit. If anything, it makes two men use the same suit without both ever being in it at the same time; and what is important (as the two men in question are externally indistinguishable) *it alone* decides which one is which, and which one is at any point of time in occupation of the suit.

We have here once again – but this time in an entirely modern idiom – one of those tacit theories of knowledge which is naïve realist for its own views, and reductionist for those of others. But the explanation of why and how either of the two alternative gentlemen takes over the suit, is intricate, and a central part of the overall theory itself. The reduction-worthy gentleman is enslaved to his own unconscious compulsions of which he knows nothing, and his views can consequently be disregarded and explained away. His rival co-tenant, however, sees the world rightly (above all, sees *himself* rightly), having understood and neutralized his own unconscious compulsions. The theory itself, possessing a monopoly or near monopoly of understanding the Unconscious and of its ways, can decide whether it is Dr Jekyll or Mr Hyde that happens to be in the suit. (Remember – externally they are indistinguishable, and Mr Hyde's cunning in impersonating Dr Jekyll knows no bounds.)

Imagine a card game in which one of the players holds a Joker, such that if he holds it one way up, the cards of the player whose turn it is count for him; but if he holds the Joker the other way, the very same cards count against that player. Needless to say, the one who holds the Joker cannot possibly lose. The fact that any view can either be the product of unconscious resistance, or on the contrary the fruit of that cognitive licence granted to those effectively analysed and free of inner handicap, is the precise logical equivalent of the possession of a Joker card of that kind.

One can use another simile. A skilful glider-pilot can actually cause his glider-plane to rise, and to travel long distances, notwithstanding the fact that he is devoid of any means of propulsion. He will find currents of rising warm air and go up with them; if he wishes to descend, he will switch to areas in which cold air is sinking. Similarly, a skilful analyst can reach any conclusion, by 'rising' with the authentic insights, and 'falling' with the reduction-worthy self-delusions. But he has one great advantage over the glider-pilot: it is he who decides, and only he, (unless of course he is quarrelling with another analyst), whether hot air is going up or cold air coming down.

The implicit naïve realism which grants unlimited cognitive licence to those that are pure of heart (i.e. have been effectively analysed and hence are inwardly unhampered) has a curious, very conspicuous, and on reflection not very surprising consequence. Cognitive licence, like most things, is habit-forming. Anyone who has been in unchallenged possession of it for too long is liable to end up using it with less and less restraint, and in the end perhaps with no restraint at all. Cognitive licence corrupts, and absolute cognitive licence corrupts absolutely. He who thinks he has it may well end up with little capacity to distinguish between having an idea, having an idea that has any precise meaning, and knowing it to be true. The metaphysical extravagances of the old Freud (such as the Death Wish) suggest that something of this kind happened to him. But the thinker who has gone furthest in this direction was probably Wilhelm Reich. But, as Rycroft's splendid intellectual biography of the man makes plain, what is remarkable about him is not the extreme absurdity of his views, but the fact that there were no logical constraints within the system to prevent anyone else reaching similar absurdities. The puzzle is not why Reich went the way he did, but why so few others went the same way, or quite as far.[7]

Perhaps the boundary between the *reducible* and the *authentic* cannot now or ever be drawn coherently. It is a very messy and inherently indeterminate business. It is one of the perpetual points of stress in our thought about man and his place in nature. All this is relevant to psychoanalysis for the following reason: psychoanalysis positively flourishes in the conceptual milieu in which this stress is endemic, and benefits enormously from it. The area of mental illness and compulsive irrationality, which after all is its natural habitat, leads one constantly to bang one's head against this problem. An anguished person cannot but ask: when am I deluded, what can I trust?

The problem of the reducibility of human conduct is elegantly harnessed to the structure of the ideas and practices of psychoanalysis. Like a mobile which is only an apparent *perpetuum mobile*, but which depends on air movements or temperature change for its perpetual motion, this too is an energy-capturing system, and one of the important sources of energy which it taps, with great efficiency, is precisely the frictional heat generated by the rubbing of authenticity against reducibility.

This system of ideas harnesses both our sense of heteronomy, of dependence on forces we do not understand and cannot control, and our hope that autonomy, authenticity should be feasible. For once the contradictory hopes of control and of freedom are both of them satisfied. We hope for universal causal order so that we can control nature: we hope for exemption from that order so that we should not ourselves be controlled. It is hard to have it both ways. The feeling of dependence or heteronomy does of course have a double source: the abstract sense that a causal order does obtain in general, and the more specific perception that the realm which concerns us most, namely that of personal relations, does somehow seem tightly constrained, though we cannot normally manipulate those constraints to our advantage.

Psychoanalysis links the dual-condition Angst to a promise of delivery, a soteriology, a technique of liberation, a delayed and conditional autonomy, a liberation controlled and administered by a well-defined guild, and to a theory of the *pays reel* of the kind which, as indicated, has a great initial plausibility, and calls forth a powerful *click* of recognition. Yes, of course our conduct and our feelings and so forth are reducible: the forces which control or generate them are now mapped, at least in outline, by a high-powered theory linked to medicine and thereby to science in general, in other words to that corpus of knowledge which has demonstrated its capacity to unravel the causal mechanisms of nature, certainly with greater effectiveness than any other corpus. It indulges wholeheartedly in the sense of a tight determination of things, as do many primitive thought systems. Nothing in our psychic life is left to chance. Disregarding the fact that the complexity of causation makes many events quite indecipherable as symptoms, it treats them all as omens or portents, available for decoding. Admittedly this can be done only by members of the guild of shamans, and one shaman's interpretation can always be trumped by another's. But we do, it appears, live surrounded by a plethora of omens, there to be read, though we cannot read them unaided. This vision has a marked similarity to a certain kind of paranoia, in which the sufferer sees *all* events as menacing and significant, and credits himself with the intuitive power of reading their significance. In this form of paranoia, our pattern-seeking sense of causation seems to become overactive, unrelenting and compulsive.

But, happily, we are not doomed to remain in a 'reducible' condition for ever. Authenticity, liberation is possible. Admittedly, it is not normally accessible to the unaided individual: self-analysis, the Pelagianism of depth psychology, though not absolutely declared invalid and inadmissible, does not seem to be much encouraged or favoured. It seems only to be an exception, allowed above all so as to explain the mystery of how the saving truth initially entered the world at all, as a heroic and virtually solo performance by the Founder; and being for this reason admitted in principle, the possibility of an occasional repeat performance is somewhat grudgingly allowed. But the true, approved, grace-assisted path to authenticity lies through proper submission to the technique.

REALITY REGAINED

AN EMACIATED WORLD

The point of entry to the understanding of the great appeal of psychoanalytical ideas, was the fleshy, realistic *feel* of human nature as presented by them, in contrast with the unrealistic, emaciated, ethereal Bundleman, engendered by conscientiously empiricist psychology.

That is a relatively familiar story. What is less familiar, at any rate in connection with Freudianism, is this: empiricism had not merely emaciated man, but it had, just as disastrously, emaciated the *world*.

The world, as seen through a correct theory of knowledge, is intolerably thin, cold, and cardboard-like. It is so intolerably cold and thin that it is psychologically impossible to be consistent and to believe in it in daily life, even if one endorses the theory of knowledge which engenders it. David Hume confessed as much in a celebrated passage.

Why is this so? The basic tenets of a sound theory of knowledge, which does alas entail this refrigeration and emaciation of the world, are quite simple. Neither we nor the communities of which we are members, really possess any *a priori*, absolute certainties. What we know, we know only because the evidence, so far, happens to have pointed that way. So far, so good: this simple formulation of empiricism doesn't sound as if it were so very disastrous. But it is. Its immediate corollary is: everything in the world is simply conjectural. Future evidence, and we are now committed to respect evidence alone, may abrogate it or transform it out of all recognition. Descartes had thought that his method of doubt led him, *pro tem*, to a *par provision* self; but we are now for ever doomed to live in a *par provision* world. Hume thought the self was a bundle of perceptions; but we now live in a world which is a bundle of conjectures.

Bismarck had rightly observed that a common market is not a homeland. Similarly, a bundle of conjectures is not a habitable world. So, once again, we are doomed to conceptual schizophrenia. Just as our double status as free observers and agents on the one hand, and as unfree objects of observation on the other, led us to see ourselves from two incompatible viewpoints, so here once again we are irresistibly led in two directions. The sovereignty of evidence, to which we are committed when on our best cognitive behaviour, and because we like the fruits of the technology which depends on genuine knowledge, leads us to a cold and insubstantial world, within which nothing is solid enough to allow us to lean on it; our need for repose, rest and support leads us to slip back to a solid world offering some support. We live by an uncomfortable inconsistency, and many of us are uneasily if obscurely aware of it.

Note that this is a new predicament. Traditional societies are not empiricist. The general framework of reality, as far as they are concerned, is fixed and absolute, it dovetails with and underwrites their values and hierarchy, and vice versa. Not for them the separation of fact and value, which is such a pervasive theme in modern philosophy, and an inevitable consequence of the sovereignty of evidence and the conjecturalization of the world. On the contrary, for them truth and goodness are two mutually supporting pillars of a single edifice. They are not insensitive to facts: but facts come in only through a certain limited number of licensed apertures. They do *not* constitute the edifice as a whole. The edifice is independent of them and not at their mercy.

One way of seeing the ideological achievement of Sigmund Freud is to understand that he has constructed a solid, non-conjectural, support-providing world, something that had disappeared from our life; that he invented a technique for supplying this commodity made-to-measure for individual consumers; *and that he had erected it using exclusively modern, intellectually acceptable bricks.*

THE SERVICING OF REALITY

To understand this achievement, we must first of all sketch out in a generic and abstract way how a reality is serviced, how the social construction of reality generally operated in the past.[1]

The basic framework of such a habitable world is *given*. It dictates both the pattern in which specific facts are perceived, and the moral code by which they are to be judged. This socio-conceptual and moral framework is perpetually serviced and maintained by a corps of guardians, who attend simultaneously to its theoretical articulation, and its invocation in the crises and anguish of daily life. The framework does not merely organize the general pattern; its doctrines also define access to the deep controlling realm in which the fates and fortunes of individuals are decided. Thus the guardians are not merely theoreticians, they also dispense solace, aid, salvation. They have monopolistic access to both the crucial truth and to salvation (specific and generic, that is, recovery from individual ills, and a general affirmation of the moral acceptability of the individual). In terms of the theory itself, those who challenge it and its guardians are possessed by evil forces.

Now the really important thing to notice is this: in such a world, reality is *solid* – and not at all conjectural. The solidity is achieved by its multi-strand nature. It is woven into a hierarchical, simultaneously salvation-promising and menacing system of concrete, personal relationships, with the hieratic personages who mediate both truth and salvation. Fact, theory, value, relationship, hope, fear, are all interwoven and hold each other in place. To ask a person within such a thick texture to doubt it, is to ask him not merely something he simply cannot do: it is to ask him something quite incomprehensible, to deny his own identity and the surrounding world which defines and sustains it.

Contrast such a person with the condition of a paradigmatic, perhaps a little overdrawn, modern man. The theoretical background vision of his world is indeed theoretical – distant, unconnected with his hopes and fears, unmediated by any hieratic personage, unanchored in any personal relation, and the whole is open to revision, conjectural, technical and semi-intelligible. For succour he must go to a series of disconnected specialists. He knows fact and value to be distinct: his values, so his philosophers tell him, he can sustain only by his own feelings, or by his own decisions . . .

In quite a genuine sense, he is reality-deprived. A world with a genuine feel of reality needs to be serviced and sustained, its various aspects must interlock and sustain each other. Most of mankind had lived in such worlds, but some of us do so no longer. These services are no longer provided, or only by a demoralized skeleton staff.

Generally speaking, for various reasons which are beyond the compass of this book, but which include the complex and mobile division of labour and the related need for economic and hence sustained cognitive growth, a world with such a feel of reality normally is not available under modern conditions. But psychoanalysis *has* created such a world, and it has done it with modern, currently acceptable elements, and against a backdrop of modern intellectual doctrines, and with rituals and institutions compatible with our social organization.

To say all this is in a way to bring out an important corollary of the customary accusation of dogmatism which is made against the movement. Of course, this criticism is valid: its central doctrines (sometimes, indeed, its minor refinements) seem quite beyond the reach of even tentative doubt for its adepts. They sin, certainly, against the prime rule of modern cognitive comportment, the capacity to see any and every idea as a conjecture, to be capable of isolating it and seeing what evidence would sustain it and what evidence would damn it, to see it, in brief, as vulnerable. For them, the central ideas are not conjectures, they are solid realities.

What in effect they have done, however, is simply to restore, and in an astonishingly modern idiom to boot, the old condition of humanity, such as it was prior to pervasive scepticism, prior to the conjecturalization of the world, to the subjection of things to doubt and evidence. They have restored, for some men at least, a properly serviced reality, in which facts, hopes, the moral hierarchy, and the crucial personal relation(s) once again form a mutually sustaining system, endowed with the feel of reality.

A HABITABLE WORLD

The world erected by psychoanalysis is a cosmos, a moral order, built to the most demanding specifications, and easily the equal of those traditional orders for which our romantics express so much nostalgic regret. Let us recapitulate the nature of this world and the manner of its construction and maintenance.

In its sub-basement there is an awe-inspiring realm within which our fates are decided. Traditional worlds do generally possess such sub-basements. It reflects the sense we have that there is indeed a fatality, there is a pattern about the events which concern us, which we sense but can't greatly control, but which we can occasionally appease, propitiate and approach. That realm in this case is the Unconscious, and it is there that the fate of what really concerns us (namely personal relations) is decided.

Access to this realm is mediated by a delimited, duly authorized, separate and demarcated guild, whose members are in a different sacramental condition from ordinary people, and who are in a special cognitive state which alone makes access to the realm in question possible. They, and they alone, can provide effective pastoral care, solace, support and comfort, for they alone can genuinely enlighten, for only they are licensed to know and heal. What confers authority on their intuitions is their sacramental state confirmed by the guild, which cannot be subject to extraneous, independent checks. The doctrine in terms of which all this is articulated is, at the very least, acceptable and incorporated in the wider pantheon of contemporary knowledge.

There is also a middle realm in which we live, distant

perhaps from the basic realm where real decisions are made and dependent on it, but fully and properly recognized and thus authenticated by the guild, and incorporated through its doctrines in the wider cosmology of the society. The world we really live in and are concerned with, for it contains personal relations, a kind of Middle Earth, is thus confirmed by and linked to accepted wider belief. For many other areas of science, the world of daily life, while not totally denied, remains something shadowy, irrelevant, uninteresting.

Deeper initiation, the techniques administered by the guild, provide insight for the initiate both into the deep realm of control and into the mechanics of the Middle Earth, and above all into their interconnection.

The initiation is intimately linked to an intense personal relation (to the Initiator), and explores all the other intense relations of the initiate, by reliving and reinvoking them, if not actually re-enacting them in the 'therapeutic relationship'. Knowledge, emotion and personal relations are thus welded into an organic whole. Middle Earth is recognized, revalidated, and also reorganized after a certain suspension. The strongest personal emotion becomes intertwined with the most important conviction, with the greatest fears and profoundest hopes.

But more than this: morality, cognition, and reality are similarly fused. The language in which this reality is explored and confirmed is also the language of moral self-discovery, of the confirmation of legitimate moral direction; after all, the undergoing of analysis is a kind of moral battle with the internal but elusive and ambiguous enemy, a battle which if successful leaves the victor in assured possession, not only of knowledge of how those things which most concern him truly stand, but also of his own true values. Victory is gained over oneself, in the name of the true self, but only at the end of the therapeutic process do the inner goodies and baddies stand revealed. Adjustment, or identity, is attained. Such virtue through true knowledge also constitutes a guarantee, if not of happiness, at least of the absence of 'neurotic unhappiness'.

All this is attained at the considerable price of initiation – in time and money. But then, no one values a condition attained without a painful and costly *rite de passage*. Things are valued in accordance with the personal investment they require.

One must repeat and stress: the knowledge here acquired (if such it be) is not isolated and abstract – it is linked with a sustained and intense personal relationship which provides support and continuity. It is linked indirectly, but very intensely, to all the other important relations of the person's life, for they were relived in the course of the analysis. The manner in which knowledge was attained required exploration and recollection, often with redoubled force, of all past emotion. Analysis is emotion recollected, but not at all in tranquillity. The early period of this exploration was one of delayed and painful pattern-deprivation, and moreover a period of humiliating and total moral undressing and of admission of all weakness and past humiliations. At the same time, the conditions in which this was done established the total discontinuity between this intense situation and the rest of life; but it was all necessary in the interests of securing access to that frightening and powerful sub-world, the Realm of Control. Yet the humiliations were thereby in the end erased, and some propitiation of the dread realm secured. In brief, the Absolute was glimpsed, and Absolution obtained.

Now compare all this with what is available in the outside world, in that appalling open market – for ideas and salvation – of modern secular, disenchanted society.

Another guild of professionals whose duties include pastoral care for people in distress – especially, perhaps, people in moral, emotional distress – does survive. But they are organized in the name of a system of beliefs surviving from pre-scientific and pre-industrial society, which virtually no one (including members of the guild itself, and its leading prelates) takes very seriously. The doctrine is regularly reinterpreted as a 'symbolic' affirmation of the latest wave of new beliefs, or as an expression of the continuity of the community and its folklore, or curiously enough as both of

131

these things at once. This clerisy in effect becomes a society for the preservation of collective folklore, somewhere alongside the National Trust and the Arts Council. In brief, members of this clerical guild are only linked to a version of the Realm of Control which few any longer take very seriously, and which inspires neither fear nor hope. Hence pastoral attention by members of this guild has virtually no efficacy. Ironically, if they wish it to have any charisma, they add something like psychotherapy to their equipment, and in any case eagerly imitate its style and stance. In fact, there is a well-organized system of 'religious counselling', which blends the old faith with the new depth therapy. It squares the circle, by combining the passive acceptance of the Voice of the Deep (inherent in this kind of therapy), with the old stance of guardianship of revealed, authoritative values. In practice, this is presumably done, by discreetly nudging the Voice of the Deep to show some respect at least for the old rules, in return for a generously liberal interpretation of their requirements.

On the other hand, our society also possesses an impressive corpus of new background belief. But these, though inspiring awe and respect, are technical, unintelligible, unstable, abstract, and connected to the world we live in only by a long chain of obscure and indirect links. As has been noted, the world we think in, and the world we live in, are no longer the same.

It is true that there is one secular world-view which does have fairly widespread appeal, namely Marxism, which is articulated in an acceptable modern idiom, and which, though false, is not self-evidently absurd, and which also contains an implicit ethic as an integral part of itself. But, while containing a promise and a recipe for collective salvation for mankind as a whole, it contains not the slightest trace of any recipe for the relief of immediate individual anguish. Some do find personal salvation in working selflessly for the salvation of all: but most of us are not public spirited or altruistic enough for this way out, and some who are, have lost, or never possessed, confidence in the doctrinal content of this creed.

As for the Middle Earth, the lived world – it has a painfully provisional, interim status in our society. It is only indirectly and precariously linked to serious knowledge: its assumptions are suspended when *serious* business is entertained. Anyone contemplating a really weighty enterprise, involving major commitment of resources, does not plan it in the light of 'common sense', but consults experts and respects their recommendations. The experts are not consulted, like the astrologers and oracles of agrarian society, simply in order to shift the burden of responsibility, nor do they act as random arbitrators (though this may largely be what happens when experts in the social sciences are invoked). They really do know far more than is accessible to common sense. In brief, common sense and its objective counterpart, the daily 'lived world', is linked *neither* to any ultimate cosmology *nor* to any salvation *nor* to any specific solace, *nor* to effective manipulation of the world.

All this being so, there isn't perhaps such a great mystery about the impact of a movement and system of ideas which is articulated in an idiom which links it to genuinely respected truth, and which does contain both an integral morality and recipe for personal salvation, and which restores a feel of reality to the lived world.

What it gives its adherents, among other things, is a sense of genuine *reality*. A man inhabiting a Cartesian, epistemic world, in which everything is conjectural, and evidence is king, and where all values float in detachment from facts and their patterns, suspended in a limbo of a *sine die*, permanent provisionality, lives in a ramshackle and sad world. Both his world and his morality are but *par provision*. His traditional predecessor lived in a world whose basic and immediate structure was not at all conjectural but, indeed, *basic*, unutterably solid, the very foundation of everything else, and utterly permeated by the moral values of its inhabitants.

All this was of course achieved by the many-stranded nature of cognition (as of all other activities) in such a world. Any *object* was not merely constructed out of the evidence which supports it and by the categories which bind it: *that* is a fair account of what an 'object' is for modern man, and his theoreticians of knowledge have rightly told him so. No, a traditional object was far more than a conceptually bound summation of evidence; it was linked to the people who used it, to their status system, their morality, their sense of community. This is *real*, solid; and to ask someone to doubt its reality is to ask him to doubt his entire world, his self – and no wonder he looks blankly, and has no idea what it is that you are asking of him. Not every man can be his own Descartes.

Adherents of psychoanalysis tend to have the same blank look when it is suggested that they might, even just for a moment and for the sake of argument, suspend their belief. Can a man doubt the reality of anything so solid as the Unconscious? Or an experience as intense and personal as an analysis? What can he be saying – that analysis might not benefit *him*?

THE BOURGEOIS DIONYSIAC

A generalization seriously considered by social anthropologists is: societies endow that which is of vital importance for their livelihood with ritual significance. Pastoralists value cattle, agriculturalists have harvest festivals and fertility cults, hunters attach ritual importance to game and its killing, and so on.

If there is some validity in this plausible generalization, then industrial society constitutes an oddity. Though it evidently depends on industrial production for the standard of living to which it is so eager to become accustomed, there are surprisingly few ritual acts oriented towards its productive machinery. One hears of the occasional ritual attitude to a tractor in Israeli kibbutzim, and once upon a time, the Soviets made something of a fetish of the Dnieper Dam. But these examples are rare and comic rather than paradigmatic. It is true that one brilliantly successful industrial society, Japan, is notorious for its company rituals and songs: but note that this ritualization is turned towards the *company*, not its plant. We seem to be in the presence of a charismatic community, but not of a physical fetish.

Perhaps this constitutes the clue to the resolution of our paradox. Men worship not simply that on which they are dependent for their sustenance, but that which makes them feel insecure and precarious. Modern man is dependent on machines, but is not normally afraid of them.[2] What he *is* afraid of is other people. It is they who need to be appeased, for it is they, and virtually nothing else, that constitute an ever-present, menacing threat.

An analysis isn't only *about* personal relations, or a supplication of that realm which controls them: it is itself a personal relation. According to some theories internal to psychoanalysis, it is the personal relationship between patient and therapist which is essential, far more so than the unmasking of hidden facts, for therapeutic effectiveness.

Now psychoanalysis flourishes among middle classes (and above) in fairly developed societies (and perhaps among their outposts in other societies – there is certainly such a thing as comprador psychoanalysis). It behoves us to look at the nexus linking the psychoanalytic system with the individualist, bourgeois environment in which it flourishes. (One intriguing question is whether the psychoanalytic sub-culture could in principle be extended to populations made up of people who are still frightened of *things* rather than of *people*.)

Its world is, notoriously, an individualist milieu. Spiritual individualism has led to the doctrine of Every Man His Own Priest, to the universalization of priesthood and the abolition of a separate clerisy – roughly speaking, to Protestantism. On this analogy, one might expect a movement which preaches something like self-analysis – Every Man His Own Therapist – rather than, as is the case, permitting self-analysis only as the most exceptional self-starter-motor, which alone enabled the system to break out of the vicious circle engendered by its own doctrine to the effect that no one can break out of pervasive deception unaided.

135

But, in fact, there is no such cult of self-analysis. Why is this? My guess is this. Self-analysis, like solitary vice, simply isn't sufficiently exciting and convincing, and, above all, it is insufficiently reassuring. An experience, a pleasure or a conviction needs endorsement by an Other before it feels convincingly real. Who'll pay good money to join a club which lets in people like himself? Who could be rescued from deep insecurity by insight provided by someone as neurotic and unstable as himself? It is all too easy, too blatantly circular and incestuous. There is the story of the prep-school master who recommended self-abuse to his pupils on the grounds that it is cheaper, more hygienic, and you meet a much better class of person: the trouble is, though his first two points are valid, the third one is not.

Even in an individualist age, and perhaps *particularly* in an individualist age, men are other-directed. David Riesman long ago suggested something of the kind.[3] Reassurance can come only from the Other, above all the Authoritative Other. If this is so, and I strongly suspect it is, then the technique of psychoanalysis, with its intense and absorbing one-to-one relation, its privacy and insulation, is the best possible compromise, perhaps the *only* possible compromise, between individualism and our need for reassurance by the Other. Modern man, when in a state of crisis, cannot relate to a community, for he has none: there are only fluid and conspicuously uncharismatic, overlapping and shadowy communi*ties*. (The nearest thing to a sacramental community in the modern world is the nation or the nation-state, and it does have its own rituals; but it is too large and anonymous to help much in private crises, though it can provide an escape from them in times of nationalist fervour.)

But the minimal yet intense otherness, as a compromise with privacy and individualism, is not the only point at which psychoanalysis is amazingly congruent with the social requirements of our age. There are other points too at which it seems capable of squaring the circle.

Religion, if Durkheim is to be believed, requires the dualism of the sacred and the profane. The suspension of normal conventions, the heightening of consciousness, the simultaneous escape from the ordinary and the confirmation of its pervasive features, the intense emotion – all this is normally attained through the collectivity of ritual. The psychoanalytic session similarly achieves a kind of sharp and total *sursis*, a discontinuity with the rest of life, a suspension of its conventions, a heightening of emotion, and yet also presents itself as a precondition of valid comportment in the rest of life: all that it shares with intense rituals of other faiths. What distinguishes it from most of them is the near-privacy, the concentration on the individual. But it takes a special kind of individual to need and appreciate this form of contact with the sacred.

Modern man is an individualist as well as an individual, well habituated to living through inner monologue, given to manipulating meanings and people, not things. But he is also much given to order and rationality, far more so without doubt than any other species of man in history. No wonder that free association, as a kind of extreme polar opposite of his normal values, is appropriate for him as a signal of the special state, the equivalent of false noses at the carnival, the great inversion. But how is he to attain that great abandon, that trance-like emotional state, which other populations generally sought as whole collectivities? Religion has ceased to be a team game.

The psychoanalytic session is a masterpiece of combination of the requirements of a rule-addicted, orderly and individualist ethos, with those of abandon and intense emotion. It is punctilious and punctual, and strictly ruled by the clock (another patient is waiting) more so than other activities even in the most bourgeois of societies, where time-tables are occasionally bent in order to accommodate rank or very intense and insistent demands. But no train time-tables, or ordinary surgery appointments, are observed as strictly as analytic appointments. If Mussolini made trains run on time, Freud did as much for psychiatric appointments; and Freud's achievement is the more remarkable of the two. No other senior medical consultants are ever punctual. In this respect, the analytic session is the culmination, the apotheosis of the Protestant ethic.

Moreover, nothing actually *happens*, leaving aside what I imagine are relatively rare lapses of professional ethics. An intense relation and a revelation are not danced out, as primitive religion was. They are felt and spoken, but that is all. In fact, the static physical positions of the two participants are virtually prescribed and almost mandatory, and implicit in the deployment of the appropriate and famous piece of furniture, the ritual object of this faith. Whatever does happen and elicits the indisputably intense effect, happens through the transmission of words and meanings. What could be more appropriate for bourgeois individualists, whose 'work' does in fact consist of manipulation of meanings and people, not of things?

The whole situation is in fact a magnificent fusion of orderliness and punctuality of form, of individualism and the recognition of the Other, *and* of intensity and abandoned emotion: and the emotion is provoked by the invocation and inner reliving of relationships with people, i.e. that part of the environment *where the action is*, where we stand to lose and gain most, where our fear is strongest and most amply justified. There is an antinomian suspension of rules, combined with a rigid imposition of special rules, and a communication with the absolute reality that governs our fates.

VII

THE EMBOURGOISEMENT
OF THE PSYCHE

THE NEW GUARDIANS

In his *Sigmund Freud's Mission*, Erich Fromm describes how Ferenczi wrote to Freud, on 5 February 1910: '... the psychoanalytic outlook does not lead to a democratic equalizing: there should be an elite rather on the lines of Plato's rule of the philosophers.'[1] Fromm goes on to say: 'Freud answered three days later that he had already had the same idea.'

The institutional implementation came about two years later.[2] Ferenczi's scheme was reformulated:

... the ideal plan would be for a number of men who had been thoroughly analyzed by Freud personally to be stationed in different centers or countries. There seemed to be no prospect of this, so I [Jones] proposed that in the meantime we form a small group of trustworthy analysts as a sort of Old Guard around Freud. It would give him the assurance that only a stable body of friends could, it would be a comfort in the event of further dissensions.

Freud replied with lyrical enthusiasm:

What took hold of my imagination immediately is your idea of a secret council composed of the best and most trustworthy among our men to take care of the further development of psycho-analysis ... This committee would have to be *strictly secret* in its existence and in its actions ...

Eventually, there came to be seven members of the Secret Council, each one wearing a special gold ring as a sign of his status. The council naturally included the grand *padrone* himself.

Reading all this, one may well wonder whether one is studying the history of scientific association, or whether one has strayed into *The Godfather*. But the farcical aspects of it must be disregarded, conspicuous though they be. The parallel with Plato, raised by Ferenczi, endorsed by Freud and reported sympathetically by Fromm, is profoundly relevant and very apt.

Plato's *Republic* is probably the supreme philosophic achievement of the agrarian and pre-scientific age of human society. It is an heroic effort to settle definitively the problem of moral and political order, of prescribing and validating an overall morality. The background assumption is that of the availability of stable and eternal knowledge, in which fact and value are fused (which distinguishes it from our background, in which cognitive growth and the fact/value separation are and must be assumed); and the possibility of a correspondingly stable and hierarchical social order, consisting of guardians of wisdom, of warrior/administrators, and of subordinate producers, craftsmen and traders. The basic device by which Plato seeks to validate this order is by claiming that it is inscribed into the very nature of things and of the human psyche. The substantiation of this claim is carried out in a splendidly circular manner which is absolutely parallel to that of Freud: those who are good/wise/knowing endorse the vision, and their wisdom is in turn validated by it. And how is their wisdom established? The vision says that they, and only they, possess it.

The *direct* parallels between Plato and Freud are striking, obvious and important. Both solve the problem of order and health, and answer the crucial question 'who guards the guardians?' by postulating a special, powerful and monopolistically guarded and transmitted wisdom, which can engender guardians so incorruptible (by the possession of that wisdom, this being achieved and demonstrated by passing through the searching initiation/instruction) that they do not need to be guarded further (though the story of the Secret Council suggests that you can't be too careful). For each, sound cognition implicitly engenders a hierarchy

140

of authority and is impregnated with norms: though for one, these norms are drawn from the shared values of a culture but credited to the Transcendent, and, for the other, they are in fact individually negotiated and credited to a kind of naturalistic Deep. In both, valid cognition is intimately linked to the possession of the right kind of soul, to what one really *is*, rather than to the application of public and morally neutral criteria. Both opt for this kind of solution rather than accepting the verdict of an extraneous, independent, impersonal court (such as the verdict of publicly available evidence, as recommended by liberal empiricist philosophy). External evidence is corrupt, unless validated by wisdom, which in turn is authenticated only by the theory, which in turn is confirmed by the wisdom . . . As in totalitarian societies, the formal machinery of justice is trumped by substantive justice: the good do not err and need not be checked, and those who are not good cannot usefully invoke some formal rules to challenge the good.

In practice, those credited with the wisdom often in the end betray it by disobeying the leader, so extra severe authoritarian measures are required for the maintenance of discipline among the (theoretically) incorruptible guardians, as we have seen. The perpetual and hilarious internal dissensions, hatreds, feuds, fissions, denunciations and excommunications of the Freudian inner party, like the débâcle of Plato's attempt to implement his theories, may lead one to feel some doubts about the theory itself (which no doubt proves only that one is ill-qualified to judge it).

There are also numerous parallels on points of detail. Plato and Freud hold virtually the same theory of dreams. They hold all in all rather similar tripartite theories of the structure of the human soul/personality. In each case, the central piece of evidence for a personality composed of multiple and often warring elements, is the indisputable fact of inner conflict. Each of us *must* be many, if parts of us can and do defy and denounce other parts. Each offers mankind a recipe for salvation hinging on the adoption of a technique of moral regeneration/illumination patented and invented by themselves, and each has some difficulty in explaining his own unaided emergence into an as yet unregenerate world. Freud's allegedly heroic self-analysis, overcoming the cunning and all-powerful hydra of the Unconscious, which presumably was having an off-day (or perhaps was not used to opponents as heroic and penetrating as our Sigmund), is as puzzling and mysterious as the birth of a pure philosophical soul, like Plato's own, into a degenerate world, within which (according to the theory itself) there really was no longer any room for it.

But, interesting and suggestive as the direct parallels between Plato and Freud may be, what is really significant and illuminating is the *inverse* relationship between the two thinkers. In a really important sense, Freud constitutes the inversion of Plato: he is Plato stood-on-his-head.

PLATO UP-ENDED

Freud's self-given task was in effect the same as Plato's: to understand the human condition and extract the morality contained in it.

But the terms of reference within which they worked were different. Plato assumed a basically stable social order (or rather, one whose norm was stability, and within which change was pathological), with an in principle stable cognitive capital, and a fundamentally hierarchical ordering, which pervaded the soul, society, forms of pleasure, forms of knowledge and forms of being. Freud, on the contrary, lived in an egalitarian age which also assumed, needed and believed in cognitive growth, under the names of science and progress. But the most crucial difference of all was the *naturalization of man*: the need to see man as part of nature. Plato could and did assume an inherent hierarchy in the very nature of things, and his entire strategy of the validation of norms hinged upon this: the higher kinds of entity were recognized by the higher elements of the soul, appealed to the higher tastes within the soul, and then ordained, in this circular self-validating manner, the commandments which Plato communicated to his audience. He assumed a value-loaded, hierarchical cosmos, not a rule-bound, morally neutral nature.

Naturalism makes any such Platonic approach impossible nowadays. It is naturalism which sets the terms of reference of Freud's task, which altogether revises the background of the problem. The most conspicuous reflection of this is of course the difference between Plato's and Freud's treatment of the super-ego. Plato, whose perception of its psychodynamic role within the personality is much the same as Freud's, takes it and its demands at face value. The self-proclaimed tyrant within the soul is taken at his own valuation and deferentially anointed. Freud does not do this: the essence of Freudianism is that the super-ego is seen as of this world, tainted by the same ailments, and above all with the same self-deception and irrationality as anything else. This is a crucial part of the Nietzschean heritage.

Deprived of a trust in the super-ego, deprived of an inherent, metaphysical hierarchy rooted in the very nature of things which could then dictate our values, how on earth can the Platonic task, of understanding ourselves and thereby learning what we should do, be accomplished? Freud was in many ways the son, and the voice, of a bourgeois age, and the first part of the Freudian message (repeated with even greater emphasis by some of his followers) was – in the republic of the soul, *strengthen the middle class*! The old autocratic despotism of the super-ego be damned, and, above all, it is to be weakened by having its disreputable sources and its disingenuity publicly laid bare; the secret misdeeds of the old rulers are widely publicized in the interests of undermining their authority; but the unruly proletariat must still be controlled or, better still, embourgeoised: 'where id was, there shall ego be!' Where there had been an undisciplined intra-psychic mob of the id, of unrestrained blind lust, a kind of new property-owning responsible democracy of enlightened self-interest, of desires wise to themselves and the opportunity cost of satisfactions, shall be established . . . Freud's grand strategy for the psyche was in no way original, it was entirely of a piece with the typical enlightened middle-class attitude to the working classes. They are not to be suppressed; they are to be given the vote, encouraged to buy their own homes, to be responsible; but when we do so, 'we must educate our masters!' Otherwise they might well be dangerous.

Plato wanted to strengthen, purify and absolutize the aristocracy, harden it by military duty and make it rigid by what he considered to be philosophical and sustained education, and to ensure its incorruptibility, at least for as long as possible, by depriving it of wealth and kin. Freud by contrast wanted to fortify the middle class of the psyche, and extend it as much as possible, by including as much as possible of the old peremptory aristocracy, now enlightened, and of the old unruly mob, duly educated into consciousness, within the electorate of the mind . . .

So much for their psycho-morphological recipes. As far as this goes, a petit-bourgeois such as myself can hardly do anything other than whole-heartedly side with Freud.

But Freud, in doing his inverse-Plato act, reading off the nature of our salvation from the very nature of our psychic being, does face a grave difficulty which Plato did not have to face.

How on earth does one read moral injunctions off a set of facts? If those facts are inherently stratified into higher and lower kinds, as Plato believed they were, there is no problem: the higher facts give us our norms, the lower ones indicate what we should avoid. This was what Plato believed, and it provided him with an immediate solution.

But this way out is closed to Freud. For Freud and all of us nowadays, nature is both unitary and mute. It cannot speak through its own stratification, for it no longer has any. Facts are not stratified, they are all of a kind. So what's to be done? Freud did have an answer.

TRANSVALUATION OF VALUES, TO
CUSTOMER SPECIFICATION

The thinker who was most lucidly aware of this problem, and for whom it was indeed a central preoccupation, was Friedrich Nietzsche. He saw that the super-ego was not to be taken at face value, that it represented, in a viciously twisted and devious and cunning way, the very same interests as did all other psychic forces, and that it had no genuine claim to the special position which it arrogated to itself; and in particular Nietzsche loathed the pretensions of the super-ego of the Judeo-Christian tradition. As he did not like the values which this particular super-ego foisted on us (and which it was in his own time foisting on us with renewed vigour, under a novel humanitarian-socialist cloak), he recommended, to use his own phrase, a *transvaluation of values.*

There is no great difficulty in understanding what it was that Nietzsche did not like. What he did positively recommend is a little harder to specify. This engenders a perennial debate as to whether or not he was a proto-Nazi, whether he would have endorsed genocide, and so on. The debate is fatuous as well as inconclusive. The inconclusiveness is not simply the consequence of some inability or unwillingness on his part to express himself clearly. The elusiveness or ambiguity is in the nature of things, not in his prose. *Nature is mute.* It commends no values. A Platonically interpreted nature, with a human hierarchy projected on to it, may feed back to Plato and other credulous humans the answers they want to hear and which they suggested to it . . . But nature, seen as a unitary and all-embracing system, does not preach anything.

Nietzsche himself was more than half aware of it. The honesty which made him want to repudiate the devious super-ego instilled by malevolent priests, was itself one of the voices of the very tradition he wished to repudiate . . . and he knew it. Nietzsche was doomed to devour himself, and in effect did so.

Unlike Nietzsche, Freud *did* find a solution. *Solvitur ambulando.* Or rather, *solvitur analysando.*

In his explicit, written recommendations, it is no use looking for anything more specific or concrete than is found in Nietzsche. Freud recommends the absorption of the old aristocracy and of the plebs of the psyche in the middle class: both the id and the super-ego are to be made conscious and incorporated in the newly conscious body politic. But having done so, he does not tell us very much about how much we should heed their demands. We have given both of them a vote and a voice in the inner conscious assembly; we hope this moderates them a bit, but should we also accede to their demands?

Having admitted our instinctual needs to consciousness, and having done the same for our previously unconscious 'higher' moral compulsions, should we fall in with the requirements of either, or both? Freud does not really tell us. He cannot tell us. He knows we cannot get rid of our instinctual drives; and equally, the requirements of civilization do not allow us to indulge them to the full; and again, though we can see through the unconscious elements of the super-ego, as far·as I know there is no suggestion that our psychic constitution could do without it. So all we get is a little formal-stoic advice that we should recognize and accept the realities within us. The discontents of civilization will never leave us. It is not denied that inner realities are in conflict with each other, often in very bitter conflict. Apart from repeating *ad nauseam* that we should familiarize ourselves with the contestants so as not to be taken by surprise by them (and by their disguises), he refrains, like Nietzsche, from acting as any kind of Solomon in their bitter dispute.

So, at the doctrinal level, there is not much of a solution to be found in Freud either. Vulgar Freudianism consists of a doctrine of unrestrained permissiveness and a generalized anti-authoritarianism, but there is no warrant for this either in Freud's words or in the logic of his ideas. But the whole point about Freudianism is that it is not exhausted by its doctrinal level. More than that: the doctrinal level is not even the most important part of the whole edifice.

There is no formula in the doctrine, telling us just how much indulgence to show to our instincts (or which ones) in the interests of appeasing them, nor how much to respect the super-ego as a buttress of civilization. But in each individual analysis, each patient can and does obliquely negotiate his own inner contract or constitution with his own special guardian, and achieve precisely that compromise between the warring factions of his soul that fit his needs, his circumstances, his pocket, his particular moral environment . . . (The late Dr Frankel-Brunswick, returning to Vienna after the war on a research mission, found that where once agnosticism had been a criterion of a successful analysis, religious faith now played the same role.)

The Freudian solution to the inverse-Platonic problem, to the eliciting of an ethic from our psychic nature in a naturalist age, has two incarnations: one doctrinal, theoretical, verbal, which doesn't matter too much (unless of course someone indulges in heresy); and the practical, applied, real one, which is the only one mediated concretely in the contact between guardian and analysand. Each one of these concrete incarnations of the truth is individual and idiosyncratic, and adjusted to the special circumstances of the seeker after guidance. Hence there is no need for coherence from case to case. This ethical revelation is, in all its details, adjustable and adjusted to the requirements of each customer, and presumably each individual salesman.

Thus, and thus only, has Nietzsche's problem – how to extract a new ethic from nature, from a more realistic understanding of our psyche – been solved. The transvaluation of values, virtually unmarketable when Nietzsche first launched it upon the world in an impersonal and general form, is now made to measure for individual customers. Analysis is the bespoke transvaluation of values. The demand for it is brisk.

SOCRATES AND THE CAVE

The central ideological device is the same in Plato and in Freud: it is contained in Plato's parable of the cave. Until liberated by truth, man is imprisoned in the cave, mistaking the shadows on its walls for reality. Only the sage can liberate him and lead him out, and show him the true forms of that which he had previously taken to be reality. The erstwhile reality is then seen for what it is – pale, and distorted, shadows. If this is our situation, then we must indeed revere and obey the sage: otherwise, we shall continue to languish in the cave, and remain helpless slaves of our delusions.

On all this, Plato and Freud are in total agreement. The only difference is – what is the cave for one, is the outer daylight for the other, and vice versa . . . It is only natural that they should be mirror-images of each other in this way: on the one side, the great metaphysician of a hierarchical reality, the arch-anti-naturalist, and, on the other, by far the most influential (though not the most profound) psychologist and commentator of the renaturalization of man.

What is amusing is that their favoured method for eliciting the truth should be so similar and yet also inversely related. Each of them favours something that, in a generic sense, could be called the Socratic method. The truth is not outside; it is not independent; it is already inside us, though we know it not. But we do not know how to bring it out unaided: we can do so only with the help of a properly qualified midwife. Important truth is elicited not by extraneous research, but from inside, by well-qualified midwifery.

Plato did not merely take the super-ego at face value. He was also a rationalist, if of a somewhat mystical variety. He not only accepted the authority of the super-ego, but also endorsed the authority of the concepts, the *ideas*, which pervaded his culture, and notoriously credited these ideas with supra-terrestrial status. Thus the clusters of meanings, with their normative implications, which permeated the Hellenic ethos of his time, selectively reinterpreted by the philosopher in question, could be fed back to the Hellenes as supernaturally authoritative. But these ideas were supposedly apprehended by reason. So the appropriate method of eliciting these ideas, of midwifery, was the rational dialectic, roughly as practised by the Platonic Socrates in the Dialogues.

In the case of Freud, we are dealing with an inverse Platonic world: super-ego and ideas and reason are now all dethroned. Like an aristocracy after a popular revolution, their *Lettres de Noblesse* have lost all validity. They may even constitute a death warrant. The old aristos are ordinary citizens like anyone else, and with no authority whatsoever, and lucky if allowed to survive.

The new verities are not sought out by the old methods. They still have to be summoned up from the deep (rather deeper, this time), but there is no question of doing it by the specific Socratic method of question and answer. That method was fine, if one wanted an accurate profile of a given idea, by seeing what it did and did not cover. But no one is now interested in manifest ideas. It is the deep and hidden meanings we want.

Free-association is the wholly appropriate Freudian inversion of the old Socratic, rationalistic question-and-answer midwifery. Newly renaturalized man is not investigated through carefully delimiting the precise pattern of what he thinks. It is the profiles of his deep feelings, and covert feelings at that, which are being pursued and elicited, not the surface outlines of overt concepts. They will not reveal themselves to direct questions; they will, it seems, reveal themselves by free, logically unrestrained flow of unselected ideas, and then to the emotional response to 'interpretation', which is a question of a kind . . . Free association indisputably engenders strong feelings. Strong feeling can most plausibly be credited with unconscious roots. So it is plausible to see free association (like dreams) as a way of access to the Unconscious. (Unfortunately, this does not follow, though this assumption is central to the system. We cannot conclude from the above premises either that the Unconscious has a determinate content – how can it have if there are no logical constraints within it? – or that it reveals itself when summoned from the Deep by this method.)

The New Socratic Method of Free Association is wholly appropriate for the New Cave and the New Sunlight.

VIII

ANATOMY OF A FAITH

THE ERRING HUSBAND AND THE
PRINCIPLE OF RECURSIVE CUNNING

A married friend of mine was having an affair with a younger woman. His wife suspected as much, but had no idea as to the identity of the lady favoured by her husband's attentions. When however she and her husband gave a party, she did succeed in identifying the mistress: her husband was affectionately flirtatious with all the women guests, bar one. She was the one, of course.

The erring husband was cunning, but not very cunning. The coolness towards the lady in question was intended to deceive the observer but, in the event, actually provided the clue for her identification. Suppose he had been *more* cunning, taking care not to ignore her and thereby single her out for suspicion. In such a case, the wife might have needed not one, but a whole series of parties before she could identify her. In a prolonged time series, she could of course notice that all the other ladies went through the usual accidental ups and downs, occasionally being ignored by accident or for one reason or another, but that one particular one was always carefully treated with neither too much nor too little attention. Such even-handed treatment, in the long run, would itself become statistically suspect, and would eventually reveal the lady's identity. Of course, the husband might be cunning enough to counter this possibility as well, and he might take care that, over time, his mistress, when turning up at the parties, was on occasion treated too warmly and on others ignored, and thus, once again, that she fell in with a more sophisticated

150

statistical norm. Perhaps this game can be played at any level of sophistication and cunning; perhaps the regress simply has no end.

The Unconscious is like the erring husband. It aims to deceive. Deception is its business; indeed, deception is its essence. That much we know. What we do *not* know is the level of sophistication and cunning, the number of steps in the regress, which it chooses to employ. But it seems pretty definitely established (though the matter has not been formulated in these terms) that it is not bound to remain at the first, second, or *n*th level of cunning, deceit and sophistication. On the contrary, it can be relied upon to switch and jump between these various levels: that itself is part of its cunning, of its technique of deception, of its disinformation . . . The Unconscious is like some electronic homing device which can take into account *all* the counter-measures of its intended victim, and which indeed has immediate access to them all. It is, after all, part of the very mind which it deceives . . .

But the corollary of all this is that *any* disposition of the behaviour-controlling core of any given individual, is per-fectly compatible with *any* surface observable conduct by that same individual. In the Case of the Erring Husband, we do have, in principle, some direct access to data which can decide the question of the identity of the favoured lady: a detective who tailed him persistently and successfully, could eventually establish the truth of the matter. The indeterminacy which haunts the interpretation of his con-duct towards diverse ladies at his parties, once one realized the possibility of multiple-level sophistication, is effective only if the investigation is restricted to interpreting his conduct at parties, and penury or dignity preclude having him followed, and thus acquiring extraneous and independ-ent data.

In the case of the Unconscious, however, there is *only* the equivalent of party behaviour, i.e. external, manifest, 'sup-erficial' conduct. We cannot follow it to its lair (leaving aside for a moment the privileged access to the Uncon-scious, which, being unique, can once again not be checked). We depend entirely on outward behaviour, and we cannot know just how many veils and inversion camouflages are thrown over it. This may be called the Principle of Recursive Cunning. The Unconscious is privy to all the feeble decoy devices attempted by the conscious mind, and can *always* go one further along the regress.

In other words, we have here a core reality, (linked according to psychoanalytic theory with surface behaviour in a certain way which is itself prescribed by the theory), but without any specification of the number of steps linking the core reality with the surface. On the contrary: it is part of the mechanism that it can and does increase or decrease the number of those intermediate steps at will, as part of its bluff and deception. Supposing (for the sake of simplicity) that there are but two surface possibilities, say display of love or hate. (But if lukewarmness, or any semitone between it and either extreme, is allowed, the same conclusion still follows.) The surface manifestation will be either the one or the other, according to the number of steps inserted – but whatever it is, the same basic core is manifesting itself ... In other words, whatever happens, notoriously the same hypothesis remains wholly vindicated.

The central idea – a cunning Unconscious – is totally polymorphous in its manifestations in daily behaviour. Its cunning is displayed in controlling those manifestations, *and* our interpretations of them. It is this which makes the idea untestable through ordinary behaviour. (The testimony through the privileged area of therapy will be discussed separately.) It also means that *ad hoc* evasions of evidence are not really *ad hoc* within this system at all, but follow directly from its central insight, and thus have a kind of natural feel.

This is simply the most conspicuous example of that self-maintaining, self-perpetuating, falsification-evading quality of psychoanalytic ideas, which many observers have noted in the system. This is probably the basis of the most important criticism by far that can be and has been levelled against it.

BRIEF CHECKLIST AND A
MUCH WORSE MURDER

It is worth briefly going through an incomplete list of these falsification-evading devices.

The concept of Resistance. The idea that the repudiation of an intepretation or of a theory is evidence of its validity, because it shows the desire of the Unconscious of a given person not to be unmasked, is one of the neatest and best known ploys in this armoury. It is sometimes claimed in defence against this charge, that not *any* denial is counted as 'resistance'. But it must be replied, first, that unless an upper limit is placed on the cunning of the Unconscious, on the number of decoy camouflages it may use (and I see no reason whatever why there should be such a ceiling), there is no reason why *any* denial shouldn't legitimately count as resistance. Secondly, the allocation of denials to the resistance or authenticity is in the hands of the guild, and does not depend on some public criterion.

The lack of either a time limit or a publicly available criterion for successful termination of the use of the technique, reinforces this. If, after either a specified lapse of time, or after satisfying an independent criterion, a person were granted licence to repudiate an interpretation or a theory, and this could thereafter then no longer be treated as 'resistance', negative evidence could then begin to accumulate. In fact, the interlocking system of concepts employed makes this impossible.

The implicit doctrine of the cognitive state or condition (which though not formulated in these terms, pervades the whole system) reinforces all this. Resistance or its absence is a function of the sacramental state of the individual, which in turn is a function of his attitude to the central doctrine, its guild, its specific representative to whose case he is assigned. Those free of inner impediments need no evidence; those burdened by the impediments cannot be helped by evidence. Truth-attainment by Cognitive Licence replaces truth selected by evidence.

Level-twisting is another device which ensures that *critical* considerations become assigned to the realm of symptoms, of the reducible, while *assent* is part of the endorsed authenticity. In other fields of inquiry, the basic terms of reference are *given* to the investigator(s), and he or they cannot challenge them. The issues, and the criteria for deciding them, are the most important part of those terms of reference. It is of the very essence of psychoanalytical inquiry, that it turns upon the very assumptions and criteria which had initiated the inquest, that it queries the legitimacy of their sources. The presiding judge becomes the interrogated suspect. The distinction of levels is not respected, the logical strata become twisted, the levels intermixed. The terms of reference codified by modern empiricist philosophy are overturned: the subjugation of theory to evidence no longer holds all the time. Theories are not subject to facts, but facts are subject to interpretations, and interpretations linked to an unequal hierarchical relationship.

The allocation of experiences to either of the two categories, the reducible and the authentic, is under hierarchical control, and the control is exercised by and on behalf of the system. He who controls the allocation of an interpretation to the realm of authenticity or of reduction-worthiness, thereby controls the reconstruction of the world. The allocation is under control organizationally (only certificated guild-initiates may do it), and psychologically: the patient, softened by withdrawal of orientation, by concept-deprivation, is strongly predisposed to accept those which are endorsed, all the more so when at long last some picture he himself had offered is endorsed.

Freud's great discovery, it is said, was that we are not masters in our own house. This is so. But he fused that valid discovery with a claim that he knew how mastery would be restored. He who alone can restore our mastery over ourselves to us, must himself be our master, at any rate until he has restored our own control. Thus the doctrine assigns a master to us.

Criteria for effectiveness of therapy presuppose knowledge of what the patient would have been like without it, and of course one never has this information. A patient in analysis once committed a murder. The analyst was unabashed. Had the patient not been in analysis, he said, he would probably have committed *a much worse murder.* The splendid concept of a 'much worse murder' is entirely in the spirit of the most typical defence against the charge that therapy is ineffective: the patient would, it is claimed, have been in a much worse condition still, had he not been receiving therapy.

DATA AND THEORY

Generically, the falsification-evading techniques can be classified within various major types. The Principle of Recursive Cunning ensures, by postulating (quite correctly, in my view) that the Unconscious can play its game at any level of sophistication available to the conscious mind which it is bent on outwitting, that *any* empirical, behavioural data are compatible with any interpretation whatsoever.

This kind of untestability would obtain even if the language for codifying the surface, behaviour data were of a very precise kind, and if the same were true of the language characterizing the comportment of the underlying explanatory mechanisms in the Unconscious. If these languages were reasonably precise, we could say – assuming that there is no more than n-tuple bluff, we know that such and such a constellation of the Unconscious forces must result in conduct within such and such a range; or, conversely, with the same proviso, observable behaviour of such a kind and such leads us inescapably to such and such a limited set of possible depth-interpretations.

In a world blessed with precise behaviour-characterizing and precise depth-theoretical languages, a connection of the two could be established which could then lead to the advancement of our psychological knowledge. (But even in such a fortunate world, testing would cease to be possible if we abandoned the proviso limiting the number of possible levels of cunning, of bluff.)

But, in fact, we do not live in a world so endowed with two reasonably precise languages, covering the two zones in question: And that brings us to the second and quite distinct type of reason for the untestability of this belief-system, distinct because it does not depend on recursive cunning. The world we actually live in contains an incredibly rich system of characterizing the actual conduct, relations, feelings and thoughts of men. The number of sentences available to describe human behaviour is infinite; the number of behavioural possibilities is certainly no smaller.

Over this infinitely rich jungle of actual conduct, there floats a rather limited number of psychoanalytic cumulus-cloud concepts and possible interpretations, well-rounded and suggestive, but without sharply delimited boundaries or fixed relations either with each other or with the jungle below. The connections linking the clouds to classes of phenomena down in the jungle are very loose and almost entirely *ex post*. Chomsky's celebrated demonstration of the fact that behaviourist explanations of verbal competence are circular and have to invent the explanatory factors retrospectively is entirely applicable here.[1] The jungle-data are in no way pre-classified; the cloud-concepts classify them in terms of the theory which is built into the concepts themselves, and which they then illustrate at will from any data.

This weakness is perhaps specially relevant to one of the key theses, ideas or cloud-constellations of psychoanalysis – namely, the alleged role of infancy in personality-formation. The idea that certain types of infancy experiences lead to certain types of adult personality, is testable if either of the two domains (early experiences or adult personalities) is subdivided, with some reasonable degree of precision and above all of *independence*, into sub-categories. Then, *and only then*, can one say without vacuity that there is some kind of functional relation, as specified in the theory, linking members of the one domain to those of the other. In fact, of course, the sub-categorization in either domain is (1) extremely loose and woolly, and (2) entirely under the control of that very theory which is to be tested, i.e. imposed on the material by it and by the privileged practitioners/ operators of the theory and of its therapeutic associated practices. There is no question of independently established and applied early-experience-types, being linked to, once again, independently established and previously identified types of personality.

SOME OUTSIDE COMMENTS

The question of the validity of psychoanalytical ideas and practice has of course been the subject of some attention – though not very much from within the movement itself. There exists a superb, characteristically arrogant and com- placent letter by Freud, affirming that empirical testing of his views is quite redundant as their clinical confirmation is so overwhelming, but that it can do no harm. Generally speaking, however, the adherents simply find the question hard to grasp. Their mind simply slips off it, and comes to rest only on something quite different – usually, on what disreputable motives anyone might have for raising such an ill-founded doubt.

This phenomenon – an idea ceases to be a conjecture and becomes instead a very solid reality, beyond the reach of any test – is an interesting and important one, and I have sketched out what I believe to be its underlying mechan- isms. Societies possess techniques for rendering ideas so- cially constitutive, and these techniques tend to share certain formal features. It is important to remember that this is the normal condition of mankind: most ideas of most men at most times are beyond the reach of questioning.

The mechanism of this solid, indubitable sense of reality is basically the same as that which endows any part of a social order with its feel of solidity. It is many-strandedness which matters. An idea does not have simply a cognitive role, as a recipe for predictions, etc.; it is at the same time linked to a set of personal relations, to loyalties, hierarchies, sentiments, hopes and fears. To shake the idea would be to disturb all that. Most men are neither willing nor able to do that. When men speak, they thereby reaffirm the content of their shared concepts and their associations; they seldom, and only within carefully delimited spheres, exchange information not already prejudged by the terms and context of their speech. The reaffirmation and celebration of conceptual consensus and of its value loading (philosophically made explicit in Platonism) is a far more pervasive function of language than the exchange of un-prejudged information.

To test an idea, it must constitute *one* optional possibility within a wider world. The ideas of psychoanalysis are not an open possibility within a wider and solid world; they define, constitute, fill out their own world. To test them – for its adherents – simply does not make sense.

The outside world is less kind or less enlightened, and a certain number of independent inquiries into the validity of psychoanalytical ideas and into the effectiveness of the therapy based on them, have been carried out. They may not be *wholly* conclusive: statistical inquiries seldom, if ever, are. But they are fairly conclusive: the evidence supporting psychoanalytical claims is either non-existent or so feeble that it would not even justify an experimental interest in these doctrines, let alone their acceptance, were it not the case that evidently some other factors powerfully impel people to hold them or to toy with them.

For instance, an overview of *The Standing of Psychoanalysis* was attempted by B. A. Farrell, Reader in the Philosophy of Mind at Oxford.[2] This book, in fact, falls over itself in its attempts to be fair and kind to psychoanalysis, and in particular not to allow its dismissal as untestable. None the less, the following passages are typical of the conclusions:

... the case material of analysis only provides poor support for the low level generalizations of the theory ... the validity of psychoanalysis as a method of discovery is very uncertain ... the case material provides poor support for the interpretative remarks offered to the analysand ... [p.148]

'Reliable observations' are the one thing on which psychoanalytic assertions *cannot* be said to rest ... [p.149, emphasis in the original]

There is reasonably good ground to believe that those who seek psychotherapeutic help improve more than those who do nothing . . . But the difference is not a large one overall.

We have some grounds to believe that some patients with neurotic difficulties improve as the result of the analysis they receive.

There is no ground to believe that such patients do better under analysis than they do under some other form of psychotherapy.

There is some reason to think that patients with specific or delimited sorts of neurotic difficulties do better under treatment that is behavioural, rather than psychotherapeutic, in nature. [p.188]

The impact of psychoanalysis on the West cannot be justified on the grounds that it contains a body of reasonably secure or established knowledge . . . it [is] only too painfully evident that analysis does not contain any such body of knowledge.

Nor yet can the impact of psychoanalysis be justified on the purely pragmatic grounds that it works – that it is an effective method of treatment. [p.191]

Farrell's book is curiously ambivalent and, as indicated, falls over itself so as not to be dismissive of analysis. It tries to reject the argument from untestability on the, to me, quite unconvincing grounds that testability applies only to hypotheses, not to interpretations (p.85), and it plays down H. J. Eysenck's very important evidence about the relative improvement of neurotics who receive no treatment, and those who undergo analysis, on the grounds that it is difficult to ensure that the groups are truly comparable. This is certainly true, but the onus is on those who put forward claims on behalf of the technique to find themselves suitable control groups so as to monitor their own success. Who better placed to do this than those who recruit their own patients? Until they do so, the figures arduously assembled by outsiders as best they can, remain the best we have, and they also alas suggest that therapeutic success is not very significantly, or not at all, greater than spontaneous recovery.

Farrell refers to the figures assembled by Eysenck[3] and concedes that their reading suggests the following conclusion:

If we give patients psychotherapy, or if we do not treat them with any special form of psychotherapy, we do equally well for them. Their improvement rate is about the same. If we give them psychoanalysis, they do conspicuously worse than if we give them some other specific form of psychotherapy, or do not give them any.[4]

Farrell does not challenge the figures, but claims that the natural inference from them is not valid. The challenge hinges, as usual, on the interpretation and comparability of data. As the figures for psychoanalysis must have come from practitioners or patients, it is not clear why they should have been unjustifiably pessimistic, which is one element in the case against the conclusion. (Practitioners can be expected to be optimistic and to slant the figures that way, and the patients, if pessimistic, presumably have good cause.) Farrell does not appear to have dug up any figures *more* favourable to psychoanalysis (though he refers to figures more favourable to psychotherapy, and less favourable to spontaneous remission – which hardly helps). In brief, he can only suggest grounds for scepticism about these figures, but not for positive faith in some other figures or rival conclusions favourable to psychoanalysis.

So, until we get better figures based on more carefully prepared research, the sceptical figures must be treated with respect. But Farrell seems curiously eager to argue that more reliable figures are unlikely to be forthcoming. Why not? '. . . how can we ensure that [members of the no-treatment control group] receive no informal, non-professional psychotherapy in the course of the experiment?'[5] This must be one of the oddest arguments ever used. If unwitting psychotherapy is so easy that it can be performed, unintentionally, by the administrative staff of a research project in the course of recording personal data of a control group, (a kind of Evil Eye in reverse), what happens to the much-vaunted need for intensive and deep training of therapists or analysts? This argument can save psychoanalysis from Eysenck's figures, only at the cost of making all pretence at the possession of deep, exclusive and powerful insights based on patented initiation mysteries, rather ridiculous.

Farrell's overall conclusion is that psychoanalysis is like the curate's egg; though it appears that the good bits are exceedingly hard to find. He commends Jane Austen as superior to Freud for most practical purposes. Jane Austen, however, imposes no wager on her readers, and promises them nothing, and, notoriously, she encourages no romantic illusions. From the viewpoint of the advice to suffering humanity such an attitude is no doubt sensible. But if Freud is no advance on Jane Austen, why all the fuss? Where is the Darwin of the mind? From the viewpoint of the aim of this book – the understanding of how psychoanalysis came to transform our idiom ¥or speaking of man – it is more important to see that it is so constructed as to be wager-engendering, so as not to allow moderate reaction, but instead to enforce submission or offence/resistance, and then to capitalize on either.

Even more striking are the comments by Anthony Storr, a practising Jungian analyst, in a very insightful and sympathetic essay on 'The Concept of Cure', in *Psychoanalysis Observed*:

. . . the evidence that psychoanalysis cures anyone of anything is so shaky as to be practically non-existent.

During the past fifteen years, Professor Eysenck and other[s] . . . have repeatedly asserted, with some justice, that such statistics as exist do not support the hypothesis that psychoanalysis is an effective treatment for neurosis.

The American Psychoanalytic Association, who might be supposed to be prejudiced in favour of their own speciality, undertook a survey to test the efficacy of psychoanalysis. The results obtained were so disappointing that they were withheld from publication.[6]

Or, again, there is a volume entitled *Psychoanalysis, Scientific Method, and Philosophy*, in which we read

. . . I would like to mention Dr P. G. Denker's study of 500 cases of psychoneuroses treated, without psychoanalytic intervention, by general practitioners. The study finds that the percentage of improvements was as high as the ratio of improvements sometimes claimed for psychoanalytic therapy.

... on the Freudian theory itself, as a kind of doctrine for which factual validity can reasonably be claimed, I can only echo the Scottish verdict: Not proven.[6]

Or, after a complex discussion of the problems which would be involved in a serious testing of psychoanalytic theory, Michael Scriven observes in the same volume:

These are difficulties ... for psychoanalysis in justifying its claims ... Without any attempt to deal with [them], how in the name of Roger Bacon could a psychoanalyst imagine that his own hopelessly contaminated, uncontrolled, unfollowed-up, unvalidated, unformulized estimation of success has ever established a single cure as being his own work? At least the people who claim the earth is flat are giving a *nearly correct* account of a *large part* of their experience. (Emphasis in original]8

Similar findings could be multiplied. They have never been effectively controverted; the typical answers that come forth have the form of *ad hominem* denigration, or invocations of the privileged status of the inner experience of analysis (Freud himself claimed that it cannot be judged from the outside), or validations of success on the 'much worse murder' principle.

But the case for the invalidity of this system of ideas is *not* what is primarily argued in this book (though it is accepted, as the convincing conclusion of the work of others). We are trying to cope with the problem which the work of others leaves us, and certainly does not solve: why this system of ideas not merely did not sink, but why it sailed so well; why it conquered our language and, in some measure, our thought.

It is worth at this point quoting Professor Adolf Grunbaum:

In a public lecture at my University, the philosopher Michael Scriven challenged the credentials of psychoanalytic treatment. Immediately afterwards, a senior psychoanalyst in the audience turned towards me to inquire whether Scriven's father or brother was an analyst. Evidently, the interlocutor deemed it unnecessary to come to grips with the lecturer's *arguments* ...

Another colleague, concerned with ... psychoanalytic principles ... concluded that [their] purported insights ... are largely

162

all-too-facile pseudo-explanation. Professional psychoanalysts present . . . usually responded patronizingly as follows: they offered diagnoses of the neurosis that had allegedly impelled the sceptical colleague to reject psychoanalytic theory . . . the analysts in question repeatedly offered these dismissive . . . explanations with great confidence, undaunted by the fact that a Freudian diagnosis avowedly requires a considerable number of analytic sessions. Perhaps it is therefore not surprising that no two analysts offered the *same* diagnosis . . .

Far from being atypical, such . . . responses are . . . rather representative . . .[9]

THE TRICKSTER

A vigorous debate exists among philosophers whether psychoanalysis is untestable and hence unscientific, or whether it is merely false. As far as I can see, the position on this issue is very far from simple, and the same answer does not necessarily apply to each layer of Freudian theory.

Take first of all the central thesis that an Unconscious, of roughly the appropriate kind, exists (a thesis which, as it happens, I believe to be true).

'The Trickster' is the name of an explanatory concept of an unusual kind. Entities which are themselves unobservable but which account for the behaviour of observable ones, are very common. The Trickster, however, is unusual: he can and does interfere with the behavioural evidence about his own existence and his own activities. He has special links with *some* men, whom he does not deceive, or not so much, nor persistently. He delights in sustained deception of others, who tend to be the enemies of the first group. Such sustained interference and fiddling with the data is not just a minor sideline activity of his. On the contrary, it is his central preoccupation, it is part of his very essence.

It follows that if his trickery and deception are sufficiently persistent, we may never unmask them, or even suspect their presence. In fact, the reason why we are so readily persuaded of the existence of the Trickster is that, while cunning enough, he refrains, for some reason best known to himself, from being *very* cunning. He leaves plenty of suggestive evidence concerning his own doings lying about all over the place, perhaps so as to tease us.

The point is that the evasion of counter-evidence, which *other* theories have to inject *ad hoc* when in difficulties, does not need to be extraneously injected in the case of psychoanalysis. It does not need to be injected at all. It is already present. It *is* the theory itself. When is the *ad hoc* not *ad hoc*? When the idea invoked to save a part of the theory, itself lies at the very heart of the theory. The attribution of cunning to the Unconscious, and a habit of tampering with evidence, is not something added to the theory more or less surreptitiously when it flounders and is in difficulties. In all good faith, *it was always there*. The evasion is not brought in to save the theory: it *is* the theory.

The fact that this possibility of perfectly coherent and logical evasion is built into the very heart of the theory, and can always be invoked if it is desired, is in no way contradicted by the fact that it is not always invoked, that in fact Freud occasionally or even frequently changed his mind under the impact of evidence, or that experimental tests are conceivable which would at least scrutinize aspects of the theory, on a natural interpretation of it (where a natural interpretation excludes excessive invocation of the Trickster). All this is a logical point about what the theory says and means, and it is quite independent of how its adherents and practitioners actually happen to use it. It is an empirical fact that its practitioners use it quite freely, but not without some restraint.

Some observers of the system, such as Frank Cioffi, talk as if the individual ideas, taken in themselves, were testable, and as if the untestability were simply a consequence of the way in which practitioners and the Founder habitually handle them: '. . . there are a host of peculiarities in psychoanalytic theory and practice which are apparently gratuitous and unrelated, but which can be understood when once they are seen as manifestations of the same impulse: the need to avoid refutation.'[10]

This makes it sound too much as if it hinged on an *impulse* in the Founder and his followers, and suggests that somehow the impulse gives unity to those apparently unrelated peculiarities of the theory and practice. This underrates and obscures the way in which key unifying *ideas* of the system provided their own virtually irresistible impulsion in that direction, thereby facilitating the indulgence in a private inclination to escape falsification, which need not be stronger in Freudians than in other people. Individual theses within the system, formulated in isolation, may indeed be testable, and on occasion tested, as Adolf Grunbaum has recently insisted; but within the context of the system which gives them life, they can always cease to be such. I'm inclined to invert the Cioffi/Grunbaum approach: it isn't so much that testable theses can be lifted out of the reach of the testable by determined practitioners, but rather – an inherently untestable system can and does often permit a kind of *ex gratia* testing, on the understanding that this privilege remains easily revocable at will and short notice.

So the central picture is not testable, and this extends to the specific theses articulated in its idiom. This contention is not incompatible with the fact that practitioners may waive their logical right to invoke the Principle of Infinite Cunning, thereby temporarily rendering this or that contention *ex gratia* falsifiable and testable. So within the world postulated, and in a way engendered by the theory, the theory itself is immortal. No fact can ever be lethal for it.

Has it then (in its pure logical form) no Achilles' heel at all?

In fact it has, and a very interesting and central one. These are its therapeutic claims. The point is this: the strictly psychological theories contained in it, operate in a world which it itself creates and within which they cannot be falsified. On the other hand, the promise of cure is not, or at any rate *was* not, initially made with that world: it is made in our public, shared, eclectic world, whose nature and bounds are not normally or initially defined by psychoanalytic doctrine. We find ourselves once again, in one of those astigmatic, unfocused or bi-focal situations which are so characteristic of psychoanalysis, and which are of the essence of the therapeutic relation itself. What follows from this is that the evasive practices attaching to the psychology proper, and those attaching to therapy, are logically distinct. We must now look at those which cover therapeutic claims.

These devices must be different from those which cover the general theory. Those had hinged on the potentially infinite cunning (and inner power) of the Unconscious. The promise of cure hinges on exactly the opposite: on the stunning claim that, notwithstanding the great power and cunning of the beast, the beast can be, and occasionally is, tamed, and that a master lion-tamer has at long last appeared in human history and bequeathed his secrets and his skill to a carefully delimited following.

In other words, though the limitless cunning of the beast is invoked when therapies go wrong, this cannot be invoked too much or without reservation. If the beast could always win, if the lion-tamer always had to retreat, bloody if unbowed, why then – *phut* would go any therapeutic pretensions. So here, if there are to be evasions (which indeed there are), they logically *must* be different in kind.

In essence, as we have seen, they consist in the first instance of taking the patient from the public world in which he would test the efficacy of the therapy by public, extraneous criteria, to a world internal to the therapy itself, in which he may judge only when the therapy is complete, and when the (obscure and much contested) touchstone of termination includes both the consent of the therapist and the satisfaction of the client ... Even as the therapy develops, the patient loses interest in the symptoms which had been the initial cause, or pretext, of his coming at all, and this counts as good progress. But, after all, only the elimination of these very symptoms could have made possible any kind of public evaluation of the therapy! If new criteria are to be invented and agreed afterwards, such an evaluation becomes impossibly difficult, which indeed it is often defensively claimed to be. The fact that the terminal criteria are basically Stoic in character helps to ensure, as we have seen, that a dissatisfied client who had properly completed the therapy, becomes a genuine contradiction in terms. A dissatisfied client is one who has not come to terms with reality: ergo, his therapy is not complete; ergo, he may not judge its efficacy.

A second level at which therapy effectiveness is protected is by down-playing the claims made for it. Thus it was possible for an officer of an important national psychoanalytic association to announce that the association makes no claims for analysis. Had Freud announced at the start that he had discovered a new technique but that he made no claims for it, he would not have got very far. At the beginning, pump-priming big claims were absolutely necessary, and were of course made. Once, however, a belief-system is deeply institutionalized, the vested interests connected with it are such that they and the overall impetus of expectation protect it, and the system can down-grade or even wholly disclaim any doctrinal or soteriological pretensions. There are conspicuous examples of this in contemporary religion.

The criteria-shift at the termination of (and even in the course of) an analysis, is a kind of perfectly logical obverse of the discounting of the importance of the initial symptoms. From a psychoanalytic viewpoint, one could put it thus: how absurd that untreated pre-patients should be free to assess for themselves whether their symptoms (which after all they are bound to misread) warrant treatment? Those wandering over an appallingly crevassed glacier, or a mine-strewn field, with bandaged eyes, are allowed by society to decide for themselves whether they will consent to a bandage-removal! How utterly absurd. Only those who have reached the end, with bandages off at last, can appreciate the perils they have escaped, the benefits that have accrued to them by having clear sight conferred on them at last. But certificates of bandage-free vision do not seem to be issued to critics or dissatisfied customers.

But for all that, the effectiveness of therapy does probably remain the Achilles' heel of the system.

FREUD AND THE ART OF DAEMON MAINTENANCE

So, from one important viewpoint, the entire corpus of psychoanalytic theory can be divided into two parts: the theory of the existence of the Unconscious and of its characteristics and activities, and the theory of its penetration, management and at least partial mastery – in other words the theory of psychoanalytic inquiry and therapy.

These two elements are logically independent, even though ideas within each of them lend support to ideas within the other, and even if many psychoanalytic theses have implications within both areas. The first part might be called the ontology of the Unconscious, the other, its epistemology.

More suggestively, one could also call the first part the theory of the Daemon, and the second, the theory of Daemon Management.

The reason why, in practice, daemon theory does have a fair amount of empirical content, is that in the actual working of the theory, the level of power and cunning credited to the daemon, while quite high – high enough to inspire a healthy fear in its potential victims, who are also potential clients – is nevertheless not fixed impossibly high. In other words, the daemon is assumed to be strong and clever, but not so strong as never to be mastered, nor so clever as to leave no genuine clues.

Perhaps I may add my personal view, which is that he is strong and devious, but not impossibly strong and devious. But we must of course beware of complacency: the reason we think so might be precisely that he is *so* cunning that he deliberately plants evidence to suggest that he is only mildly cunning, so as to lure us off our guard.

The cognitive daemon supposition – a very powerful spirit is interfering with my logical intuitions, making the false seem luminously true, and vice versa – is never refutable, and it is not an absurd supposition. Belief-systems often invoke it to explain the unworthy doubts of their potential clientele, and to enlist those doubts as positive evidence on their own side. The secret of psychoanalysis is that this abstract, all-purpose cognitive daemon is fused, identified with the beast, the cunning perverse instinctual being within us, for whose existence there is powerful evidence, and to whose malevolent power we have become sensitized both by the general conditions of modern life, and by the failure of the Bundleman theory to conjure him away. It behoves us, not to be sceptical about the beast, but about its conflation with a daemon in control of evidence about his own doings and manifestations.

The untestability of the daemon *management* part of the theory is a much more complicated matter, a number of times over. At first sight, it would seem highly testable, in so far as it contains claims of therapeutic successes, which should be visible in *this* public world, not in the hidden inaccessible realms of the Unconscious. But whereas psychoanalytical practice has tended gratuitously to diminish the (formally quite unassailable) untestability of daemon theory, it has by contrast *increased* the untestability of therapeutic claims. Figuratively, one might put this by saying that though therapy occurs in this world, it tends as much as possible to be sucked into the monopolistically controlled world set up by the theory and the organization. Whereas the daemon has graciously consented to descend into this world (though in no way logically or otherwise obliged to do so), therapy, which inherently must take place within this world, and should be judged by its yardsticks, has to an astonishing degree succeeded in eluding this world and its judgement.

As Freud and others have insisted, you cannot judge it unless you have been through it yourself. The criteria, and their application, seem to be something that can be handled only from the inside, by initiates. When statistical studies of success rates are evaded, what is invoked is not merely the general difficulty of finding comparable groups (which haunts all such inquiries), but also the special difficulties connected with evaluating psychoanalytic therapy. Freud himself started this tradition, invoking every possible reason why the statistics would not prove anything (as if these reasons did not always cut both ways); including the splendid consideration that there were 'persons who had kept both their illness and their treatment secret, and whose recovery in consequence had similarly to be kept secret.'[11] Are the secretive analysands found only among the therapeutic successes? And is it not possible, and indeed common practice, to keep anonymous statistics, so that the figures betray no individual identities?

The rest of Freud's arguments on this subject are of a similar quality. He ends the discussion by suddenly going off at a tangent and declaring that the statistical testing is unnecessary anyway, as prejudice against the new technique, like other prejudices against techniques since found to be valid, will eventually die off. This of course characteristically begs the entire question.

The crucial though unformalized aspect of the management theory is that the technique of penetration used is *unique*. This is not formally asserted. I know of no outright statement saying that there are no ways of approaching the Unconscious other than those sanctioned by Freud (free-association, dream analysis). One might suppose that on occasion, psychoanalytical interpretations could be checked historically, by securing evidence about the real events in the analysand's youth. Most significantly, however, Freud objected to such a procedure, because it could mean that something else could sit in judgement on the process of psychoanalysis! The miraculous telescope or shaft must not be subject to extraneous checking: 'It may be tempting to take the . . . course . . . by making inquiries from the older members of the family: but I cannot advise too strongly against such a technique . . . confidence in the analysis is shattered and *a court of appeal is set up over it.*[emphasis added][12]

Part of the psychoanalytic resistance towards empirical testing of Freudian theses springs from this: if, for instance, careful records of the behaviour of young males could establish whether or not they are forming the Oedipus Complex, this would actually entail that *very* careful surface observations *can* after all detect the hand of the daemon, and that the daemon can be caught without the benefit of Freudian assistance. Thus, empirical behavioural confirmation of Freudian psychological hypothesis (as opposed to therapeutic claims) could in a way render psychoanalysis redundant. Empirical confirmation, not based on depth-interpretation, could actually count as a refutation of psychoanalytical theory!

Here the whole question of testing and validation becomes very intriguing and complex. If the point of penetration of crucial reality were literally and absolutely unique (as is indeed the claim of certain historic religions), then of course there would simply be no question of any testing. If I own an absolutely unique telescope, which alone can reach a given zone X, and if I look through it on one occasion and make my report, and then destroy the irreproducible telescope, that is that. For the rest of time, mankind, if it heeds me at all, will have to face the wager of whether or not to accept my report.

But the telescope – or should one say shaft into the underworld? – has not been destroyed. Better still: it seems to be self-reproducing. Not only has the initial telescope or shaft been used repeatedly, but also it has bred a whole progeny of others, endowed, if not with quite the same penetrative power (who could rival the Founder?), at least with power of a similar kind, if never of quite the same quality.

The telescopes/shafts could theoretically be tested *against each other*. Though devoid of an extra-shaft check or independent access to the reality in question, one could develop a kind of internal Coherence Theory of Truth, so that truth were established by a majority consensus, or some subtler form of coherence of diverse shafts. This in fact does not seem to happen. Shafts or telescopes are *not* equal. If they disagree, the theory requires that we at least be impure and thus disqualified.

So, the authoritarian and Joker card element in the tradition seems to take over, when it comes to inter-shaft non-congruence of reports on the deep. Shaft-watching is done in pairs, and moreover by hierarchically ranked, markedly unequal pairs of individuals. One of them watches and only the other one can tell him what he *really* sees. Barring the Founding Fathers, every shaft-watcher within the field has experienced both states, has been (at least once) both senior or dominant, and junior and dominated, shaft-watcher. The system of these unequal dyadic relations determines the internal organization of the guild as a whole. All this being so, any comparison of incompatible shaft-reports automatically becomes either a defiant subversion, or a triumphant reaffirmation, of the hierarchical ranking of the guild. Can such internal political conflicts, especially given the absence of external checks, be counted as *tests*, or are they rather trials by ordeal?

The Joker card prerogative – logical enough if there were but one point of access, and that one well validated – continues to be used. What happens when two Joker cards are played against each other? What indeed. There is no solution, other than a political one, decided by *force majeure*, though not physical force. Who can expel and excommunicate whom? The same, after all, happens within other systems in which a Joker card (God, the Revolution) is available, and which are built around a central, crucial revelation. Unless the revelation is strictly monopolized from the start (and, in a loosely Protestant civilization, this is difficult to perform), the moment is bound to come when two rivals play it against each other. In this movement, its use was commended from the start:

Had not Freud himself explicitly instructed his followers to treat all their scientific critics as they would an unanalysed patient offering 'resistance' (Freud/Jung Letters, p.18)? On the eve of his break with Freud, Jung spoke bitterly of just such propaganda pressures, now being directed against himself, when he complained to Freud that too many psychoanalysts were misusing psychoanalysis 'for the purpose of devaluing others . . . Anything that might make them think is written off as a complex. The protective function of [psychoanalysis] badly . . . [needs] unmasking' . . . But Jung and other dissidents were expecting too much when they sought exemption from a polemical technique that they themselves had advantageously applied – with great relish – to Freud's non-analytic critics.[13]

179

So testability does not seem to enter through the plurality of shafts, though logically it might perhaps have done so. But their hierarchical ranking – remember that all analytic relations are dyadic and strictly unequal – seems to prevent that. *Il y a toujours un qui baise, et un qui tourne la joue.* There is always one who free-associates and transfers, and one who tells him that he is *resisting*. In fact, a tendency quite contrary to cross-checking of shafts seems to be operative:

[An analyst may] vary the truth, instead of improving it through improved introspection. In other words, his resistance may acquire the form of 'dissension'. He may . . . unwittingly sidestep an as yet potential conflict . . . by selecting a school of dissension, whose very existence derives from the same predicament in its founder. For it is here that the origin of the dissension must be sought . . . the denial of any one of the basic and the interdependent facts found by Freud cannot but cause a defective crystallization of thought around the hollow nucleus of negation . . . If, at a future time, the extravagant growth of contemporary psychological teaching should be pruned back to the live stem of observation and theory of the first, the Freudian, period of its existence . . . an elaborate post-graduate education will be preventive of wasteful effort by including in its requirements that dissension be generally subjected to clearance in an analysis supplementary to the training analysis of the dissenter.[14]

The authoritarianism of this passage is so brazen as to be comic: *a priori*, all dissent is discounted as psychologically grounded, and a system of education is recommended which will penalize and correct all dissent by an additional dose of training. Elsewhere (see p.190) we quote another analyst, this time a revisionist one, H. Guntrip, who recommends a corrective dose of re-analysis for orthodox palaeo-Freudians, such as the author of the passage just cited. Each side damns the other as inadequately analysed. I am more analysed than thou!

But it should be noted that, given the overall premises of the system, all this is not illogical. That the various shaft-watchers should behave in an authoritarian way to each other, rather than comparing their observations in an egalitarian and tolerant spirit, strictly follows from the basic underlying theory of knowledge. It is *not* a matter of collating conflicting data. The shaft is not an instrument of research in the normal sense: it works by veil-removal. You can see the objective reality, indeed a kind of Absolute, through it, only because the internal delusions which inhibit vision have been removed. It immediately follows that if two shaft-watchers disagree, one of them *at least* must still be under the spell of illusion. Look for the veil, not the facts. The dissenter must be ill, *disturbed*.

There is of course the complication, alluded to by Robert Fliess, that the multiplicity of shaft-watchers are organized not in one, but several and rival guilds. Not all practitioners are quite as complacent and circular in their reasoning as R. Fliess:

> It is scarcely to be expected that a student who has spent some years under the artificial and sometimes hothouse conditions of a training analysis and whose professional career depends on over-coming 'resistance' to the satisfaction of his training analyst, can be in a favourable position to defend his scientific integrity against his analyst's theory and practice. And the longer he remains in training analysis, the less likely he is to do so. For according to his analyst the candidate's objections to interpretations rate as 'resistances'. In short there is a tendency inherent in the training situation to perpetuate error.[15]

No better account could be given of just why it is that members of the same guild tend to hand in coherent reports about what they saw down the dark shaft.

So, the plurality of shaft-watchers does not engender testability of shaft-based reports about the reality which is uniquely accessible through the shafts. Nevertheless, there is an element of flexibility and learning and correction, even in the analytic tradition. How then does it enter?

Certain entities – i.e. the success of therapy, and criteria thereof – are visible at both levels. But the confirmatory vision *down* the shaft overrules sceptical vision outside, while it can be confirmed by positive observations on the surface. If, of course, the vision down the shaft is less than confirmatory of the theory, then naturally that particular shaft is as yet insufficiently deep, and hence not yet authoritative. Shaft-vision trumps surface-vision when necessary, and surface-vision can in any case be compatible with any depth theory.

The symbiotic relationship of the two parts of the doctrine deserves note. The beast theory provides the shaft-watchers with the Joker card: the in-principle limitless cunning of the beast justifies exclusion of those deluded by the beast. But at the same time, by not using to the full the test-evading licence which is inherent in the beast thesis, the beast provides the system with that minimal element of breathing-space, of flexibility, adjustability, without which the entire system might well suffocate. But, in danger, the shutters can always be closed, the hatches fastened. The submission of the daemon to testing is a voluntary *ex gratia* concession, ever revocable and, when necessary, revoked.

ETERNAL CORRIGIBILITY

Psychoanalysts and apologists of psychoanalysis sometimes react with a sense of outrage against the charge of untestability of their doctrine and technique. It seems to them to contain a kind of imputation of rigidity, of inability to respond to new situations, and they feel in all sincerity that this is a gross misrepresentation of their intellectual experience. The course of an analysis involves constant revision and is often pervaded by tentativeness: where is that alleged dogmatism and apriorism of which they stand accused? The same is true of the history of the movement and its thought: emendations and corrections abound. So is the charge that this is an unfalsifiable, self-maintaining circle of ideas – by far the most important charge against the system – wholly misguided?

Those who are eager to press home this charge, nevertheless, tend to reply at this point that though the system accepts and incorporates correction by fact on points of detail, it is incapable of doing this for the basic ideas, the overall conceptual framework. This is so no doubt, but when the charge is reformulated in this manner, it is nowadays liable in turn to provoke a defence which has some plausibility. Ever since the publication and justified popularity of Thomas Kuhn's theory of science[16] a certain idea has gained widespread popularity: namely, that a rigidity of the basic framework of inquiry is (a) the normal condition of science, and (b) beneficial to it, and indeed constitutes a necessary precondition of scientific inquiry at most times. Thomas Kuhn is the Thomas Hobbes of science, assuring us that unless there is an Absolute (conceptual) Sovereign, known as The Paradigm, all is chaos, and the life of cognitive ideas is solitary, poor, nasty, brutish and short. Kuhn has turned the tables on scientific liberals and powerfully argued the case for Order, not merely *de facto*, but above all *de jure*. I am not a Thomasite myself, but the Hobbes/Kuhn case does deserve very respectful consideration. In any case, it is well worth while considering whether psychoanalytic apologetics can benefit from it.

The truth of the matter seems to me to be that in one very important sense, the point about psychoanalytical depth inquiry into individual minds is not that it is too rigid but, on the contrary, that in a special sense it is extremely and indeed excessively open and corrigible. Roughly speaking, psychoanalysis maintains that *all* surface data are suspect and unreliable, and many or indeed *most* depth data (i.e. analytically secured data) are also suspect. All surface data and most depth interpretations are false, you might say. Moreover, psychoanalysis maintains that there is no definitive final way of identifying the sound, veridical depth data. They can always be overturned by a further inquiry, which brings out that either analyst or analysand or both were resisting, distorting, and that consequently even deeper inquiry calls for a revision of the previous findings. This is a correct account of the spirit and procedure of psychoanalysis. So where is that alleged rigidity and untestability? Does it not turn out, on careful inspection of the matter, that far from being a paradigm of a closed conceptual system, psychoanalysis is the very model of an open one, and deserves an accolade, rather than denigration, from the prophet of the open society?

Alas, not so.

Psychoanalytical interpretations are indeed eternally corrigible, by the canons and practices of the system itself. If on not infrequent occasions some such interpretations are upheld in a rigid and dogmatic manner, this can fairly be attributed to the personal dogmatism and authoritarianism of some practitioners, and does not distinguish this field from all other areas of intellectual inquiry. It is true that what I call the Licensing Principle of Truth-identification, which pervades the implicit epistemology of psychoanalysis does indeed very strongly encourage such dogmatism; but in other fields, people often manage to be just as dogmatic without even the benefit of any such encouragement. In any case, this, as it were *personal* dogmatism, whether more common in the movement or not, is not an essential part of the crucial untestability charge.

The crucial question is: in virtue of what are interpretations corrected? The short, simple and fundamental answer is: not in virtue of any raw data (for these are never authoritative, and can be veridical only by accident, so to speak), but in virtue of further, other, deeper interpretations; and interpretations are secured only by the unique, exclusive method of depth inquiry, which is inherently hierarchical and unequal.

The consequence of all this is that there is in fact a fair amount of non-rigidity within the system, but the changes which occur are not under the control of any outside realm of fact, of any arbitrator *outside the control of the system itself.* This, it seems to me, is the real criterion of science, and one which provides a clue (not an exhaustive explanation) of the cognitive success and superiority of science.

The consequence of all this for the Psychoanalytical Movement is that there is indeed change within it, but the decision procedures actually used for determining which changes are or are not acceptable, are inherently and inescapably political, i.e. must depend on the strength of personalities and alignments within the movement. This is not due to any necessarily greater addiction of analysts to intrigue and politicking and pursuit of intellectual domination: if these facts had to be absent in genuine sciences,

177

there would be no science whatsoever in any field. It is due to the fact that, within the overall unwritten conceptual constitution of the system (and also according to the elements of a written constitution which Freud tried to impose on the movement – though this matters less), there simply is no entrenched clause which imposes extraneous, independent, factual arbitration; and there *are* important clauses, intimately connected with the central ideas of the system and indeed emanating from them, which positively militate against such external decisions. The location of the criterion of truth is determined by the ideas of the system itself: the well of truth is within the ramparts, and not outside.

This does not mean that straight, independent factual elements do not enter into the verdicts, into the conflicts between rival ideas, at all. There is nothing to prevent groups and individuals from being influenced by public, 'superficial' facts, e.g. by success rates of therapy, judged not through inside self-validating interpretations, but assessed in the same way as would be done by non-initiates, outsiders. But such extraneous validation and criticism enters and is accepted only *ex gratia*, for the system contains ample authorized, well-established principles for excluding it, if any participant in the internal debate wishes to do so.

Corrigibility, like patriotism, is not enough. Or rather, one must distinguish between mere volatility and genuine corrigibility, anchored in the end to something *not under the control* of the theory itself, or of the system of practices connected with it. But what of a system in which facts are trumped by interpretations, and interpretations by other interpretations, *ad nauseam*? In old Boston ' . . . Cabots speak only to Lowells, and Lowells speak only to God . . . '

The interpretations seem never to be obliged to heed anything other than seniors. The ranking of interpretation is subject to nothing extraneous, but only to the hierarchy of interpreters, a hierarchy engendered in part by the unequal dyadic relation which governs shaft-watching, and partly by the political organization and power relations within the guild.

THE BOUNDS OF SCIENCE

TESTABILITY

The whole issue of untestability or unfalsifiability is both tangled and important. Recently, the charge of unfalsifiability, associated above all with Karl Popper, has been challenged by Adolf Grunbaum and others.[1] The Grunbaum/Popper debate is somewhat tangential to our concerns, in so far as Grunbaum is not endeavouring to defend psychoanalysis: he is concerned to criticize Popper's criterion of science, and to establish that Grunbaum's criterion of science is superior to Popper's. The demerits of psychoanalysis are not very much in dispute, except perhaps on points of detail: what is at issue is how it should best be criticized. It is as if two toreadors were quarrelling not about whether the bull should be or has been slain, but which weapon was best or uniquely suited for the job.

The theory of science and the problem of its demarcation is not the primary concern of this book, and readers not interested in it may prefer to neglect the semi-technical points in this chapter; but at the same time this issue is so pertinent to its main argument that certain observations are appropriate. The untestability, or rather, the test-evasion charge does indeed remain the main and, in the end, valid charge against psychoanalysis; but nothing is gained, and much is obscured, if one formulates this charge in a crude, simplified, and unsophisticated form.

First of all: the entire positivist/metaphysician debate, in the form in which it has become familiar to the academic public, is gravely misleading, because it draws its examples and above all its key image from a rather special and untypical historical period, namely our own. The historical background of the society in which modern science and philosophy emerged is one much given to a very distinctive theology, one postulating a unique and hidden God. In other words, it had a vision in which the transcendent and the mundane are sharply and conspicuously separated. This vision may indeed have made a major contribution to the emergence of science. The sharpness of this boundary was subsequently echoed in philosophy: latter-day metaphysicians have tended to be logically well behaved, and when they brought news of the Absolute or the Transcendent, under one name or another, they tried not to cheat, and made plain when they were indeed talking about the transcendent, and did not mix it up with the immanent. As in a well-run kosher kitchen, separate pots were used for the milk of the noumenal and the meat of the empirical. By so doing, they made the task of the latter-day positivist-puritans easy. Their work had really been done for them in advance. They needed only to say, in effect (though at great length): what use is the transcendent if it does not enter our actual experience? Consign it to the flames!

So far so good. But the whole point is that mankind in general is seldom if ever conceptually kosher. The transcendent is *not* neatly and conscientiously separated off from the empirical. Most traditions are appallingly unfastidious about their conceptual crockery. Many, perhaps most, concepts are multi-purpose, messy, and the purposes they serve include, on the one hand, the preservation of the shared conceptual wealth, consensus and hierarchy of a given community, and on the other (but much more rarely), the singling out of factual constellations. Concepts claim transcendent validation, while at the same time affirming earthly material.

So, normally, when a given affirmation within most systems, or the system itself, is open to the accusation that it is not liable to be *overturned* by facts, this does not mean or require that each element within it is also totally insensitive to fact, that it fails to interact with facts, or that it does not have a fair amount of empirical content or suggestiveness.

In connection with psychoanalysis, Frank Cioffi observes: 'A pseudo-science is not constituted merely by formally defective theses but by methodologically defective procedures.'[2]

No doubt this is so. But this is quite normal in the conceptual life of mankind, which at most times consists of little else but methodologically defective procedures. It has been overcome, in some measure, only in that uniquely cumulative cognitive activity known as science.

The great empirical suggestiveness, and even partial truth, of important elements in the entire psychoanalytic structure, need not be in doubt. Of the two great quasi-formal elements in the system, the cunning beast theory is largely true, and becomes untestable only if no upper limit is placed on the cunning; the other, the unique shaft theory, is *interestingly* false, but again becomes untestable only if one exploits to the full certain requirements contained within it, that shaft reports (depth interpretations) be deemed valid only in certain circumstances, notably when the unequal dyadic relation of the paired watchers is respected, and the senior watcher is duly authorized by the guild which in turn is defined by adherence to the doctrine itself. But of course these two infallibly test-evading elements need not, and are not, invoked all the time; and when they are not, empirical/testable material is kept within the theory in much of its daily life. 'All hands to the test-evading pumps' is not a cry heard all the time, it is reserved for emergencies. If all hands were at the pumps all the time, though the ship would not sink, it would not sail far either. It is part of the normal working of the ship, and of its attractiveness, that though the pumps *are* available, they are *not* in perpetual employment.

Cioffi says about psychoanalysis: '. . . there are a host of peculiarities of psychoanalytical theory and practice which are apparently pernicious and unrelated, but which can be understood when once they are seen as manifestations of the same impulse: they need to avoid refutation.'[3] But he cannot mean that Freud deliberately and consciously set out to avoid all falsification. His expressed conviction that

181

he was in possession of the truth was only too patently sincere. Nor would there seem to be much point in turning Freud upon Freud and insisting that he was 'unconsciously' guided by a desire to deceive. I do not believe this to be true, or a useful way of looking at the matter. It is the *system of ideas and procedures* which is endowed with the cunning, not those who use it; and it is that system which needs to be understood.

The Grunbaum testability-of-Freudianism thesis hinges on the so-called double-conditional theory of therapy. Veridicity of analytical interpretation plus its recognition by the patient is presented as a necessary condition of cure. Grunbaum has singled out this thesis to highlight the testability of psychoanalysis for at least two reasons: this idea is indeed central to the whole system, and, as quotations used by Grunbaum show, Freud himself singled out this part of the doctrine when stung by one of the earliest formulations of the untestability taunt. The conditionality of cure on (a) validity of interpretation, and (b) its recognition by the patient, Grunbaum calls the 'Tally' argument.

In fact, the situation is more complex even than Grunbaum allows (see diagram, p. 224). The unique echo-sounder of psychoanalysis probes from the surface (1) and locates the present depth-situation of patient (2). This cross-relates to the *past* depth-situation of patient (3), a connection which in turn must presumably be veridical. But in most versions of the theory, this depth-situation in turn relates to a public and past objective situation (4), the actual traumatic event(s) which had initially engendered the patient's condition.

Where does testability occur in all this? The testability of an assertion depends in a great part on whether the terms occurring in it have a meaning that is (a) reasonably precise and fixed, and (b) independent of the theory that is being tested, and of the guild of those committed to it. Terms imposed on reality, so as to confirm the theory, terms which are the shadows, faithful poodles of the theory rather than its judges, do not help much.

Items (2) and (3) are not directly observable and hence

not independently checkable, in principle. Testing of assertions about them is precluded, first by the uniqueness of the psychoanalytic tool of inquiry (a theory says an object can be seen only through one peep-hole, and the theory controls that peep-hole) and secondly by the inherent tendency of the unique telescope to engender hierarchy and unequal authority of interpretations: the analyst trumps the analysand, and the analyst is trumped by a better analyst or later analysis. There is simply no question of taking a large number of readings and following the majority, discounting the dissentient findings as due to experimental error.

Item (4) is very questionably observable. The fact that it occurs 'on the surface', or rather, that it *had* once occurred on the surface in the dim distant past, would seem superficially to make assertions about it testable. A little reflection shows that this is highly questionable. First of all, there is the enormous difficulty inherent in identifying events which occurred long ago, and at the time were not recorded and may not have seemed significant. *Ex hypothesi*, one participant in the event was very young, lacked the equipment for precise conceptualization, and was only too well endowed with motives for distorting them; the adult participants, on the other hand, may well be dead, and, at the time, the event(s) not being important *for them*, probably lacked motives for storing them in memory. But, above all, what mattered was not public events, but their *meaning* for the patient. The same meaning was presumably compatible with a large number of external events, many of them quite insignificant by external criteria. So was any external event required at all? Freud rather revealingly repudiated the relevance of historical reconstructions of the public event, on the grounds that, by invoking independent witnesses, it imposed an external judge on the process of analysis!

All this must naturally lead one to conclude that (4) is really quite redundant for the theory. The role played in Freud's intellectual development by the realization that seductions in infancy were often subjective, fantasy events rather than 'real' ones, is well known, though the account has recently been challenged. None the less, psychoanalytical theory has not on the whole proceeded to a total disavowal of the relevance of (4). If a man were discovered who had an Oedipus Complex and the appropriate recollections (whatever they may be), but who as a matter of objective historical fact had neither a father nor anyone who could plausibly be credited with a paternal role, this might put some mild strain on the theory; and to this rather marginal extent, contingent on rather implausible contingencies which are most unlikely to be well documented, *past*, historic, objective reality does make its small and dubious contribution to the testability of the theory.

It is an interesting fact, which hinges on all this, that psychoanalytical theory tends to develop in two rather contradictory directions: either the amputation of (3) and (4) and hence reduced relevance-area, so to speak, of the theory, which then restricts itself to the here-now and to therapy; or on the other hand of a further extension of (3) into the past, on the principle presumably that if you invoke the irrevocable and subterranean past, you might as well go to extremes. But the links (4)-to-(3), and (3)-to-(2), can easily be amputated and abandoned, like a lizard's tail: when firmly passed between the fingers, they tend to come off and continue to wriggle in one's hand while the lizard makes off.

Does, then, testability enter through the present and the future, through assertions about (1) and (2) and their therapeutic effects? As indicated, (2) on its own engenders no testability, owing to the uniqueness of the shaft and the inequality, the hierarchical ranking of shaft probes and of all shaft-probe-partners. Therapeutic effectiveness, and above all the denial of therapeutic effectiveness to other modes of inquiry and cure, would however *seem* to be testable. But this ceases to be so if the therapeutic ore brought up from the shaft, *and* the ore excavated by rival shafts, can properly be assessed only by the doctrine and guild itself, as appears to be the case (see quote from Anna Freud, p.188).

Moreover, the veridicity of shaft-reports can always be reassessed in the light of their therapeutic success: if they

fail, this shows that either the formulation was not really, properly internalized (mere intellectual assent is insufficient), or that it was not veridical after all. Veridicity is an ever-revocable ascription within this system. Therapeutic success by rival techniques can be, and is, discounted as superficial, and of course a whole variety of techniques is available for discounting failure of the favoured technique itself. Neither veridicity nor cure being fixed, the relation between them is hardly a good testing point. The real technique never fails, and its rivals never prosper.
See Appendix A.

TESTABILITY VINDICATED?

Grunbaum's work offers little solace to apologists of psychoanalysis, but it does claim to rebut Popper's view that psychoanalysis is untestable. Grunbaum's argument is rich, complex and important, and requires and deserves much fuller treatment than can be given it here. Nevertheless, its main point can be summarized and dealt with briefly. He rightly picks out one central doctrine in Freud for examination, and claims, disputably, that it is testable. In Grunbaum's own words: 'Now Freud enunciated a two-fold *causally necessary condition* for the analysand's conquest of neurosis as follows: only psychoanalytic interpretations that "tally with what is real" in the patient can mediate veridical insight, *and* such insight, in turn, is causally necessary for the successful alleviation of his neurosis.'[4]

Now testability does not enter here, as Grunbaum of course realizes and makes clear, merely through the positive promise of a cure. As Grunbaum observes: '. . . Freud was usually loath to attribute therapeutic *failures* to the incorrectness of his interpretations and blamed the patient's resistance instead.'[5]

No: testability does enter not through any promise of cure, but through the affirmation of an exclusive, unique path to a cure.

If the doctrine can correctly be interpreted in this way, it becomes testable by the simple device of seeing whether other methods (which include the absence of any method at all) can sometimes achieve a cure. Theoretically, even a single instance of either spontaneous recovery, or cure by some method other than psychoanalysis, would thereby refute psychoanalysis, while however also restoring it to science by Popper's criterion, by rendering it untrue but scientific; and all this would also establish Grunbaum's philosophical point against Popper. In practice, most of us would be loath to put such a burden on a single instance, however well authenticated, and would prefer to be presented with a whole class of such cases, large enough to be convincing.

There is of course no need to wait for such a class of cases. There has been a great deal of research both on spontaneous remission and on the effectiveness of other forms of therapy. Whether this research establishes that no treatment at all or other therapies are equal to, slightly worse, or slightly better than psychoanalysis, is still a matter of dispute and interpretation and will probably remain so for some time; but what is beyond any dispute whatsoever is that sometimes and indeed quite often, spontaneous recovery *does* occur, and that sometimes, and indeed rather often, other therapies *are* effective. This clearly establishes (*if* Grunbaum's interpretation of Freud's doctrine is correct), that psychoanalysis is both testable and false. This can be no great source of joy to Freudians, but could at the same time be a source of sorrow to Popperians.

I do not think, however, that Grunbaum's interpretation is really defensible as an accurate account of Freudian doctrine. What Grunbaum has in effect done is to take an admittedly important, fascinating and central thesis of the Freudian corpus, isolated and circumscribed it, cleaned it up so to speak, and has thereby gone some way towards rendering it testable. But in doing so, he has torn it out of the context of the entire system within which it functioned and which gave it life. The corpus as a whole is of course full of interesting ideas which, if this is done to them, also become testable. The untestability charge never made any sense if directed against single ideas in isolation and properly cleaned up. Cioffi comes closer to the truth of the matter when he claims that the untestability of psychoanalysis is procedural rather than doctrinal, and says: 'We could express this mnemonically by saying: the notion of a pseudo-science is a pragmatic and not a syntactical one.'[6] For the benefit of those not familiar with this piece of philosophical jargon, one should say that syntactics are concerned with the formal structure of proposition, seen in isolation, whereas pragmatics are concerned with what the users concretely *do* with the proposition. But Cioffi's formula is not quite right. It makes it sound as if the pragmatics were arbitrarily added to the content of the doctrine, when the doctrine is in trouble. But in fact the pragmatic strategies are direct and manifest corollaries of the central ideas of the doctrine! The pragmatics protect the doctrine, but the doctrine also engenders, produces, protects, guarantees the pragmatic practices.

The logical machinery with which Grunbaum surrounds his argument (the double necessary condition, etc.) is really quite unnecessary. To show that the thesis which Grunbaum has picked out of the Freudian corpus is testable, only one operation, and a very simple and easily intelligible one at that, is necessary: *cure* must firmly, unambiguously be a concept applicable and applied *in the public domain*. In other words, its meaning and application must be governed by criteria which can be applied impartially by any reasonably intelligent and well-informed person, irrespective of the sacramental status ascribed to him from within the guild. Once 'cure' has this kind of public meaning, any predictions about cures will immediately, and for obvious reasons, become testable.

There is still a complication: the assertion 'X produces a cure' may still remain untestable (even though 'cure' in the sentence satisfies my condition), if the identification of X itself remains under guild control. The neatness and importance of Grunbaum's example hinge on the availability of the proposition '*Only* X can effect a cure'. Thereby he makes its testability quite independent of the guild control of the meaning of X. The proposition 'Only X can effect a cure' is testable quite independently of the meaning of X, by seeing whether procedures *other than* X also do so. This seems to me the very core of the alleged demonstration of the testability (and incidentally, of the falsehood) of psychoanalysis. After that, the only falsification-evading technique which remains is to reinterpret 'other than X'. This is of course used: the very characteristic quotation from Anna Freud (see below) attempts precisely that, and we have seen Farrell, strangely enough, suggesting that the administrators of control groups may quite unwittingly be practising therapy on the members of the control group.

But Grunbaum, while concentrating on all kinds of nuances and complexities which do not put his argument in peril, does not sufficiently concentrate on the crucial fact that his argument hinges on a normal, public domain meaning of 'cure'. If this meaning be granted, then indeed his entire demonstration promptly follows, without further ado.

All this is very strange, for Grunbaum is in fact in possession of conclusive evidence concerning the manner in which the rest of the corpus will be deployed to save the system from falsification through the evidence to which it here becomes vulnerable (i.e. effectiveness of other therapies or of no-therapy-at-all). In the very same article, a few pages earlier he quotes Anna Freud (once described by her father as his only son) as writing: 'In competition with the psychotherapists they [analysts] are justified to maintain that what they have to offer is unique, i.e., thorough-going personality changes as compared with mere superficial symptomatic cures.'[7] In brief, therapeutic successes of other techniques (so crucial to the Grunbaum demonstration that psychoanalysis is testable) are disqualified, by a semi-tacit redefinition of 'cure', which in effect places the notion of 'real cure' under guild control. In other words, 'cure' looks like a public word, and of course remains such when public evidence is favourable; but if the evidence ceases to be such, the term undergoes a tacit transformation which preserves the system as a whole.

It is eminently questionable whether the crucial 'double necessary condition' of cure thesis really can be credited to Freud. In a sympathetic account of Grunbaum's position, Edward Erwin writes about the studies of the effects of other therapies and of no-therapy, and holds it relevant that '. . . the aforementioned evidence was not available to [Freud]. It is doubtful that there was *any* good evidence before the 1960s for the effectiveness of any non-psychoanalytical therapy.'[8] But Freud could not but be aware of spontaneous remissions, and Erwin notes the evidence which shows that Freud was indeed aware of this. He then, however, allows for the possibility that spontaneous remission occurs only in a sub-class of neuroses, so that psychoanalysis would still remain a strict condition of cure for the other kinds of neuroses, and thus would remain testable.

But it is inconceivable that there is *any* class of neuroses for which spontaneous remission *never* occurs, and Freud could not have had any illusions about that. There is no class of neuroses, antecedently defined, which is known to be an illness from which one cannot recover without aid. But the thesis that psychoanalysis is a necessary condition of a real cure can of course still be maintained, by the double strategy of distinguishing between real and superficial cures, and between neuroses which do and do not fit the thesis, and restricting the thesis to the sub-class defined, precisely, by the fact that it satisfies the thesis . . . In brief, an examination of the very part of Freudianism which Grunbaum selects as paradigmatically testable, illustrates and supports exactly the opposite conclusion: that the system is so constructed as to evade falsification.

The main device employed here for this achievement is merely one instance of a general principle which pervades psychoanalysis and is central to it, and which we have also discussed in other contexts. It can be called Selective Reduction and Authentication, or the Double Language syndrome. In this particular instance, it works through the dual meaning of 'cure', which can either be a concept operationalized in the public realm and with a public meaning, or can have its meaning bestowed on it and controlled through the privileged access granted to guild members in virtue of their ability to gaze into the unique shaft. $Cure_1$ and $Cure_2$ are not openly distinguished, and they are, as you might say, each other's shadow concepts. $Cure_1$ is in use in public discussion and the movement's publicity, $Cure_2$ if evidence is unfavourable . . .

The general principle underlying the operation of the two languages, and above all their symbiosis and mutual dependence, should be obvious. It may be worthwhile giving some examples of such shadow concept-pairs.

Language 1	*Language 2*
superficial symptomatic cure	real cure
neurotic unhappiness	ordinary unhappiness
resistance	rational criticism
authoritarian conscience	humanist conscience

An amusing example of the use of the second pair can be found, for instance, in an article by the late H. Guntrip, a fairly influential psychoanalyst, writer and therapeutic practitioner, in which he tries to grapple with the philosophical objections to analysis. Referring to Sir Peter Medawar's formulation of the standard charge that psychoanalysis makes itself impervious to criticism by invoking the notion of resistance, he says: 'Medawar's . . . criticism is based on a simple mistake . . . Medawar simply confuses "resistance to analytic therapy" with "criticism of theory".'[9] This could only be a mistake (let alone a simple one) if some independent criterion existed for distinguishing the two, if the switch allocating the very same behaviour to one or the other of the two labels were not claimed by the guild as its monopoly. Bizarrely, Guntrip illustrates this on the very same page, when he tells us how theoretically misguided analysts should be handled: 'If an analyst becomes too rigidly orthodox, one would feel that a too blind acceptance of a too palaeo-Freudian theory called for psychoanalytic treatment.'[10] The palaeo-Freudian, as we have seen from another quotation, (p.173), feels exactly the same about the innovator. I am more analysed than thou! Guntrip provides a splendid example of how non-conformist moralistic pastoral zeal can acquire a new lease of life by adopting Freudian terminology and techniques.

It is interesting to find another analyst, trying on an earlier occasion to answer the 'untestability' charge, instinctively employing exactly the same argument as Guntrip's. Of course error can occur, and analysts do make and recognize mistakes, and hence their ideas are testable and indeed tested! But how does the error arise, and how is it corrected? Only because of an inadequacy inside the analyst, to be corrected by going deeper into himself, purifying himself:

> There is, then, some justice in the analyst's contention that no one who has not been analysed can assess his work. But he is not . . . infallible . . . He may fail to infer a motive in someone else for something which 'rings no bell' in himself . . . Or he may have a bias in himself which makes him over-ready to impute his own motives to others.[11]

So, an analyst with a sufficient range of inner bells, and no bias, will not make mistakes. Guntrip's and Money-Kyrle's reactions to the testability problem illustrate one of my crucial contentions: that one of the logically unconscious bases of psychoanalysis is a curious version of conditional naïve realism, the assumption that truth is self-evident, provided certain conditions (the appropriate inner purification, in the gift of the guild and its theory) are satisfied.

Guntrip was quite given to invoking resistance where rational criticism might have seemed more appropriate. He knew that an earlier book of mine had provoked virulent denunciation, because its critics (perhaps quite rightly) thought it an atrociously bad book. In the course of a prolonged conversation, he urged me to explain their attitude by their resistance. He was clearly puzzled when I declined to take up the idea, and I could see in his eyes that he thought that I had foolishly failed to avail myself of a powerful tool.

A further example is drawn from the work of another of the men who had worked hard to give it some philosophic coherence – Erich Fromm.[12] Drawing the natural conclusion from the overall psychoanalytic picture of man – that the super-ego should no longer be taken at face value – Fromm finds that, after all, one cannot altogether manage without a sense of inner obligation. So a supposedly new kind of conscience is commended . . . But this can do its job only if it possesses some psychic force over and above whatever rational considerations can in any case be invoked on behalf of its recommendations. But how does this vectorial force and its direction differ from the other and repudiated kind of inner compulsion? My conscience is humanist but that of my opponents is authoritarian . . .

The point about this duality of language, the paired shadow concepts such that one of the pair is authentic and the other reduction-worthy, is of course that the speaker controls the switch, and can throw it one way or the other. There is not and never can be an external, independent decision procedure for determining which of the two members of the pair can, at that moment, rightly be invoked. He who controls the switch can then decide the boundary between authenticated truth and compulsion-spawned delusion.

THE NATURAL TRANSCENDENT

The various middle-range theories within psychoanalysis are linked to reality through the cunning beast and the shaft: in other words, their empirical content is to be found either in ordinary observations of human behaviour, or in clinical reports from practitioners of shaft-watching. The potential contained in both ensures, as indicated, that they need never face disastrous factual confrontation and the methods employed in both probably have the consequence that their meaning is less sharp than that of ordinary, commonsensical formulations about human conduct and inner life; but it does not mean that they are not interesting, suggestive, and on occasion true.

It may seem a curious and paradoxical fact that two theories, one of which (when its evasion-potential is not fully exploited) is true, and the other (on a similar assumption) is false but extremely interesting, should jointly generate a world which is impervious to testing. But it is so. And one must stress once again that this result is secured not by invoking *ad hoc*, in other words extraneous, aid but, on the contrary, through ideas central to the system itself and parts of its core inspiration.

The neat and sharp separation of nature from the transcendent was an achievement of the modern philosophy of the last three centuries. From one viewpoint, the achievement of psychoanalysis was to invent or discover or postulate a new transcendent, the Unconscious, which at the same time is unambiguously a part of nature. It isn't smuggled into nature as some kind of alien and distant element, like some meteorite from outer space composed of extra-terrestrial elements – quite the reverse: its main appeal is that it is so very gloriously part of nature, that it provides us with a language for seeing ourselves as akin to animals and not to angels.

It has all the properties of the old familiar semi-transcendent realms (semi-operationality of concepts, self-maintenance, needs-satisfaction, confirmation of social cohesion and hierarchy), but it is at the same time unambiguously part and parcel of nature as we now conceive her. *This*, above all, is why the concept has such an appeal and is so easily, so appealingly usable. Note that the Freudian theory of slips and dream interpretation is a reformulation of the old beliefs in omens and portents. The endless ambiguity and volatility of interpretations ensures that these theories can never be falsified. What was wrong with omens and portents was that they presupposed a kind of supernatural realm which is no longer in fashion. When rooted in a *naturalistic* transcendent (the Unconscious) they recover all their old attractiveness.

The difference between a psychoanalytical *seance* and a spiritualist one is this: the spirits and ghosts called up by the latter are not respectable, by the norms dominant in the mainline academic high culture of our time. Psychical research is only marginally tolerated in respectable intellectual circles, even when it fastidiously observes all the formal empiricist proprieties in its statistical methodology. Spiritualist communication with the Other World is even less well regarded, notwithstanding the fact that in its claims to unique access to its favoured realm, it has a clear formal resemblance to the logic of psychoanalysis, with its privileged and exclusive telescope, as the practitioners have called it, directed at *its* special realm.

And just this of course is the clue, the explanation of the difference. Psychoanalysis has postulated an Other Realm which has all the crucial properties once possessed by the supernatural world (*that* is where our precarious fates are decided, and where propitiation is best directed) but at the same time, is entirely compatible with the contemporary naturalistic vision of the world. Nay, it is far more than merely compatible: the naturalistic, biological vision of man positively *requires* it, and it was sadly defective and incomplete before this realm had been supplied to us by Freud.

Once Darwinism had established that we were animals, we clearly needed a name for that part of us in which the dark lower forces make themselves felt, an area previously uncharted and virtually unnamed by polite language, or only castigated by the earlier religious idiom. The need for an adequate, or at least usable and suggestive language for speaking of this region, arose both from the renaturalization of man, *and* from the conceptually confused sense of the darkness within us which we all felt, but did not know how to speak about, and which previously had to be left to romantic writers specializing in the nocturnal aspects of man.

Religions often tell their acolytes that reason must be suspended. Psychoanalysis can also and does require such a suspension, but in the name of force or forces, the Unconscious, which looks like being entirely, indeed paradigmatically, naturalistic, wholly of this world, of the domain of biology and medicine. Religion may well envy such an cogent appeal to suspend reason, issued in the name of nature.

In brief, the old religious or metaphysical transcendent is withering away not because it is transcendent, but because it is the wrong *kind* of transcendent. A *naturalistic* transcendent (and the Freudian Unconscious is nothing if not that) is alive and well, and Freud is the Plato of naturalism.[13]

SWICHENS

A certain phenomenon has become very familiar in the psychology of perception. If one draws a cube *without perspective*, it tends to 'jump' in one's vision in a certain way: the square which constitutes one of the cube's six sides, first looks as if it were the front of the cube, and then as if it were its back. Many other visual patterns can be constructed which present two or even more rival interpretations.

What is less familiar, and has been far less explored, is that such interpretative jumps can and do occur not merely in visual patterns, but equally, and perhaps more significantly, in *conceptual* ones. The same as it were 'raw' material can assume this or that shape in succession, each seeming compulsive and exclusive for a time, yet each liable mysteriously to give way to the other. Despite its importance, the phenomenon seems to have no name. The term 'paradigm', as introduced into the philosophy of science by Thomas Kuhn, has some but certainly not all of the characteristics that are required. Paradigms are compulsive, and they organize a domain, but they lead only to a jump to another paradigm under the impact of *new* material, which gradually makes the old paradigm less and less attractive, and eventually leads to the crystallization of a new one.

By a *swichen* (a term invented and derived from switch-vision) I mean one of two or more alternative ways of conceptually interpreting a given domain, such that each of the swichens is more or less equally attractive and more or less equally compatible with the material. No accretion of new evidence is required to stimulate a jump. The two or more mutually exclusive but equally domain-compatible swichens I would then call a swichen-group.

These neologisms seem to be necessary if one is to give anything like an adequate account of the overall conceptual strategy of psychoanalysis. Human conduct and experience comes to be seen through at least two rival swichens, under the impact of psychoanalytic theory and practice. First, there is the public swichen or *Lebenswelt*, which analytically oriented people share with the rest of mankind, or at any rate with those of a similar background culture. Within this vision, the cunning beast is clearly much in evidence, men do indeed suffer incomprehensibly, and do not understand the patterns and compulsions which govern their relationships. The beast is far more than a mere conjecture: though imprecise, it is nevertheless a very highly plausible idea, and one which, in some form or other, we know to be almost certainly valid. In this world also, the shaft idea, the theory concerning the technique by means of which the precise habits of the beast can be identified and mastered, is a highly interesting, though also most questionable hypothesis. (The basic attraction of psychoanalysis is simple: it gives an account of the beast, and we do know that the beast is indeed within us; and it promises at least partial delivery from torments imposed by the beast.) This is Swichen 1.

Swichen 2, to which some men jump in certain circumstances, is different. Within it, both beast theory and shaft theory cease to be hypotheses or conjectures and become constitutive, pervasive, world-defining, and constitutionally entrenched and fundamental truths. The constitutiveness is achieved by linking them to an intense and slowly maturing personal relationship.

Psychoanalysis consists, in effect, of a systematically induced, assisted and medically sanctioned jump from Swichen 1 to Swichen 2, (and much more questionably back again). It would not occur if it were not for the indisputable fact that the beast theory (shared in some measure by both swichens) is overwhelmingly plausible within the first and public vision, and if this did not imply a crying need for a remedy: and if the shaft hypothesis, though risky and unproven (and, as it happens, false) had not had at least a good minimal plausibility even within

Swichen 1. Within Swichen 2, both conceptual and social-emotional constraints operate to ensure that neither beast nor shaft can be tested *and* found wanting.

THE THREE-HORSE RACE

Formally, the truth of shaft theory (access to Unconscious by the technique, plus therapeutic effects) is really settled by the existence of non-psychoanalytic cures (either spontaneous or by means of other therapies). In so far as the shaft is unique, it can be tested only by its one manifestation in the public realm, i.e. the therapeutic success. Notoriously, therapeutic failure slides off it like water off a duck's back, but it is more vulnerable to the success of other therapies (and of none at all), if the system is firmly committed to excluding this possibility.

But these rather formal arguments have less impact than evidence about the relative success or otherwise of psychoanalysis, of *other* methods, and of *no methods* at all.

For instance, Seymour Fisher and Roger P. Greenberg's massive *The Scientific Credibility of Freud's Theories and Therapy*,[14] comes out fairly favourably on the side of Freud's general theories, though they note with a touch of surprise that 'an important part of the scientific data giving substance to Freud's oral and anal personality typologies is based on conscious-self reports elicited by questionnaires'.[15] If so, this would seem to support substance at the cost of undermining claims for the allegedly unique depth-telescope: surface observations suffice after all for probing the deep!

While providing some partial support to what we have called beast theory, they provide none for shaft theory.

Some may argue that the failure of research to demonstrate the superiority of the analytic approach is due to anti-analytic bias . . . It is our speculation that the failure to find support for a uniquely superior psychoanalytic therapy cannot be attributed simply to bias and a lack of appropriate sensitive measures of behavioural and intra-psychic change.

In a sense, it is hard to imagine that psychoanalysis could, as a general inquiry, be found superior to other approaches, since the evidence indicates so clearly that there is no one conception of what psychoanalytic therapy is. The field is filled with vagueness, appeals to authority rather than evidence, lack of specificity in the definitions used, and unreliability in the application of techniques ... The vagueness and heterogeneity of clinical practice have translated into an amorphous research literature.[16]

The failure to find any evidence of superior therapeutic effectiveness is conceded. In my terminology, the claims for the shaft, though fascinating, lack any substantiation. Their general finding that the beast theory (or NM) may contain ideas that are not merely interesting but partially true, seems to me overwhelmingly plausible and acceptable. But what these authors say about the low conceptual level of clinical practice and its research shadow, highlights another supremely important point: as long as the concepts and ideas of beast theory remain linked to reality and opera-tionalized through shaft-watching, (as psychoanalysis in-sists they should be – sometimes that this should be the *unique* link), there will be no hope of sorting out truth from falsehood. Owing to the slipperiness of these concepts – which is inherent in the very logic of dual shaft-watching, not in some inherent logical feebleness of practitioners in their prior existence – psychoanalysis remains an absolutely hopeless retrieval system for whatever depth-truths, or for that matter surface-truths, it may stumble upon.

The literature on this subject is by now considerable and will no doubt continue to grow.[17] There is not much point in going over it here in detail, in as far as the overall pattern in this three-horse race is rather clear.

Spontaneous Remission, when ridden by that outstanding jockey H. J. Eysenck (unquestionably the Lester Piggott of this course), attains astonishing speeds, sometimes in the neighbourhood of sixty-five per cent. Other jockeys have raised complaints against the methods used by this rider to hasten this steed, and even to hold up those of others, and these complaints may or may not be upheld by the racing board. If they are not, it looks as if *Spontaneous Remission* may well win. If, however, the protests are upheld and this horse is slowed down, the picture is different, but far from conclusive: *Spontaneous Remission* is then somewhat behind but not disastrously so, with *Other Therapies* leading *Psychoanalysis* by a length or so. The distances involved, however, are small enough to ensure that anything may yet happen in the home stretch. A recent report[18] rather favourable in attitude and findings to *Psychoanalysis*, claims that it has recently diminished the distance separating it from the leader *Other Therapies*, but does not claim that *Psychoanalysis* has caught up, let alone overtaken, *Other Therapies*.

The only thing which could really sustain the claims of *Psychoanalysis* would be if it had a clear and unmistakable lead. One thing which emerges from the entire literature, without any shadow of doubt, is that this is not so. Hence the problem arises – how can one explain the confidence of the rider of *Psychoanalysis* and of those who have put their money on him? This question allows of but one answer: that steed is riding in two races at once, one public and the other private, and in the private race, all other mounts are disqualified.

BEAST, SHAFT AND TEST

The intriguing question of the testability of psychoanalytic ideas and claims has no simple and straightforward answer. The situation can perhaps best be summed up as follows.

The system contains two central claims, which may be called P and Q.

P is what we call the doctrine of the beast, the view that our conduct, feelings and thoughts are dominated by forces and processes of which we are not properly conscious, and within which instinctual drives are of the first importance.

Q is what we call shaft theory. It affirms that in properly supervised free-association, psychoanalysis possesses a privileged or perhaps unique mode of approach to the realm of the beast (possibly supplemented by subsidiary techniques such as dream analysis), which can, when properly applied, disclose the truth about that realm, *and* be therapeutically effective.

Essentially, psychoanalysis consists of the conjunction of P and Q. But it is most important to note that this is not a simple, mechanical additive conjunction. The two propositions are not simply asserted alongside each other. Their links with each other are far more intricate, complex and many-sided.

Nevertheless, let us first of all consider each in (admittedly artificial) isolation. P is true. In its strongest possible formulation, it is also untestable: a really all-powerful malignant daemon can control everything, and notably evidence about himself, and also the adoption and rejection of theories about himself. It follows that no evidence which suggests his non-existence can ever be conclusive or even weighty. It is well within his powers, *ex hypothesi*, to fix just such evidence for his own ends.

But in practice, P is not normally affirmed in its strongest possible sense. It is normally asserted and interpreted at some unspecified, loosely defined point well below its maximum strength. On such an interpretation, it is not only true but also testable.

By contrast, Q is interesting, suggestive, plausible and false. The alleged telescope into the depths does not provide accurate information, nor is the possession of the alleged information which it brings, effectively therapeutic. Were it so, the evidence would by now have accumulated, but the evidence which is available is woefully inadequate, and cannot sustain these claims. What is true is that sustained free association probably does reveal *some* area of affective import to the free-associating individual, and if carried out in the prescribed manner, does often engender a powerful 'transference'.

Q, if interpreted as a claim made in the public world, i.e. a claim to therapeutic success recognizable by the general public, by all and sundry, is false. That is of course its 'normal' interpretation. Q can, however, be reinterpreted with the help of notions such as 'superficial symptom removal' and 'real insight', where these become not public concepts, but concepts employable only by a selected sub-population, selected by the theory and its associated guild. On that interpretation, Q ceases to be false and becomes untestable.

So, in different ways, both P and Q fluctuate between testability and untestability, though on the most natural interpretation (which makes each of them testable), one of them is true and the other false.

Moreover, the corpus of the theory engenders a whole host of more specific propositions, refinements or specifications or alleged applications of both P and Q, which inherit the status-fluctuation (between testability and untestability) from their two logical parents. They are not strictly speaking corollaries of P and Q, in so far as they are not simply deducible from them by a straightforward logical operation. Rather, they are specific assertions about psychic processes, made in the general style of P and Q and within their framework, but excogitated in a clinical context by Freud and his intellectual progeny. Their links both with their theoretical premises and with their empirical foundations are too loose and pliable to allow them to be assigned firmly to truth or falsehood, though no doubt some of them may tend strongly in one of these two directions. Part of the general linkage between P and Q arises precisely from the fact that these more specific doctrines appear to be applications of both of them: they invoke both the general substrate of the Unconscious and its manifestations in all behaviour, and the data of clinical, therapeutic experience.

But there are other and supremely important links between P and Q. Psychoanalysis generally presents Q as the means by which the truth of P was discovered in the first place! Q is the Columbus who discovered America. The indisputable existence of America does not strictly speaking entail the historical reality of Columbus: documents might yet turn up in Genoa or Madrid or Cadiz, showing that no such person had ever lived. America would still be here, its existence unimpugned. But in our case, the barely disput-able reality of America, of our unconscious new found land,

somehow seems to guarantee the authenticity of the discovery and the discoverer. The inference is faulty, but it has
been made to seem persuasive.

Equally fallacious, but enormously persuasive, is a kind
of argument from moral and emotional need. If America
exists, then we also *need* Columbus. For the Columbus we
are dealing with in this case is not merely its discoverer: he
is, far more significantly perhaps, also its conqueror, its
lion-tamer. The Unconscious continent now discovered is
not merely a reality, it is, above all, a terrible peril to us all.
If it exists, life is hardly bearable, thinkable, without the
availability of some protective measures. Happily, he who
discovered it, *also* found the counter-measures to the deadly
perils it contained . . . How terrible it would have been had
he not only discovered it, but then announced that it
contained forces which could not be contained or controlled! But no, happily it is not so. Christopher Sigmund in
fact discovered the dangerous continent only at the very
moment – indeed, by the very same means – as he also
found the effective counter-measures to its formidable
threats. Miraculously, the tool of discovery was, at the very
same time, also the weapon of conquest and mastery. A
most fortunate coincidence for mankind.

A further link between P and Q is the fact that Q, while
validated as discoverer of P, and as the fulfilment of an
insistent need engendered by the very existence of P, at the
same time possesses the monopoly or near-monopoly of
authenticating reports about the specific outline of P.

And here we come to a really central point. The existence
of the Unconscious looks like a hypothesis, comparable to
the affirmation of oil deposits in the Bristol channel, or an
archaeological site under the foundations of a modern
building, or an extra, hitherto undetected planet in the solar
system. It may, in part, be analogous to such ideas. But it is
far, far more than that.

The affirmation of its existence does not merely consist of
a claim that a certain kind of object or entity is to be found
in a given realm. On the contrary, the existence of this
entity totally transforms the status of all evidence and of all

choice and abandonment of theories. The entity has a unique relationship both to evidence of its own existence (found in daily or clinical conduct), and to the events describable as the acceptance of or resistance to theories about itself. These, and these above all, are the areas in which it displays and disports itself. This totally transforms the rules of the game. It automatically engenders a hierarchy (of those with and without access to the entity) and of an associated strategy of salvation. And it does all this in a way which has drastic and obvious implications for testability.

X

LA THERAPIE IMAGINAIRE

FLOAT AND SAIL

In *The Experimental Study of Freudian Theories* H. J. Eysenck and G. D. Wilson, the editors, say: 'A theory which fails consistently to predict . . . may nevertheless survive, due to the vagaries of the *Zeitgeist*.'[1] Eysenck and Wilson are, quite legitimately from the viewpoint of their concerns, not very interested in the *Zeitgeist*, and invoke it as a *deus ex machina* to account for the survival of psychoanalysis despite its persistent therapeutic failures and despite the success of spontaneous remission (inadmissible for Freudian theory). *Zeitgeister* come and go, it would seem, and if one of them hampers the advancement of knowledge, we may just have to wait a bit for it to disappear, like a spell of bad weather.

In a sense, the present book is more interested in our *Zeitgeist* than it is in psychoanalysis.

The crucial strategic position occupied by Freudianism in the social and intellectual history of mankind, makes it possible for us to learn a vast amount from it about, on the one hand, the general anatomy of belief-systems and, on the other, the special conditions prevalent in our age.

If we have answered the question of why this system serves our age so well, we shall have gained a great deal. In part, obviously, we shall have learnt much about the nature of belief-systems in general. But, more significantly, we shall have learnt much about our age and its quite distinctive social and intellectual terms of reference. The belief, organizational and soteriological system with which we are concerned is quite unthinkable in any age other than our own; and within our age, its impact, vitality, and its up-market, quality catchment area – it is the opium of the intellectuals *par excellence*, more so even than Marxism – makes it virtually unique, and perhaps absolutely unique.

TRUTH AND IDEOLOGY

It is worth noting and stressing here that truth is not an advantage in producing a burning faith – contrary to Gibbon's highly ironic observations. Imagine for a moment that the crucial contentions of therapeutic effectiveness of the method were valid, that a very high proportion of patients, far higher than those which recover spontaneously, were genuinely cured. Given the terrible amount of neurotic suffering in the world, the demand for cures would become overwhelming. Psychoanalysis does not only serve the idle rich, but also many who are in acute distress (and no doubt some who fall into both categories). Given the passionate faith and enthusiasm of believers, any therapeutic successes would be rapidly and effectively advertised. In no time, the sacred fire would be stolen, and would spread round the world in the hands of those who had seized it. One thing is certain: if analysis worked, the Japanese would long ago have adapted it, and flooded the world market with cheaper, quicker and more efficient analysts.

The point is this: truth is unpatentable. Once out, and once the one important secret of *effectiveness* is out – whether it be industrialization or science in general, or nuclear fission, or whatever, attempts to protect and monopolize it are, in the modern world, totally unavailing.

But whereas truth is unpatentable, a certain kind of falsehood – the kind we have described as wager-engendering, by containing both some genuine bait and some genuine offence – is self-patenting, and constitutes the very stuff of which burning faiths are made. Compare two techniques, A and B, such that A cures eighty per cent of patients by a publicly testable method, and B cures only twenty per cent by an esoteric and invisible unspecifiable method which is accompanied by intense emotion. A will spread like wildfire, but the very publicity of the method will ensure that no magic attaches to those who peddle it. It can and will be freely emulated. It generates no offence, no transference.

B generates both. It will make its enemies among disappointed patients who do not fall into the lucky twenty per cent; but those within that fortunate group will not merely feel cured, but *bound* to the method and its practitioners. The very fact that there is no way of picking out the twenty per cent in advance, makes B untestable, but that in turn ties adherents to their therapists by faith. If they spread the word and, once again, twenty per cent of those whom they treat again become converts, given the consequences of exponential growth, the movement will grow considerably and prosper, though it will also feel under siege, which will help its morale and discipline.

'WELCOME HOSTILITY' writes H. Guntrip, thus in capitals and goes on: 'A recent 600-page textbook on "Clinical Psychiatry" by Maye-Gross, Slater and Ross (1954) provides further welcome reassurance that psychoanalysis has not yet lost its power to arouse emotional opposition. The work of Freud will never be safer than when it evokes hostility.'[2] Guntrip, who had a plural faith, but deplored the current inability of religion to engender offence, regretfully warns his readers that: 'What happened to Christianity could equally well happen to psychoanalysis.'

Ironically, technique A, with an eighty per cent success rate, will become common property and engender no movement at all. This elementary consideration must be borne in mind, whenever we attempt to deal with any specific case of Gibbon's problem.

It is sometimes asserted that the real trouble with psychoanalysis, even if valid, is that it is intolerably expensive, labour-intensive. This does not seem to me to be so, or at any rate, were psychoanalysis valid, it would not constitute a serious problem. Assume that the world at present contains 1,000 analysts (and it certainly contains far more).

Assume an analyst can train six new analysts every five years, and so as to allow for mortality, that having done so he trains no further analysts at all. On these rather modest assumptions, a simple calculation will show that the entire population of the earth could consist of nothing but properly trained analysts, within about half a century.

This is not at all impracticable: the daily hour is perfectly compatible with full-time other employment for the analysands, as is well known, and initially the age-structure of this global analysis programme could be so arranged that the analysts themselves would be close to retirement age anyway. Very soon, however, as a kind of demographic equilibrium were approached, each analyst would only on average be training 1. N trainee analysts (one to replace himself, and N to allow for wastage, where N would be a fairly low digit). By that time, neither the analyst's nor the analysand's other profession would suffer, and so world production would not drop significantly as a result of this global morally educational and therapeutic programme, which could be run by UNATO (United Nations Analysis and Therapy Organization), with elegant headquarters in Vienna. If analysis gives us insight into, and the capacity to neutralize, irrational hostilities and compulsions, then, given the appalling danger which mankind now faces from international conflicts, the programme would seem to be more than worthwhile. If it is not adopted, this cannot be justified by any appeal to some inherent economic unfeasibility.

THE WELL

Freud did not discover the Unconscious. What he did do was to endow it with a language, a ritual, and a church. The general spirit of the language, which conveys that our instinctual needs are central to us, and that they operate in a hidden, devious and cunning manner, seems to me unquestionably sound. The more specific doctrines articulated in that idiom seem to me questionable, unproven, and above all inherently elusive: if true by chance on one occasion or another, there is no way of retaining or retrieving the truth or stiffening the link between assertion and fact, given the loose and slippery nature of the assertions. The obverse of the evasion of all contrary evidence, is that when analysis does stumble upon truth, the elusiveness of its concepts, their fragile links to reality, prevent any *retrieval* of the truth in analogous circumstances.

Whether a better idiom, from this viewpoint, could be found, would seem to be an interesting and open question. It may be that the astonishing complexity of human situations, their dependence on highly diverse social contexts, makes it impossible to find genuine specific generalizations, other than either trivial or slippery ones. But though inclined to be sceptical about the possibility of psychological advances in this direction, I certainly would not wish to be dogmatic in my scepticism.

The part of the corpus which is at best totally unproven, and on available evidence appears to be quite false, contains certain specifically Freudian doctrines which are in his system firmly welded on to the idea of the Unconscious, but are in fact quite independent of it. The most crucial ones among them are the following:

1. The view that the Unconscious can best (or at all) be approached by the method of free association.

2. The idea that the psychoanalytic method is also therapeutically effective.

The basic picture presented by Freudianism is that the Unconscious is hidden behind an unscalable, impenetrable Wall; and that there is one legitimate and well-authenticated Checkpoint Charlie at which one can get through, namely psychoanalysis; and hence that, by using this exclusively controlled point of penetration, ailments rooted in our Unconscious (and without any doubt, there must be many such) can only or best be cured by availing ourselves of the good offices of the guards who are in control of Checkpoint Sigmund, as it should properly be called.

It is a very essential feature of psychoanalysis that it does not distinguish – and indeed does everything to obscure –

the utter distinctiveness of the two theses: (a) the Wall exists, there is indeed a powerful and cunning Unconscious, and (b) Checkpoint Sigmund is an effective and trust-worthy communications-point. (a) is true; (b) is not.

The truth of the matter seems to me that, indisputably, the Wall does exist. It is not, at all its points, quite as high or quite as unscalable as psychoanalysis asserts in its efforts to sustain the monopolistic claims of Checkpoint Sigmund. On the contrary, I am inclined to think that it has become a crumbling ruin in some places, and its penetration by unaided common sense and intelligence is not always impossible. In any case, it had better be possible, for Check-point Sigmund seems to be nothing but a source of sustained disinformation.

For various reasons, the amount of unconscious self-deception, by both partners, in the psychoanalytic thera-peutic relationship, must be far greater even than that which is normal in most other intimate human situations. The reason why this must be so is that it has been so constructed as to be largely free of the normal extraneous and independent checks which in other situations help limit our self-deceit, and which alone are capable of doing it, while the incentives impelling the participants eventually to agree on a negotiated interpretation, optimally favourable to their self-images, are very strong.

It is indisputably true that prolonged free association in the prescribed situation engenders powerful emotions. It is also very plausible to suppose that intense emotion is connected with continuous and unconscious attitudes and conflicts. But it does *not* follow from these two propositions that free association reveals *truths* about the Unconscious, *or* that the recognition of such truths is therapeutically effec-tive. It is probably true that this method reveals some emotionally septic areas; it is not at all evident that it either reveals *all* of them, or that it reveals truths *about* them, or that this process *cures*. The contrary inference is the central *non sequitur* of psychoanalysis.

The interesting but curious doctrine that in the Uncon-scious, all contradictions are allowed, raises the question of

209

whether or in what sense it can be credited with having any determinate content at all. If one discovers that it contains a given element, its freedom from logic does not allow one to conclude that any other and contrary element is not also present. But how can there be any tension, in that case? Moreover, the Unconscious appears to understand and utilize the logical fastidiousness of the conscious mind, in so far as it panders to or plays upon the incompatibilities which our conscious minds feel only too acutely.

THE PINEAL GLAND

Apart from conferring a language and a sustaining ritual and organization on the Unconscious (plus a baseless therapeutic promise), Freud also achieved something else. Quite unwittingly – for this was not his main or conscious purpose – he elaborated a system which solved, or alas 'solved', some of the most important, persistent and haunting problems which face us. He constructed a system which, were it valid, would dissolve many of the major, emotionally disturbing conceptual strains of our society, *and* solve some of the main problems of philosophy.

Strictly speaking, there is no need for any 'and': the two things are the same. Serious philosophy (not always identical with academic philosophy) must nowadays be concerned with the emergence of science, of a secular order, mass leisure and industrial production, and the way in which we can handle our new and wholly unprecedented situation. The present volume does not aim at explaining just how this great revolution in our thought-styles about ourselves came about. But it does aim to highlight the manner in which psychoanalytic ideas relate to those other great transformations of our collective situation. Within psychoanalysis there is a tradition of low philosophical sophistication; hence one must bring out and make explicit the ideas which are pervasive implied in psychoanalysis, but remain in a kind of logical unconscious, and which most analysts would not be capable of formulating themselves. I feel no inhibition about claiming to know better than they do themselves, what they implicitly think. They have, after all, set a good precedent for such a practice.

It is possible to sketch out only very briefly the astounding set of fundamental problems which find their *en passant*, semi-conscious (but consequently all the more effective) solution in Freudianism, and which would now be finally solved were Freudianism valid.

1. The Plato/Nietzsche problem of extracting an ethic which would genuinely correspond to our real nature and its needs and possibilities. (This is of course a problem faced by very many thinkers; I have simply singled out the two who are most relevant.) Plato, working against the background of a stability-seeking and hierarchical society amenable to metaphysical belief, had no difficulty in extracting an ethic from a supposedly hierarchical structure of the soul, society, cognition and reality. Nietzsche, wishing to do the same against the background of a renaturalized world, found it much more difficult. Freud completed Nietzsche's endeavours in this direction, by inventing a technique for individualized, private, yet expertly assisted and validated solutions, an individual-customer-adjusted re-establishment of a cosy link between Is and Ought.

2. The Cartesian problem of mind–body interaction, which is closely related to the problem of the relation of our 'humanistic' self-knowledge and 'scientistic' understanding of nature. It is also the problem of the communication between our blind passions and our powerless, abstract concepts. Descartes supposed that mind and body met in the pineal gland.

Freud's new pineal gland is an enormous improvement on Descartes, and incidentally on Hume, or at any rate it sounds much more plausible. Our dark lusts and our meanings meet in the middle ground of the Unconscious. That sounds a good deal more plausible than the pineal gland. It has always been difficult to see how the crude destructive passions could mesh in with our complex and fragile, porcelain-like conceptual structures. Freud provided the answer. The Unconscious houses the dark powerful forces, but at the same time it speaks English – like a drunk. The crude, a-logical, uncategorial language spoken by the Unconscious, a kind of Pidgin-Human, is on the one hand crude enough to be understood by the dark forces and to act as their spokesman and ambassador, yet close enough to real human speech to exchange coded messages with consciousness . . . It all somehow has a certain plausibility. Hume had thought (absurdly) that our passions spoke polite eighteenth-century English, and could mesh in with ends and means articulated in such an elegant idiom. Freud's version is much more credible. (However, Freud's theory of cathexis is, for once, strikingly parallel to Hume's vision of passions attaching themselves to emotively colourless facts.)

The problem has its social or cultural complement. Is man to be handed over to impersonal scientific explanation or understood in his own terms and in his full individuality? Psychoanalysis ensures that the answer is both/and. Man is part of the biological world, and his animal instincts receive full recognition: but their specific constellation in the heart of any one man is only approached individually, and by human *meanings*, not neurological or similar entities . . . All's well.

As Donald Davidson puts it: 'It seems then, that there are two irreconcilable tendencies in Freud's methodology. On the one hand he wanted to extend the range of phenomena subject to reason explanations, and on the other to treat these same phenomena as forces and states are treated in the natural sciences.'[3] Indeed; and various philosophers have been eager to help him be consistent and to eliminate one or the other element, to become more physicalist or more hermeneutic. But his system would never have possessed its great appeal, had it not been ambiguous or, if you like, ambivalent on this point. Dark forces without meanings are blind, meanings without drives are impotent. In the Unconscious, one can have *both*. A purely hermeneutic psychoanalysis would not sound like science, confer no power, and few men would turn to it in distress; a purely physicalist or biological psychoanalysis would have been too much like science, and no fun. But the plausible-sounding fusion of both is very different, and most attractive.

3. The Cartesian problem of the trustworthiness of our knowledge. How do we know we are not deluded? We do know that others delude themselves, and that their delusions are accompanied by the greatest assurance; why should we assume ourselves to be exempt?

Descartes invented the malignant daemon who deceives us, but it was, for him, only an intellectual, experimental device, a supposition. Freud discovered the daemon for real, not as a supposition to bring home that we *might* be deceived, but as a bitter reality which explained just how we *were* indeed deceived.

But he accompanied his discovery with a closely linked technique for outwitting him, for sorting our deception from truth, and for recovering full and, for the first time ever, *justified* confidence.

4. The Kantian problem of a reduplicated self, arising from the fact that in an age of effective science we see ourselves both as free agents and inquirers responsible for our decisions and conclusions, *and* as objects, parts of nature, subject to its laws and thus devoid of freedom and responsibility. Instead of the stressful and unbelievable doctrine that we are each of these two things simultaneously, Freud told us that we were one or the other, not simultaneously, but according to whether or not we submitted to his technique of liberation . . . Autonomy, which for Kant had to spring from inside, could now be assisted (nay, *had* to be assisted), possibly even on the Health Service.

5. The Weberian problem of a 'disenchanted', cold, impersonal world. The modern world is in fact bound to be such: cognitive growth goes jointly with specialized, single-strand cognitive inquiry, which inevitably separates the intellectual exploration of the world from personal relations, values, and the hierarchical ordering of society. Freud restored a form of cognition which, while articulated in an impeccably modern idiom, and seemingly part of medicine and science, was firmly locked in with a

hierarchical and comforting personal relation, and with values and the hope of personal salvation. Thus a reality is re-enchanted, and its enchantment is permanently serviced, albeit at a price.

This is an aspect of Freudianism which is generally neglected by those who concentrate on its failure to be scientific. Of course it is fair to raise that criticism, in so far as the doctrine does loudly claim to be a science, and in so far as this claim is essential to its success as a belief-system. Nevertheless, if one looks at it only as a system of scientific claims, one is liable to miss altogether most clues to its real functioning.

It is not *a* hypothesis, located in a wider world, whose fate and applicability is to be decided by the higher court of evidence. On the contrary, it sits in judgement on facts and decrees how they are to be interpreted (and only other interpretations of its own can sit in judgement on interpretations). Its truth, if it be such, does not modify a bit of the world: it is constitutive of the world, it pervades and defines it. It is not attained through evidence but by a deep inner experience, an inner revelation which is also a moral regeneration.

6. The Durkheimian problem of reuniting cognition, ritual, and social order. Psychoanalysis has or is an astoundingly effective ritual, adapted to an individualist age, engendering all those affective consequences which Durkheim associated with ritual, and indeed separating the sacred and profane with all the neatness which that theory postulated.

To offer a persuasive solution to so fundamental a set of problems, and to offer them in a way that the solution is *lived* out rather than merely thought, ratified by both ritual and an intense personal relationship, and generally not consciously thought out at all, is an astonishing achievement.

I say all this with no irony whatsoever. I am not claiming that the average middle-class educated man in Western society is knowingly preoccupied with the problems contained in the works of Plato, Descartes, Hume, Kant, Nietzsche, Durkheim and Weber. Rather, I am saying that the problems faced by these thinkers are those which also emerge from the inherent and pervasive intellectual tensions of our society and its thought-styles. Hence a theory which, with its accompanying technique/ritual and organizational underpinning, appears to solve them all, above all through the deployment of that very technique/ritual, and which offers adjustable, customer-specific salvation, is bound to have a great impact.

CAPTAIN OF HIS SOUL

It is natural to ask what kind of man was capable of this astonishing achievement. He has often been accused of being authoritarian, dogmatic and intolerant, and of having some considerable difficulty in distinguishing between loyalty to truth and loyalty to himself. He ran a scientific association in a manner which bore a fair measure of resemblance to the administration of the Mafia or of a Leninist party. He constructed a belief-system within which doubt of the system itself appeared to have little standing other than that of a neurotic symptom. He provided this system with an admirable organizational base, whose members were recruited by means of tempting implicit promises, whose fulfilment, however, could not, within the rules of the system itself, be queried.

All this appears to be so, but may perhaps miss the heart of the matter. Dogmatism is not uncommon among creative intellectuals, even or especially among those who preach liberalism. Freud was not unique in these traits, but only in the scale of his impact.

More serious may be the low level of his capacity, or inclination, to indulge in genuine doubt about his central position. It is serious because it is profoundly ironic. His achievement is sometimes summed up, by Freud himself as well as others, as the completion of the naturalization of man, the culmination of the progression Copernicus–Darwin–Freud. The first removed man from the centre of the universe, the second assigned man back to nature and among the other animals, and the third showed man that he was not even master in his own house. And so it is.

What is so odd is how little he applied this insight to himself and above all to his own ideas. When he made Jung promise him that he would uphold certain doctrines, when he organized a secret inner party to watch over the loyalty of the other members, when he asserted that he was sure of possessing the truth, and that it could not be judged from the outside by those who had not submitted to the technique he had himself invented, the idea that he himself might be deceiving himself does not seem to have crossed his consciousness (nor, evidently, his Unconscious, given that he had such good access to it). There is not the slightest reason to suppose that statistics of clinical success, had he kept them, would have been less disappointing at the time than they turned out to be later, when such records were kept. The personal histories of the early initiates do not generally make happy reading. Yet he could assert there was no need for empirical confirmation, because the clinical evidence was so overwhelming. This would suggest a person capable of some persisting indulgence in self-delusion.

But above all, unlike Nietzsche, he never had any sense of the self-devouring quality of his central ideas. On the contrary, the self-devouring monster allowed Freud, at any rate, to continue to live in an astonishingly stable, solid house, and plainly to remain full master within it. He invented a technique which devours and digests any external terms of reference or criteria, which could have judged the technique itself; but the technique, lethal to critics, never turned in on itself, its own premises and foundations.

His concept of the Unconscious is a curious offspring of Descartes' Daemon, Kant's Thing-in-itself, and Schopenhauer's Will. Freud in effect took the daemon, whose original role had been to inspire us with doubt, endowed him with flesh and turned him, by a strange but potent alchemy, bizarre but most effective, into an instrument of certainty and confidence. By firmly seizing control of that key switch which consigns all else either to reduction-worthy delusion or to authentic perception, he turned the daemon into a Joker card to be used against all comers.

But the renaturalization of man, the discovery of his animal status, of the cunning, deceitful, covert and animal nature of even the putatively 'higher' aspects of man, and indeed especially of them – these discoveries are in fact self-devouring. He who makes them, saws off the branch on which he sits. Nietzsche knew this full well. His bitter irony, his whole style, the structure of his thought, are all built around the recognition of this.

Not so with Sigmund. He who discovered, or popularized, the idea that we are not masters in our own house, appears to have been firmly, unquestionably, and somewhat complacently master in his own, not to mention those of many others. The fact that he dominated the house of others ought not perhaps to be held against him: other thinkers do that, and there seems to be much eagerness to be so dominated. What is a little harder to view with sympathy is his continued and total mastery within his own. Like Gustav von Aschenbach, the hero of Thomas Mann's *Death in Venice*, he '... taught a whole grateful generation that a man can still be capable of moral resolution even after he has plumbed the depths of knowledge ...'

It isn't that, in doing so, he was breaking some moral code. Quite the contrary. Most moral codes recommend strength of character and the overcoming of doubt. They do not condone Hamlet's conduct. No, what Freud was sinning against was not some moral code, but the logic of his own ideas.

No Hamlet he. Conscience made no coward of him. On the contrary, it seemed to endow him with great confidence, and he proved most royally. He ended as king of a movement which transformed the thought and speech of mankind. So the man destined to play and be king, and who was unfitted or disinclined to play Hamlet, unwittingly devised a routine for turning others into Hamlets.

In a strange kind of way, however, these formula-produced Hamlets are rewarded with a glimpse of the Absolute. Their previous world is entirely suspended, it stands still, while they temporarily leave it. All their previous convictions and ideas, including their motives for entering into this state of *sursis* itself, and the criteria for re-emerging from it, are suspended by the technique which requires that all this be re-examined, on the assumption that it might be the façade, the front-man of the daemon/ Unconscious. It is an emotional operationalization of Descartes' method of universal doubt. The idea of the Unconscious entails a suspension of trust in all the inner intuitions of our reason: one which many religions must envy. What survives or re-emerges from these guild-controlled searching fires is Real, and determines what is and is not genuine. It is an Absolute-by-residue.

History had played an odd joke on Europe in making Nietzsche a German, and Freud a Jew. It could hardly have gone further in inverting customary stereotypes. Nietzsche, bitterly, sardonically self-ironizing, fully aware of the way in which his own problems and solutions were rooted in his own past, of the way in which efforts at transcending it were but one further example of its power, aware of the way in which such self-knowledge undercut itself, was gnawing steadily at his own innards; Freud, sturdily, beefily confident, never applying the acid of his own ideas to those ideas themselves, never adapting the devaluing explanations which he applied to others to his own central positions, his values barely shaken when their foundations were removed, untroubled by or unaware of the circularity of his own reasoning . . .

Having given the most powerful body-blow to the foundation of our values, to the picture of man which had sustained them, he inclined to uphold them with astonishing freedom from giddiness. The fact that such confidence meant granting himself exemption from his own theories, bothered him little: the exemption was easily granted.

When he did turn in on himself it was only, it seems, to find confirmation. His own Unconscious obligingly corroborated his own theories, and his own theories showed how well he understood himself and others. Nietzsche ended in madness, which has a certain fittingness and dignity in one who had undercut the bases of rationality and hence of any defensible criteria of sanity. Freud died clinically sane, with confidence undiminished, and evidently allowing himself ever wilder speculations. The licence he had granted to his own vision after his self-analysis some four decades earlier had come to be used ever more freely.

CONCLUSION

Our primary aim has been to summarize and explain a major intellectual revolution, to provide a basic model of its intellectual and social organization and functioning, which highlights its inner life and movement, its place in the wider conceptual economy of our tradition, and which helps explain its appeal.

It is of course of the very essence of psychoanalysis that it tells others more about themselves than they consciously know, and more than they consciously think. It is too much to hope that it will gladly allow others to do unto it what it loves to do unto others. A much more likely reaction, and one well in keeping with the traditions of the movement, will be to discount the model as an expression of unconscious hostility and resistance to the insights of the movement. (Either the author has not been analysed, in which case (a) he is disqualified from talking about it, and (b) is resisting his unconscious awareness of his need for it; or alternatively, and exhaustively, he *has* been analysed, in which case clearly the book is a reflection of an unsuccessful and uncompleted analysis, broken off because the author was afraid of what he would find out about himself, etc.)

But while our primary aim has been to explain the success of a movement rather than to assess its doctrines, the two tasks cannot (other than ironically) be separated. True as well as false beliefs require explanation, as Gibbon insisted; none the less, the strategy of explanation must take into account whether or not the beliefs are true. Either way, the assessment must be included in the account.

This being so, it may be both natural and useful to end with a brief summary assessment of the claims of the movement.

The general vision of human conduct, motivation and relations which can roughly be summed up in what I called the Nietzschean Minimum, the affirmation of its instinctual base, deviousness, covertness, persistence over time, lack of proportion, focus on personal relations, and the incorporation in all this of the supposedly 'higher' aspirations – is almost certainly correct. Its seemingly specific doctrines above all implicitly convey the more general, unspecific but important insights of the Nietzschean Minimum. If made precise enough, and unslippery enough, to acquire a *stable* empirical content, some of them may also be specifically true. Nothing in my argument hinges on whether or not this is so.

Freudian terminology is an easy-to-learn, plausible jargon which sensitizes one to this truth, and to that extent constitutes an improvement on other and older idioms. Here there is a striking parallel with Hegel (and his disciple Marx). He too invented an easy slide-off-the-tongue idiom which decoded not so much the psyche as history. He too returned meaning and hope to a disenchanted world, rejoined fact and value, saved the world from cold inquiry and handed it over to facile humanist peddlers of salvation. Just as Hegelian-type doctrines, notably Marxism, have succeeded in restating social and political issues in the context of the recognition of deep and persistent historical change, which see man as part of *history*, so Freudianism has succeeded in offering a vision, ethic, and technique of pastoral care, which firmly place man in the context of *nature*. At the same time, however, it sins against another modern requirement: the need for cognitive growth, which in turn presupposes that each intellectual system be judged, in the end, by data *not under its own control*. Freudianism systematically controls its own data base.

Are the more specific Freudian doctrines, or some of them, within this style of thought, valid? Charitably, one might suggest that at least by accident, some of them must have alighted on the truth. Uncharitably, one might say that within the general conceptual ambience of psychoanalysis, with its appallingly low level of operational definition of concepts, they do not remain anchored to any truth which they may accidentally hit on, but float away again. No retrieval of empirical content is possible, when the links between theory and fact are so loose, and under the control of that switch which consigns data to reducibility or to authenticity at will.

The Unconscious is, among other things, a name for a certain relationship between substance and evidence. This daemon controls his own manifestations, the evidence about himself, and he is purposive and cunning. This relationship ensures both the persistence of the substance, and the loosening (to any required extent) of all operational precision of subsidiary theories.

Whether psychological generalizations at this level are in principle available at all, or whether attempts to find them will always founder on the complexity of the material and the diversity of social and semantic contexts in which the behaviour occurs, is an interesting question, and not one to be solved here. Suffice it to say that while psychoanalysis may often alight on truth by chance in individual cases, its middle-level generalizations are at best suspect. They float anchorless in a nebulous realm governed by its own loose laws; often beyond the reach of any test, they sometimes do indeed sail into the realm of fact, but even when they brush up against truth, they float away again long before bearings can be taken with precision.

Much more important, however, because both contentious and of great importance for suffering humanity, is the assessment of psychoanalytic claims of privileged and unique access to this Unconscious, and the closely associated claims of being able to use this access therapeutically.

Here, scepticism would seem to be indicated and indeed seems to have been in part shared by the Master in his old age. There was in any case a great oddity about a unique peep-hole to a special realm, uncheckable by any others – but only, at best, by its therapeutic success. (The shift of stress from *therapy* to *truth*, begun in Freud's lifetime, seems to have been accompanied by continued insistence on unique and privileged access to truth: so the progression was in effect from public therapy to private truth.)

Given both the poor nature of the statistical and common-sense observation evidence in support of therapeutic success, and the bizarre inner logic and some internal absurdities of the whole privileged access theory, one cannot really come out with any positive conclusion here. The decisive consideration here seems to me this: if there is any therapeutic effectiveness in this technique, the supporting statistics should, and indubitably *would*, long ago have been collected by the guild itself – if they were available. The perfectly genuine methodological problems connected with assembling such statistics cannot convincingly be invoked to explain their absence. They haunt all complex fields of inquiry, and do not elsewhere seem to present an insuperable obstacle.

Two Nobel prize-winners have put their assessment on record:

... I believe men will look back on our age as an age of superstition, chiefly connected with the names of Karl Marx and Sigmund Freud.[4]
[F. A. Hayek]

... psychoanalysts will continue to perpetrate the most ghastly blunders just so long as they persevere in their impudent and intellectually disabling belief that they enjoy a 'privileged access to truth' (M. H. Stern, *International Journal of Psycho-analysis*, 53, p. 13, 1972). The opinion is gaining ground that doctrinaire psychoanalytic theory is the most stupendous intellectual confidence trick of the twentieth century.[5]
[P. Medawar]

The impudence to which Sir Peter Medawar refers, the supposition of privileged access to truth, is conspicuously present. But basically the indisputable *chuzpah* inheres not so much in people, but in a system of ideas and practices which has a marked unity and which needs to be understood. The claim to cognitive privilege has been made not only by practitioners, but also on occasion endorsed by philosophers.[6]

The provision of human warmth and solace, much in demand in our society, is uncertain and precarious. In this situation, the vacuum principle operates: *something* must fill this crying need. It is psychologically impossible to tell sufferers that no help is available, even if it is true. And even if one told them, most of them would not be willing or able to accept it. A doctrine and organization which confidently implies a promise of relief through the implication of its key ideas, and whose doctrinal orchestration and prima facie plausibility is greatly superior to that of its rivals, cannot but be heeded, especially when the technique itself supplies eagerly sought human contact and reassurance as part of the profound cure, and excludes critical assessment of itself by the implicit rules which succour-seekers must obey if the amelioration of their condition is to be attained. Once established, the Principle of Institutionalization also operates very effectively. Any doctrine and practice which acquires a good institutional base, can thereafter survive even if its doctrinal claims are not substantiated, and, interestingly enough, even if it itself, *sotto voce* and in small print, disavows all its own erstwhile striking claims and promises. There are other very good examples of this.

In brief: the news of the plague which is upon us and of its character is, in rough outline, true. The news brought us about the cure is not. *C'est la thérapie, et non pas la maladie, qui est imaginaire.*

APPENDIX A

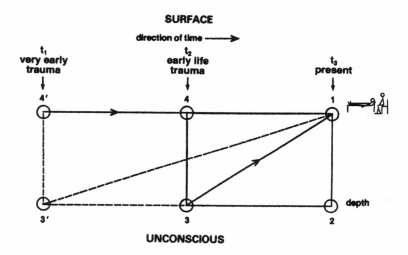

The diagram illustrates the processes of depth therapy as conceived by its practitioners.

The horizontal dimension, moving from t_1 to t_2 and to t_3, represents the flow of time. t_3 is the present. t_2 indicates early youth, the period during which according to the standard psychoanalytical theory, the character-forming episodes or states of mind occurred. t_1 indicates an earlier period still (say early infancy or the birth trauma), the period during which according to some radical revisionists, the really decisive events took place.

The vertical dimension has only two positions: the upper one represents the observable world of public events. The lower one represents the realm of the Unconscious.

The theory of therapy is ambiguous; and involves either a triangular or a quadrilateral circuit: 1, 2, 3, 1, or 1, 2, 3, 4, 1.

224

In the latter case, the therapist probes the present state of the patient's Unconscious, proceeds through it to recover its past state, and also refers to the past objective, external situation, which had interacted with the past Unconscious. However, the past objective situation can be held to be irrelevant, in as far as its *meaning* to the Unconscious, rather than any objective features, was what matters and mattered. As that meaning is independent of the objective situation, the latter can be disregarded, which is what Freud in any case recommended.

Two types of revisionism are to be found in the movement: those who insist on going further back into the past, invoking 1, 2, 3', or 1, 2, 3', 4'; and those who insist on the 'here-now' as sufficient, and eliminate the past altogether, restricting themselves to 1, 2, 1.

Note that all items at the lower level are correctly identifiable only by means of a procedure which is itself a corollary of the overall theory, which in a sense repeats it, and which is under control of the practitioners. This, in conjunction with the fact that the practitioners also try to retain control of evaluation of success of therapy, casts doubt on the testability of the central thesis that recovery of unconscious mental contents (2, 3, or 3') has therapeutic effects. This is the thesis singled out by Grunbaum in defence of his claim that psychoanalysis is testable (though unsatisfactory).

NOTES

CHAPTER 1

1. W. H. Auden, 'In Memory of Sigmund Freud', *Collected Shorter Poems* (London: 1950).
2. This term, literally Display-Gentile, was in current use to describe a Gentile figurehead of a Jewish firm, set up to ward off anti-semitic feelings towards the establishment in question.
3. References in A. Grunbaum, 'Epistemological Liabilities of the Universal Appraisal of Psychoanalytical Theory', *Nous*, Vol. XIV, No. 3 (September 1980).
4. Jeanne Favret-Saada, 'Excusez-moi, je ne faisais que passer', *Les Temps Modernes*, No. 371 (June 1977), and Sherry Turkle, *Psychoanalytic Politics* (London: 1979).
5. Fulke Greville, *Mustapha* (1609).
6. See, for instance, J. P. Stern, *Nietzsche* (Cambridge: 1979).
7. Edmund Leach, 'Time and False Noses', in *Rethinking Anthropology* (London: 1961) p. 132.

CHAPTER 2

1. Keith Thomas, *Religion and the Decline of Magic* (Harmondsworth: 1980) p. 5 *et seq.*
2. David Hume, *The Natural History of Religion* (1757) Ch. V.
3. *Ibid.*, Ch. VI.
4. Nigel Balchin, *Mine Own Executioner* (London: 1945) p. 7.

CHAPTER 3

1. The allusion is to the characteristic theatrical device employed by the playwright Luigi Pirandello, in plays such as *Six Characters in Search of an Author*, or *Tonight We Improvise*. The device consists of deliberately breaking down the distinction between actors, producers and the author of a play on the one hand, and the characters *and* the audience on the other.

Characters discuss the further development of the plot with each other and with the audience (or other actors pretending to be parts of the audience). The confusion which this engenders in the mind of a member of the audience depends in part on the fact that he does not know which convention is operative – is the actor talking inside the play, or outside it?

The person who does not know which convention is operative at any given moment is at a hopeless disadvantage. The person who does know, who decides, who can throw the switch one way or the other to determine whether one is within or outside the play and its conventions, is in charge and can easily dominate.

2. The content-flexibility of psychoanalytic concepts is illustrated from perhaps the most celebrated of such notions, that of the Oedipus Complex. Sidney Hook reports: '. . . I asked psychoanalysts . . . what kind of evidence they were prepared to accept . . . that a child did not have an Oedipus Complex . . . I asked it innumerable times . . . Dr Ernst Kris . . . replied that a child lacking an Oedipus Complex would be one who acted like an idiot' (in S. Hook (ed.), *Psychoanalysis, Scientific Method and Philosophy* (New York: 1959, p. 214).

   Others were perplexed or denounced the question as sophistical or meaningless. By contrast, the leading analyst Winnicott seemed to have no trouble at all discerning an apparent lack of the Oedipus Complex: '. . . Winnicott twice remarked: "You show no sign of ever having had an Oedipus Complex." My family pattern was not Oedipal.' (Harry Guntrip, 'My Experience of Analysis with Fairbairn and Winnicott', *International Review of Psychoanalysis*, 2, 145 [1975] p. 148).

3. S. Freud, *Introductory Lectures on Psychoanalysis*, The Pelican Freud Library, Vol. 1 (Harmondsworth: 1973) pp. 507, 508.

4. Cf. Michael George Briant, *Fact and Value in Psychoanalysis*, London University Ph.D. thesis (1973).

5. Else Frankel-Brunswick, 'Perspectives in Psychoanalytic Theory' in H. D. David and H. Von Bracken (eds.), *Perspectives in Personality Theory* (London: 1957).

6. Penelope Balogh, *Freud: a Biographical Introduction* (London: 1971).

CHAPTER 4

1. Ernest Jones, *The Life and Work of Sigmund Freud*, edited and abridged in one volume by Lionel Trilling and Steven Marcus (London: 1962) p. 327.

2. Janet Malcolm, *Psychoanalysis: the Impossible Profession* (London: 1982) p. 88.
3. *Ibid.*, pp. 166, 167.
4. *Ibid.*
5. J. Marmor, 'Psychoanalytic Therapy as an Educational Process', in *Psychoanalytic Education*, Vol. 5 (New York: 1962). Quoted in F. Cioffi, 'Freud and the Idea of a Pseudo-science', in R. Borger and F. Cioffi (eds.), *Explanation in the Behavioural Science* (Cambridge: 1970).
6. J. W. Miller (ed.), *Freud: the Man, His World, His Influence* (London: 1972).

CHAPTER 5

1. R. Wollheim credits Freud, though with a qualification, with holding that only *another* instinct can repress an instinct (*Freud*, [London: 1971] pp. 146, 158).
2. Cf. Noam Chomsky, *Reflections on Language* (London: 1976).
3. Originally published in *Language*, Vol. 35 (1959) pp. 26–58, and frequently republished.
4. Wollheim, *op. cit.*, p. 166.
5. See F. Cioffi, 'Freud and the Idea of a Pseudo-science' in Borger and Cioffi, *op. cit.*, p. 493.
6. R. E. Money-Kyrle, *Man's Picture of His World* [London: 1961] p. 188.
7. Cf. C. Rycroft, *Reich* (London: 1971).

CHAPTER 6

1. The phrase is that of Berger and Luckmann, and constitutes the title of their book. The basic idea is similar, but the details differ considerably. But the difference in approach is this: I approach this process in the third person and ironically: this is how the *illusion* of reality is engendered in traditional social orders. (For brevity of exposition, the disclaimer is not constantly repeated.) P. L. Berger and T. Luckmann, *The Social Construction of Reality: a Treatise in the Sociology of Knowledge* (New York: 1966).
2. There was an interesting outburst of animism in the RAF during the Second World War, when engine failures came to be connected with *gremlins*. Whereas normally, well-maintained engines are reliable enough to inspire trust, in the specially stressful conditions of wartime flying, the risks and

tensions they engendered were evidently such that spirits needed to be invented who could then be inwardly supplicated or appeased.

3. D. Riesman, *The Lonely Crowd* (New Haven: 1961).

CHAPTER 7

1. E. Fromm, *Sigmund Freud's Mission* (London: 1959) p. 85.
2. *Ibid.*, p. 88.

CHAPTER 8

1. Chomsky, *Reflections on Language*.
2. B. A. Farrell, *The Standing of Psychoanalysis* (Oxford: 1981).
3. H. J. Eysenck and G. D. Wilson (eds.), *The Experimental Study of Freudian Theories* (London: 1972) Ch. 21.
4. Farrell, *op.cit.*, p. 178.
5. *Ibid.*, p. 179.
6. Anthony Storr, 'The Concept of Cure' in C. Rycroft (ed.), *Psychoanalysis Observed* (London: 1966) p. 58 *et seq.*
7. Professor Ernest Nagel in Sidney Hook (ed.), *Psychoanalysis, Scientific Method, and Philosophy* (New York: 1959, 1964) pp. 54, 55.
8. Michael Scriven in Hook, *op.cit.*, p. 249.
9. Adolf Grunbaum, 'The Role of Psychological Explanations of the Rejection or Acceptance of Scientific Theories', in *Transactions of the New York Academy of Sciences*, Series II, Volume 39, (24 April 1980) 2713. (A *Festschrift* for Robert Merton.)
10 In F. Cioffi, 'Freud and the Idea of a Pseudo-science', in Borger and Cioffi, *op. cit.*
11. S. Freud, *Introductory Lectures on Psychoanalysis*, p. 515.
12. Quoted in Cioffi, *op. cit.*, p. 480.
13. F. J. Sulloway, *Freud, Biologist of the Mind* (London: 1980) p. 487.
14. Robert Fliess (not to be confused with Wilhelm Fliess) in the Foreword to R. Fliess (ed.), *The Psychoanalytic Reader*, XV–XVII (New York: 1948), quoted in Grunbaum, *op. cit.*
15. R. Fliess, 'Research Methods in Psychoanalysis', *The International Journal of Psychoanalysis*, 33 (1952) pp. 403–9. Quoted in Sulloway, *op. cit.*, p. 486.
16. T. Kuhn, *The Structure of Scientific Revolutions* (Chicago and London: 1962, 1968).

CHAPTER 9

1. Prior to the appearance of his book, one of the best sources for A. Grunbaum's arguments was 'Epistemological Liabilities of the Clinical Appraisal of Psychoanalytic Theory', in *Nous*, Vol. XIV, No. 3 (September 1980).
2. Cioffi, *op. cit.*, p. 471.
3. *Ibid.*, p. 473.
4. Grunbaum, *op. cit.*, p. 321. Emphasis in original.
5. *Ibid.*, pp. 322–3. Emphasis in original.
6. Cioffi, *op. cit.*, p. 471.
7. Grunbaum, *op. cit.*, p. 317.
8. E. Erwin, 'The Truth about Psychoanalysis', in *The Journal of Philosophy*, Vol. LXXVIII, No. 10 (October 1981) p. 551.
9. H. Guntrip, 'Psychoanalysis and Some Scientific and Philosophical Critics', *British Journal of Medical Psychology*, 51 (1978) pp. 207–24.
10. *Ibid.*, p. 216.
11. Money-Kyrle, *op. cit.*, p. 18.
12. The distinction between the two kinds of conscious is put forward by Fromm in *Man for Himself* (London: 1949). The idea is also formulated by him more briefly: 'Freud . . . saw that the super-ego was originally the internalization of an external and dangerous authority. He did not distinguish between spontaneous ideals which are parts of the self, and internalized commands which rule the self . . .' (Erich Fromm, *The Fear of Freedom* [London: 1942, 1960]).
13. In my youth, I attended for a couple of years a seminar run by the leading logical positivist thinker of the period. The young lecturers and graduate students who also attended it were impeccably with-it, by the standards of the time, and their intellectual world was defined by positivist empiricism on the one hand, and on the other by psychoanalysis. I could never understand how they could fail to sense the strain between the sustained reverence for verifiability on the one hand, and equally sustained indulgence in a technique manifestly indulging in communication with the Untestable. All I can say is that this problem did not seem to bother them at all. The fact that both doctrines were currently fashionable seemed good enough to establish that they were compatible.

In this connection, I recall the late Dr Frankel-Brunswick reporting the remark made of a similar world in pre-war Vienna, to the effect that psychoanalysis had been the religion of the logical positivists. When I consulted A. J. Ayer about this – who after all had studied in Vienna at the time – his comment was that this could not be so, because logically the two doctrines were not compatible (and that some kind of behaviourism would have been an appropriate psychology for the Vienna Circle). No doubt: it doesn't establish however, that psychologically they could not and were not embraced jointly, just as I observed them jointly and uncritically embraced in the London of circa 1950.

14. S. Fisher and R. P. Greenberg, *The Scientific Credibility of Freud's Theories and Therapy* (Hassocks, New York: 1977).
15. *Ibid.*, p. 397.
16. *Ibid.*, pp. 411, 412.
17. See for instance H. J. Eysenck and G. D. Wilson (eds.), *The Experimental Study of Freudian Theories* (London: 1973); S. Rachman, *The Effects of Psychotherapy* (Oxford: 1971); R. B. Sloane, F. R. Staples, *et. al. Psychotherapy versus Behaviour Therapy* (Cambridge, Mass. and London: 1975). (Contains an interesting survey of attempts to collect and evaluate data in this field.)
18. D. A. Shapiro, 'Science and Psychotherapy: The State of the Art', *British Journal of Medical Psychology*, Vol. 3, Pt 1 (1980) pp. 1–10.

CHAPTER 10

1. Eysenck and Wilson, *op. cit.*, p. 393.
2. H. Guntrip, 'Centenary Reflections on the Work of Freud', *University of Leeds Medical Journal*, Vol. V, No. 3 (1956), pp. 162–6.
3. D. Davidson, 'Paradoxes of Irrationality' in R. Wollheim and J. Hopkins (eds.), *Philosophical Essays on Freud* (Cambridge: 1982) p. 292.
4. F. A. Hayek, *The Three Sources of Human Values* (London: 1978) p. 30.
5. P. B. Medawar, 'Victims of Psychiatry', *New York Review of Books* (23 January 1975).
6. Wollheim, *op. cit.*, p. 17; or James Hopkins, in the Introduction to R. Wollheim and J. Hopkins (eds.), *Philosophical Essays on Freud* (Cambridge: 1982) p. xli.

SELECT BIBLIOGRAPHY

Badcock, C. *The Psychoanalysis of Culture* (Oxford: 1980)

British Journal for the Philosophy of Science, Special issue on psychoanalysis, Vol.VII, No. 25 (May 1956)

Brome, Vincent, *Ernest Jones. Freud's Alter-Ego* (London: 1982)

Brown, J. A. C., *Freud and the Post-Freudians*, (Harmondsworth: 1961)

Carotenuto, Aldo, *A Secret Symmetry: Sabina Spielrein between Jung and Freud* (New York: 1982)

Cioffi, Frank (ed.), *Freud* (London: 1973)

Clark, Ronald W., *Freud. The Man and the Cause* (London: 1980)

Eysenck, H. J. and Wilson, G. D. (eds.), *The Experimental Study of Freudian Theories* (London: 1973)

Farrell, B. A., *The Standing of Psychoanalysis* (Oxford: 1981)

Fisher, Seymour and Greenberg, Roger P., *The Scientific Credibility of Freud's Theories and Therapy* (Hassocks, New York: 1977)

Frischer, Dominique, *Les analysés parlent* (Paris: 1977, 1981)

Fromm Erich, *Sigmund Freud's Mission* (London: 1959)
  The Fear of Freedom (London: 1942, 1960)
  The Crisis of Psychoanalysis (London: 1970)
  Greatness and Limitations of Freud's Thought (London: 1980)

Grunbaum, Adolf, *The Foundations of Psychoanalysis* (New York: 1984)

Hook, Sidney (ed.), *Psychoanalysis, Scientific Method and Philosophy* (New York: 1959, 1964)

Jacobi, Russell, *The Repression of Psychoanalysis* (New York: 1983)

Jones, Ernest, *Free Associations* (London: 1959)

Bibliography

The Life and Work of Sigmund Freud, edited and abridged by Lionel Trilling and Steven Marcus (London: 1962)

Journal of Philosophy, Symposium: Psychoanalysis, Vol. LXXVIII, No. 10 (October 1981) pp. 549–72

La Pierre, Richard, *The Freudian Ethic* (New York: 1959)

MacIntyre, A. C., *The Unconscious* (London: 1958)

Magee, Bryan, *The Philosophy of Schopenhauer* (Oxford: 1983)

Malcolm, Janet, *Psychoanalysis: The Impossible Profession* (London: 1982)

Marcus, Steven, *Freud and the Culture of Psychoanalysis* (London: 1984)

Masson, J. M., *The Assault on Truth: Freud's Suppression of the Seduction Theory* (New York: 1983)

Miller, J. W. (ed.), *Freud: the Man, His World, His Influence* (London: 1972)

Money-Kyrle, R. E., *Psychoanalysis and Politics* (London: 1951)

Man's Picture of His World (London: 1961)

Obholzer, Karin, *The Wolf-Man Sixty Years After* (London: 1982)

Rachman, S., *The Effects of Psychotherapy* (Oxford: 1971)

Roazen, Paul, *Freud and His Followers* (London: 1976)

Robert, Martha, *The Psychoanalytic Revolution* (London: 1966)

Rogow, Arnold A., *The Psychiatrists* (London: 1971)

Rycroft, Charles (ed.), *Psychoanalysis Observed* (London: 1966) *Reich* (London: 1971)

Sloan, R. B., Staples F. R., et. al., *Psychotherapy versus Behaviour Therapy*, (Cambridge, Mass. and London: 1975)

Storr, Anthony, *Jung* (London: 1973)

Sulloway, Frank J., *Freud, Biologist of the Mind* (London: 1980)

Turkle, Sherry, *Psychoanalytic Politics. Freud's French Revolution* (London: 1979)

Wisdom, J. O., *The Unconscious Origin of Berkeley's Philosophy* (London: 1953)

Wollheim, Richard, *Freud* (London: 1971) and Hopkins, J. (eds.), *Philosophical Essays on Freud* (Cambridge: 1982)

INDEX